INDONESIA

INDONESIA

State and Society in Transition

Jemma Purdey,
Antje Missbach,
and Dave McRae

LYNNE
RIENNER
PUBLISHERS

BOULDER
LONDON

Published in the United States of America in 2020 by
Lynne Rienner Publishers, Inc.
1800 30th Street, Boulder, Colorado 80301
www.rienner.com

and in the United Kingdom by
Lynne Rienner Publishers, Inc.
Gray's Inn House, 127 Clerkenwell Road, London EC1 5DB

Library of Congress Cataloging-in-Publication Data
A Cataloging-in-Publication record for this book
is available from the Library of Congress.

ISBN 978-1-62637-851-3 hc
ISBN 978-1-62637-852-0 pb

British Cataloguing in Publication Data
A Cataloguing in Publication record for this book
is available from the British Library.

Printed and bound in the United States of America

The paper used in this publication meets the requirements
of the American National Standard for Permanence of
Paper for Printed Library Materials Z39.48-1992.

5 4 3 2 1

Contents

Acknowledgments

WE AIM TO ADD TO THE RICH BODY OF SCHOLARSHIP ON INDONESIA by bringing together in one volume aspects of Indonesia's history, politics, international affairs, economics, and society to provide an overall picture of this complex nation. Having observed Indonesia closely for more than two decades, we have published research on the history, politics, and peoples, and together we share a keen desire to communicate and educate more people around the world about it. By engaging both our own research expertise and intensive analysis of recent specialist literature, we offer a comprehensive and up-to-date view of state and society in Indonesia.

We thank Lynne Rienner and her team for guiding us smoothly through the production process. Our gratitude is also due to Richard Chauvel, who read every chapter and greatly enriched the book by sharing his insights and critical feedback. Many thanks to Rachel Salmond for helping us get the manuscript into shape.

1

Indonesia:
An Underrated Country?

THIS BOOK IS A STUDY OF THE CONTEMPORARY POLITICS AND society of Indonesia, the world's largest Muslim-majority nation, with approximately 270 million people. Only China, India, and the United States have larger populations; India and the United States are the only two democracies larger than Indonesia. Unique among countries of its size, Indonesia is an archipelagic state. Consisting of more than 17,000 islands, Indonesia straddles the Pacific and Indian Oceans, and some of the world's busiest shipping and trading routes pass through its waters.

Indonesia's size and unique geography mark it as a country that merits attention beyond its borders, particularly as the balance of geopolitical and economic heft continues to shift from the West to Asia. Yet Indonesia is rarely included in lists of emerging powers and economies, of which the BRICS (Brazil, Russia, India, China, and South Africa) grouping is probably the best known. Its absence is in contrast to the global role the country played at the peak of its international influence in the 1950s and 1960s, when it initiated the Non-Aligned Movement (NAM) as an alternative to the Western and Soviet blocs of the Cold War and positioned itself at the helm of an anti-imperialist bloc of new emerging forces.

What accounts for Indonesia's much more modest international profile in contemporary times? Is it simply that Indonesia is in fact "one of the most underrated and under-appreciated countries in the world," as former senior Singaporean diplomat and academic Kishore Mahbubani (2018) posits? Or has Indonesia's influence genuinely waned, because of various characteristics of its domestic affairs? In this book, we seek to equip readers to respond to these questions by

1

presenting a comprehensive survey of contemporary Indonesian politics, society, and culture, and its relations with the outside world.

No academic observer would contest the view that democratic Indonesia is beset by various shortfalls spanning politics, economic development, and society. Twenty years after the end of authoritarian rule, Indonesia faces many challenges, ranging from enduring poverty, rising inequality, and endemic corruption to increasing illiberalism, erosion in the protection of basic rights, and failure to address past instances of state violence, all of which are addressed in detail in the following chapters. How we interpret these deficits depends in large part on the comparative lens we adopt, with possible points of comparison being the Indonesia of twenty years ago, its neighbors in Asia Pacific, other so-called third-wave democracies, and its fellow members of the G20 (Group of 20), perhaps its most prized international forum, which is made up of the twenty largest economies in the world. When measured against such points of comparison, it becomes clear that Indonesia's performance in various spheres of governance is broadly typical of countries with similar political pasts and income levels, diminishing the case that it has been egregiously underrated.

In political terms, present-day Indonesia is unrecognizable when compared with the period of authoritarian rule by President Suharto that ended in May 1998. All legislative representatives and executive heads of government in Indonesia, from the village level up to the presidency, are now directly elected in competitive elections. Indonesia's party system has also transitioned from stage-managed competition between three regime-approved parties to one in which ten or more parties of differing and often loosely defined ideologies jockey for voters' approval, albeit with vote buying persisting as an important part of their candidates' electoral strategies. Critical commentary on political candidates by the media and civil society is widespread. More fundamentally, Indonesia's amended constitution establishes a separation of powers and a clear basis for democratic competition. The document also establishes a new bill of rights, mostly modeled on the International Convention on Civil and Political Rights, although the implementation of these rights has been inconsistent.

Following its postauthoritarian transition and two decades of democratic consolidation, Indonesia similarly stands out within its immediate region. Among its Southeast Asian neighbors, no other country has consistently maintained democratic status since the year 2000. Among those countries that have been democratic for part of this time, the Philippines is considered by scholars to have temporarily regressed into authoritarianism (Diamond 2015, pp. 145, 151), whereas Thailand has oscillated between democratic and military rule. Transitions in Myanmar (Burma) and, most recently, in Malaysia may yet add to the community of democracies in the longer term, but for the most part Indonesia's attempts to promote democracy within Southeast Asia have been a lonely endeavor. Concerning Asia as a whole, Edward Aspinall (2015) observes that the average Freedom House democracy index score for his list of eighteen significant countries in the region was 3.83 in 2015—a score that is significantly closer to the authoritarian end of the Freedom House index spectrum, which scores the most democratic at 1 and the most authoritarian at 7. Indonesia rated a somewhat better score of 3. For the most part, therefore, Aspinall notes, Indonesia has maintained its democratic status, despite the absence of so-called spillover or neighborhood effects from other nearby democracies.

If we change the lens to compare Indonesia to other so-called third-wave democracies (that is, countries that have become democracies since the mid-1970s, such as the Philippines, South Korea, and Taiwan [Huntington 1991]), we find that Indonesia's deficits as a democracy appear to be quite typical at worst, and at best well above average.[1] Certainly, Indonesia has not succumbed to a reversion to authoritarianism, even though various observers perceive this to remain a risk. After all, this is a fate that democracy scholar Larry Diamond (2015, p. 144) calculates to have befallen almost 18 percent of democracies worldwide in the first fifteen years of the twenty-first century. Erosion of the quality of Indonesia's democracy over the same period similarly complies with a global decline in the degree of freedom (Diamond 2015, pp. 147–148). In 2017, the Freedom House index found seventy-one countries, including Indonesia, to have suffered a decline in political rights and civil liberties; only thirty-five registered an improvement. Thus 2017 was the twelfth consecutive year of decline in global freedom, leading Freedom House to declare that "democracy is in crisis" (Freedom House 2018). V-Dem data also show levels of liberal democracy to have declined somewhat from a peak level in 2006–2008, although by this index Indonesia's current levels of democracy remain comparable to its early transition (Coppedge et al. 2019).

It is only in comparison to its peers in the G20 that Indonesia's democratic deficits stand out. In 2017, Indonesia was ranked fifteenth out of nineteen member countries in The Economist Intelligence Unit's Democracy Index (2017), the lowest of any democracy in the grouping. (Turkey, Russia, China, and Saudi Arabia are the G20's authoritarian members.) Even then, Indonesia's position is not especially anomalous once income is taken into account. The nine top-ranked G-20 members in this index, including all five countries ranked simply as "democracies" as opposed to "flawed democracies," are all Organisation for Economic Co-operation and Development (OECD) members with much higher per capita incomes than Indonesia.

When we shift to the economic sphere, we can observe that Indonesia's development deficits again appear in sharpest focus when compared to the OECD countries of the G20. Inequality, for example, has emerged as a major development challenge for Indonesia during the democratic era. Despite consistently rapid economic growth of around 5 or 6 percent per annum since its recovery from the deep economic crisis that precipitated the end of Suharto's rule, inequality has risen steadily. Indonesia's Gini coefficient, a common measure of inequality, rose from 0.33 in 1998 (just after the Asian financial crisis) to 0.41 in 2015 (Yusuf and Sumner 2015, p. 338), although it then declined somewhat to around 0.384 by 2018 (Aisyah 2019). The twelve OECD members of the G20 had much lower Gini averages—around 0.35 in the late 2000s—benefiting from the higher average social spending of advanced economies (Lustig 2016, p. 28).[2] Indonesia compared more favorably with the non-OECD G20 countries, whose average Gini coefficient of 0.47 in the same data set exceeded Indonesia's score of 0.41. Indeed, a comparison of Indonesia with six other middle-income countries based on 2010 data produced a decidedly mixed report card for Indonesia. Economist Nora Lustig (2016) observed that Indonesia not only had the lowest absolute level of income inequality in her sample, but was also doing the least through its social and fiscal policy to address this issue. Overall, she found Indonesia's fiscal policy had no redistributive effect, with the country spending roughly the same on health and education for poorer and richer citizens.

Indeed, Indonesia's modest social spending and failure to redistribute wealth through its fiscal policy places that nation only in the middle of the pack in its region with regard to inequality. For a nation of 270 million people, significant challenges remain to bridge the still significant gap in income levels and to lift those millions still in poverty out of that position.

To reiterate, Indonesia's performance in the political and economic spheres has been typical of nations of similar standing. Indonesia's chief advantage is its size, a major factor in its emergence as a country of significant regional economic clout. But as the data also show, following the devastation of the Asian economic crisis in 1997–1998, improvements have not necessarily touched all Indonesians and have not been as rapid as many would have wanted. In political terms, Indonesia's success as a stable democracy places it above many other similar nations. However, for those in Indonesia striving for stronger protections for human rights, including those of minority regions, ethnicities, and sexualities, there have been worrying signs in recent years of a backward slide toward less, rather than more, freedom.

We posit that Indonesia's predicted economic growth, demographic and geographic significance, and relative democratic stability mean that although not underrated as a nation, it is less understood than it should be. We aim in this book to delve into the historical, political, social, economic, and cultural orders in contemporary Indonesia to illuminate and enable deeper critiques of what life is like for Indonesians, the successes and ongoing challenges the nation faces, and what the future holds.

Continuity and Change

Since 1998, Indonesia has experienced an extraordinary shift from authoritarianism to democracy, and from economic crisis to a rapidly growing economy. In this period the people of Indonesia have witnessed episodes of sectarian and separatist violence, major reforms of national institutions, decentralization of the political structure, destructive natural disasters and terrorist events, and government by five presidents, including four elected in democratic and peaceful ballots.

A clear picture emerges from this book that even after so much tumultuous change, Indonesia's transition is ongoing. In twenty years, Indonesia's economy will very likely be much larger than it is today and, by some estimates, among the top four or five in the world. Even though most regard Indonesia as a relatively successful democracy today, many long-term observers, both inside and outside Indonesia, hold a negative view of the nation's future. They do not believe that the risk of falling back into authoritarianism has been fully overcome.

To better predict the trajectory of ongoing change in Indonesia's governance and society, it is necessary to have a clear understanding of the longer-term context of present events. Studying Indonesia's past helps us to better comprehend the forces shaping its present and to appreciate the enormity of the past and continuing endeavor—the imagining and eventual realization of a nation-state uniting an enormous diversity of ethnic and language groups (Ananta et al. 2015). To this end, the book opens with two chapters on the nation's history, covering the precolonial and colonial periods and Indonesia's postindependence slide from parliamentary democracy to authoritarianism toward the end of founding president Sukarno's rule (1945–1965) and continuing into Suharto's long New Order regime (1965–1998).

These earlier periods continue to shape the choices made by Indonesia's leaders and broader society as they face contemporary challenges. For example, the strength of Indonesian nationalism and the particular and enduring appeal of both Pancasila, Indonesia's state ideology, and Sukarnoism remain key pillars for the majority of political parties; both of these elements were exhibited by the candidates in the 2014 and 2019 presidential elections. The Indonesian military's central place in the national story arises from its conception as a revolutionary army of nationalists and freedom fighters under the Dutch and Japanese occupiers. In contemporary Indonesia, this legacy means that for the people and for the institution itself, the military is still considered a vital element of the nation-state. Moreover, the history of the Dutch-sponsored federated-states strategy to resist full Indonesian independence also helps us understand why federalism continues to remain impossible in Indonesia, even during the period of far-reaching decentralization after Suharto.

We recognize the continuity of actors between the authoritarian and democratic periods as a consequence of the long-term persistence of a social order that emerged under Suharto's rule and supported nepotism, cronyism, corruption, and patrimonial networks of power. This order still permeates business and politics and lies beneath a tendency to return to authoritarian strategies in facing current political crises, in turn curbing freedoms. The continued resonance of imaginings of the role and influence of pre-independent Indonesian kingdoms and Sukarno's postindependence prominence in the Non-Aligned Movement can also be recognized in thinking about Indonesia's present-day place in the world.

In order to evaluate the political change and remaining risks to a democratic future in Indonesia, we then examine the vast political reforms of the early post–New Order years. We pay special attention to the instability that accompanied this change, including sectarian violence and separatist conflicts in various parts of outer Indonesia. We also inspect the political structures in contemporary Indonesia and the role of elections and political parties—in sum, the machinery of parliamentary democracy that has gradually been put in place since 1998. In many ways still under negotiation, Indonesia's political and judicial institutions remain vulnerable.

We offer a detailed examination of the drivers of social and economic inequality, including the demographic challenges of improving access to employment, and to health and education services for the nation's large, overwhelmingly young and geographically scattered population. Since the end of the New Order in 1998, although enormous effort has been directed toward improving the quality of life for ordinary citizens in Indonesia, complex challenges persist and growing inequality and poverty are hard to ignore. While the nation experiences rapid economic growth and the accumulation of wealth, the gap between rich and poor is widening. We ask if the present level of growth and development is sustainable when so many are being left behind.

The role of civil society and human rights issues reveals one of the most significant contradictions within this democracy. Some gains have been made for human rights protections, but the failure to deal with past crimes against humanity enacted under the New Order and subsequent governments is viewed by victims, survivors, and their supporters as undermining any commitment. An increase in attacks on human rights organizations and agents by fundamentalist Islamic groups indicates new levels of intolerance and harassment. As we explore this context of growing intolerance in Indonesian society, we examine the situation of religious, ethnic, and gender minorities that are becoming increasingly marginalized.

Young people—those between the ages of eighteen and thirty— make up the single largest group in Indonesia, so a significant number of people were born after the fall of the New Order or have no real memory of it. To better understand this crucial demographic and its interests, values, and outlook, we take a closer look at key elements shaping this generation. How are popular culture and the media shaping Indonesia's future? How open and free is the media in post-1998 Indonesia? Many deem Indonesia to be in the middle of a turn in society toward a more conservative practice of Islam, so we explore the role of religion in the lives of Indonesians today. In shedding light on the everyday politics and cultural tastes in Indonesia's society, we reveal a culturally rich society—one that also employs advanced technologies to remain highly connected globally and is persistently outward-looking.

Indonesia's history shows us that the inhabitants of the archipelago of islands that make up this nation have long been globally connected and open to teachings, religions, languages, and foods from around the world (Gelman Taylor 2013). Indonesia has occupied a strategic position within the maritime and trading world and within international politics. With its growing economy, geostrategic regional significance, and membership in the G20, contemporary Indonesia is seeking more attention on the world stage. Indonesia has long been seen as the leader within the Association of Southeast Asian Nations

(ASEAN), but how does Indonesia see its role as a nation both regionally and globally, and what is the status of its relationships with neighbors and key international partners?

Like other rapidly developing and evolving democracies, Indonesia is an incredibly dynamic and exciting nation where, on the one hand, innovation and progress in business, education, and technology are encouraged and supported, yet on the other hand, there continues to be ongoing negotiation and debate over the rights of the individual, including those of minorities, women, and young people. By exploring these levels of contemporary Indonesian state and society, we hope to reveal the complexities and tensions within this nation. The question is, can Indonesia resolve these tensions? Can Indonesia achieve its potential as a thriving economic power and democracy in its region and beyond?

Notes

1. This is also the case when Indonesia is compared with other Muslim-majority countries. The Economist Intelligence Unit Democracy Index (2017) rates Indonesia (6.39) below India (7.23), where Muslims are a minority group, and significantly above the next three largest Muslim-majority countries—Pakistan (4.26), Bangladesh (5.43), and Nigeria (4.44). Elsewhere, Pepinsky (2014) argues that Indonesia is a "typical Muslim country" in terms of economic, social, and political indicators based on a data set of fifty-two Muslim majority and Muslim plurality countries.

2. Gini coefficient averages calculated from International Labour Organization et al. (2015).

2

Preindependence Indonesia

Firstly: we the sons and daughters of Indonesia declare that we belong to the motherland, Indonesia.
Secondly: we the sons and daughters of Indonesia declare that we belong to one nation, the Indonesian nation.
Thirdly: we the sons and daughters of Indonesia uphold as the language of unity the Indonesian language.
—Youth Oath, October 28, 1928

AT THE SECOND YOUTH CONGRESS CONVENED BY THE BUDI UTOMO organization in Jakarta, October 27–28, 1928, the Sumpah Pemuda (Youth Oath) adopted by its members was the first clear expression of the nationalist awakening underway in Indonesia. How did Indonesians get to this moment 300 years after the Dutch arrived in the archipelago to trade and, eventually, to administer the Indonesian archipelago as a part of their empire? How did they eventually achieve a declaration of independence on August 17, 1945?

As Indonesia scholar and political scientist Ben Anderson describes it, the adoption of the Sumpah Pemuda was the beginning of the construction of an "imagined community"—Indonesia—made up of an archipelago stretching from the northern tip of Sumatra to Papua in Melanesia. It was a nation in the image of the colonial state, imagined as a coming together of diverse cultures, languages, and inherited structures of aristocracy, calling for complex negotiations between and across all of them. As in other postcolonial states born in the twentieth century, such imagining was possible because of the shared colonial experience, with its common language, administration, and currency, which bound

9

together an otherwise diverse collection of fiefdoms, kingdoms, and sultanates that had often been in conflict over trade and land disputes.

Indonesia's preindependence history is not that of the cohesive and united archipelagic state that we know today but is instead the story of its constituent parts, which had looked outward, welcoming traders and teachers from other lands and absorbing the cultures and religions they brought with them.

Early Indonesia and Dutch Colonialism

Kingdoms, Religions, and International Commerce

In the first 1,500 years of the Common Era, the forces of trade and religion defined Indonesia's history. As early as 500 BCE, Chinese records document trade between southeast China and Java's northern coast of such commodities as rice from Java and spices from the eastern islands of the Indonesian archipelago. By the first century BCE, Indonesia was linked into a trade route connecting China to the Roman Empire via the Straits of Melaka (Malacca), and the goods traded along the route had expanded to include sandalwood and cloves from eastern islands including Maluku. There was also demand from the Arab states for spices such as mace, cloves, and nutmeg from the eastern islands. The Indonesian archipelago also became an important stop on the sea trade route between China and India. By the fourth century CE, the archipelago was experiencing an international trade boom that was to shape its future thereafter. By 1000 CE, Chinese traders had settled in enclaves in the archipelago's ports. The boom in international trade had two important effects on the archipelago's peoples—the importation and spread of new ideas, religions, and philosophies, and an injection of wealth and power that allowed its kingdoms to expand into pseudo-states, with vassal states and trade and economic systems that extended through the region.

Records show that Buddhist monks from China passed through the archipelago along the trade routes as early as the fourth century CE on their way to and from their studies in India. Scholars seeking to understand how Hindu-Buddhist culture arrived in Indonesia conclude that it was the consequence not of Indian religious scholars coming directly but rather of the scholars traveling through the region from China and of traders from India who brought religious teachings along with the goods they traded. The work of Édouard Chavannes (I-Tsing 1894) and, more recently, Michel Jacq-Hergoualc'h (2002) documents the travels and studies of Chinese scholar Yijing at the end of the seventh century CE. On his first trip to the holy places of Buddhism in 671 CE, Yijing stopped in at Srivijaya (Palembang, the capital of modern-day South Sumatra) to study Sanskrit and returned to study there for a longer period. His letters depict Srivijaya as a major center of Buddhist teaching in the late seventh century.

The Srivijaya kingdom, given its strategic position on the Straits of Melaka, took advantage of the trade boom to launch its political expansion, thus laying the foundations for its dominance over this part of the archipelago for the next 600 years. As Indonesia's first "state," we have some knowledge of Srivijaya as having a military force, including a strong naval force, and significant potential for raising revenue by taxing the traders passing through the Straits. The state's reliance on international trade to sustain it eventually led to its decline in the thirteenth century.

The earliest forms of written Malay came from Srivijaya, which is credited with promoting the spread of Malay language variants across the archipelago as a lingua franca and trading language. First recounted by French scholar George Coedès in the 1920s (Coedès 1975) at the time of Indonesia's national awakening, the story of Srivijaya became "evidence of early greatness, of archipelago unities" and was often referenced by the nationalists (Gelman Taylor 2003, p. 26).

Meanwhile, as Srivijaya dominated the west of the archipelago, the kingdom of Mataram, based in central and eastern Java, was also expanding. Following its merger in the early eighth century with the Ho-ling, a trading port on Java's north coast (probably between Pekalongan and Semarang), the Mataram kingdom had adopted significant Hindu-Buddhist influences (Kumar 2012, p. 112). The merger enriched Mataram's trade connections with China, and its aristocracy also saw in Hindu-Buddhist cosmology "a way of exalting their own positions" (Cribb 2000, p. 194). Through the eighth and ninth centuries, powerful families initiated the building of extraordinary temples in central Java— first the Borobudur temple by the Buddhist Sailendra family, which went on to take power in Srivijaya in the ninth century, and, soon after, the Prambanan temple by the rival Hindu Sanjaya family.

A UNESCO (United Nations Educational, Scientific and Cultural Organization) World Heritage Site since 1991, Borobudur is situated near Yogyakarta in Magelang, Central Java. Constructed between about 780 and 833 CE, it is the largest Buddhist temple in the world, consisting of nine stacked platforms, six square and three circular, topped by a central dome. The temple is decorated with 2,672 relief panels and 504 Buddha statues. It is thought that the temple was abandoned following the fourteenth-century decline of Hindu-Buddhist kingdoms in Java and the conversion of the Javanese to Islam. Sir Thomas Stamford Raffles, lieutenant governor of British Java, sparked Western interest in its existence in 1814. Borobudur has been preserved through several restorations, the largest being that undertaken between 1975 and 1982 by the Indonesian government and UNESCO.

In 1016 CE, the two great states of Mataram in Java and Srivijaya in Sumatra, having grown in wealth and power and linked by family ties, went to war, from which Srivijaya emerged victorious. Airlangga, Mataram's last major ruler, is thought to have been the son of a Balinese king and Javanese princess whose union had marked the cultural and political coming together of Java and Bali. Airlangga was a strong cultural figure, during whose rule the epic poem Arjunawiwaha (marriage of Arjuna) was commissioned and is retold as the story of Airlangga's life.

From the defeated Mataram kingdom a new Javanese empire emerged 200 years later, which encompassed East and Central Java as well as Bali—the mighty Hindu-Buddhist Majapahit kingdom. Under Hayam Wuruk, its ruler from 1350 to 1389, and his prime minister, Gajah Mada, the kingdom's influence extended from East and Central Java to coastal areas of Kalimantan, Sumatra, Maluku, and Bali. The expansion and success of the trading kingdom rested largely with growing demand from China and Europe for spices, especially nutmeg, mace, and cloves from Maluku and pepper from Sumatra and West Java (Brown 2003, p. 27). The trade relationship was so important to China that it sent a series of trade-diplomatic missions to the archipelago in the early fifteenth century, seven of which were led by Zheng He (Cheng Ho), a Muslim. The first of these, in 1405, consisted of 300 vessels carrying crews of over 27,000 (Cribb and Kahin 2004, p. 507). No doubt aimed at asserting Chinese hegemony in the region, the expedition set about destroying pirate fleets in the Melaka Straits. The Majapahit kingdom also returned to the aesthetic and cultural heights of its Mataram antecedent in the eighth century, with great achievements in architecture, art, and literature. It collapsed in 1527, following its defeat by its rivals in Java's first major Muslim state, Demak. Although Demak was a strong military power, its defeat of the Majapahit kingdom resulted in a power vacuum and triggered a long period of conflict and struggle between different holders of power in the archipelago. Because it had sustained 300 years of military and trade success, the Majapahit kingdom, alongside Srivijaya, became a model for Indonesian statehood in imaginings of nationhood in the early twentieth century.

The Coming of Islam, Circa 1200–1700

Historians describe the coming of Islam to Indonesia as "a process of assimilation" over three centuries, beginning in North Sumatra in the thirteenth century and progressing through Central and East Java, where it was more or less established by the sixteenth century.

By the ninth century, trade between Sumatran ports and Arab states had been established, and by the thirteenth century, Muslim traders from South Asia, the Middle East, and China lived in settlements in the major Indonesian ports (Gelman Taylor 2003, p. 93). Islamic teachers came to these settlements and mosques were built, establishing a community that expanded to include locally born Muslims. Entries in the diary of explorer Marco Polo on a visit to Sumatra in 1292 provide early evidence of Islam in the state of Perlak and probably also in neighboring Pasai, both located in what is now Aceh. Moroccan scholar and adventurer Ibn Battuta visited Pasai in the mid-1300s, noting in his record of his visit: "The sultan of Jawa, al-Malik az-Zahir, is a most illustrious and open-handed ruler and a lover of theologians. He is constantly engaged in warring for the Faith [against the infidels] and in raiding expeditions, but is withal a humble-hearted man who walks on foot to the Friday prayers" (Ibn Battuta 1929, p. 274).

Throughout the 1400s and 1500s, local rulers (*rajas*) converted to Islam, taking on the title of sultan and compelling their subjects to follow their new faith, thus embedding Islam in the governing political structures. These early Islamic sultanates were located mostly along the trade routes, at first in the small but strategically important port cities on the western and eastern fringes of the archipelago, such as Aceh in the west (ca. 1515) and Ternate (ca. 1460) in the east. Most coastal communities of the Indonesian archipelago had converted to Islam by the early seventeenth century, but historians point out that the spread was not "a continuous rolling wave of Islam" (Ricklefs 2001, p. 7) but a slow and complex process in which trade played an essential part.

There is debate and speculation about the reasons for the steady conversion to Islam through the 1400s and 1500s. One of the arguments put forward is that Islamic commercial law provided a better framework for trade and commerce than traditional or Hindu-based laws. Those engaged in trade also found that conversion to Islam gave them access to a valuable international trade network, with additional benefits such as access to credit, whether they were simple traders or the sultans, who also enjoyed the prestige of contact with the Ottoman Empire.

The rulers of the inland states adopted Islam a little later, with the state of Mataram in Central Java, which emerged in the sixteenth century and took the name of its eighth-century antecedent, not adopting Islam until the seventeenth century under Sultan Agung, who ruled from 1613 to 1646. The version of Islam practiced by the inland sultans was still in keeping with the traditional Hindu-Buddhist beliefs that regarded the ruler as the closest to god. The sultans were attracted to the teachings of missionaries of the Sufist mystical Muslim sect, whose claims of super-natural powers perhaps fitted well in Javanese court circles familiar with mysticism within Hinduism and Buddhism.

European Influences and the Dutch Traders

By the sixteenth century, booming markets for Indonesia's spices and other commodities in Europe precipitated the first European forays into Southeast Asia in attempts to bypass the Chinese and Middle Eastern mid-dlemen traders. In 1509, the Portuguese established a post at Melaka on the Malay Peninsula, already a major trading center at the entrance to the sea trading route. Initially expelled by the sultan of Melaka, the Por-tuguese returned to recapture the port of Melaka in 1511. This city was a strategically important point from which to control all trade from China through Southeast Asia to the Middle East and on to Europe. The Por-tuguese went on to establish significant settlements in key spice-trading ports in the Indonesian archipelago at Ternate, Ambon, Timor, and Tidore. Meanwhile, Melaka proved to be no great gain for Portugal, as Asian, British, and Dutch traders who did not want to do business with them sim-ply moved their business elsewhere, first to Aceh and later to Banten in West Java and to Makassar, South Sulawesi. The rivalry among the Eng-lish, Spanish, Dutch, and Portuguese to monopolize trade in the region set a course for major changes for the peoples of the Indonesian archipelago.

The Dutch sent their first trading fleets to the archipelago in the late 1590s and met with some success, but increasing demand in Indonesian domestic markets and an oversupply of tradable goods in Europe reduced their trading profits. Their response to declining profits was to merge several independent operators into the Dutch East Indies Com-pany (Vereenigde Oost-Indische Compagnie [VOC]), which was formed in 1602 and given the official right to the monopoly of all Dutch trade east of the Cape of Good Hope and west of the Magellan Straits, together with the right to exercise sovereignty in that region on behalf of the Dutch state (Cribb and Kahin 2004, p. 130). A governor-general was appointed to administer the company, whose headquarters were established in Batavia, Java, in 1619. From its beginnings, the VOC had expansionist and monopolistic ambitions. In 1641, the Dutch drove the Portuguese from Melaka, then took over Makassar in the 1660s and prevented foreign traders from operating in Banten. The VOC was quickly establishing a monopoly on the spice trade, enabling the Dutch to extract whatever commodities and revenues they could from the archipelago, sidelining and destroying traditional processes as they did so.

The expansion encompassed not only the trade routes but also the territories of the archipelago as it took advantage of inter-sultanate wars and rivalries. The sultanates had profited greatly from the spice trade by collecting revenue from export duties, but rivalries within and between sultanates resulted in power vacuums in which the VOC intervened actively (Locher-Scholten 2004, p. 39). Between 1670 and 1755, the VOC brokered a truce between rival siblings, which divided the Mataram kingdom into the sultanates of Surakarta and Yogyakarta. By the eighteenth century, the VOC was drawing revenues, or tributes, from these royal courts and, until the early nineteenth century, hired out VOC mercenaries to sultanates in successive wars against each other, thus acquiring further territories and concessions from the sultanates. By the early nineteenth century, Dutch attitudes toward working with the local sultanates in pursuit of their trade and increasingly territorial goals had shifted; they had come to recognize "the impossibility of constructing a colonial realm with indirect rule, based on weak local rulers and fluid Malay structures" (Locher-Scholten 2004, p. 44) and confirmed their desire to take over as colonial rulers in the fullest sense. It was to take almost another century before the Dutch achieved this scale of intervention in the archipelago.

As far as religion was concerned, however, the Dutch had no interest in proselytizing. Some local people converted to Christianity in the Dutch trading centers, such as Batavia, Ambon, Minahasa, and Roti in the east, but Islam continued to spread throughout the archipelago through the eighteenth and early nineteenth centuries. The sultans showed little interest in Dutch language and culture, and they continued to focus on Islamic scholarship. Thus, the Dutch became Christian rulers of a Muslim country.

Despite the successes of the VOC in the archipelago, it declined under the weight of growing administrative costs and increased market competition and was declared bankrupt in 1799. The company was nationalized and handed over to the Dutch government in 1800. Meanwhile, in late eighteenth century Europe, the rivalry of the Napoleonic Wars between Britain and France dominated politics. Napoleon overran Holland, creating a royal house with his brother Louis (Lodewijk) Napoléon as king in 1806. Over the next decade, as a consequence of the wars in Europe, the Dutch

East Indies experienced a period of rule by the French (1806–1811) followed by a period of British rule (1811–1815).

European Power Struggles and the Colonies

In 1808, King Lodewijk Napoléon appointed H. W. Daendels as governor-general of the Dutch East Indies, who in a relatively short time established major infrastructure and made legal changes. Notably, Daendels oversaw the building of the Great Post Road along the North Java coast and the construction of a new settlement at Batavia, using mostly indentured slave labor. Built at great expense and under cruel conditions for its indentured workers, its completion reduced the time for a letter to get from Batavia to Surabaya from two weeks to six or seven days (Cribb 2000, p. 110). In his dealings with the warring local rulers, Daendels was notoriously harsh, alienating many. In one instance, he sent the sultan of Banten into exile on Ambon and absorbed the territories of his sultanate for the Dutch East India Company (Vereenigde Oost-indische Compagnie [VOC]).

After five years in the Dutch East Indies, the French were replaced in Java by the British in 1811, following British domination of the French in the Napoleonic Wars. Sir Thomas Stamford Raffles was appointed lieutenant governor of British Java and largely continued Daendels's programs of administrative centralization and subjugation of the sultanates. Under Raffles, conflict with the sultanates escalated, reaching its climax in 1812 when British forces stormed the *kraton* (palace) in Yogyakarta, looted its archive, and sent the sultan into exile, replacing him with his son. Raffles was a passionate historian and, under his rule, significant historical sites, such as Borobudur, were drawn to Western attention and documented. His book *The History of Java* was published in 1817, two years after the colony was handed back to the Dutch in accordance with the Anglo-Dutch treaty signed at the conclusion of the Napoleonic Wars.

In 1825, what was essentially a civil war between supporters of Prince Diponegoro of Yogyakarta and other royal courts was precipitated by several factors, including a dispute over succession to the Yogyakarta sultanate. Up to 250,000 people perished in the Java War before it ended in 1830, when the Dutch intervened, using their superior military capabilities to dictate the terms of settlement, which included drawing up new boundaries for the Yogyakarta and Surakarta sultanates. In its aftermath, the aristocracy was forced under the rule of the Dutch as they ushered in their Cultivation System (Cultuurstelsel) policy, which required a portion of the colony's agricultural production to be export crops. By the mid-1800s, the Dutch had gained full economic and political control. The sultans of Yogyakarta and Surakarta no longer reigned; instead, they served the colonizer.

Imperial Expansion and the Cultivation System

At the end of the nineteenth century, the Dutch administration of its interests in the Indonesian archipelago was a complex bureaucratic structure, and subordination to the state varied from region to region. Some regions maintained significant autonomy in political, trading, and social affairs. The VOC had shown little interest in making territorial claims unless they were deemed necessary for business purposes. As a small European country, the Netherlands lacked the resources for a more concerted colonizing effort. Until steamships plied the trade route starting in the mid-1840s, it took many months for correspondence to travel between the Netherlands and the archipelago, allowing colonial administrators and local leaders alike some level of autonomy in decisionmaking (Locher-Scholten 2004, p. 53). As the nineteenth century drew to a close and Dutch imperialism extended into the next century, new levels of control were applied in new areas of life within the colony and existing controls were tightened.

Historians describe this period of modern imperialism in the Dutch East Indies as the period in which the Dutch sought to extend their influence beyond trade to the control of the means of production and to make territorial gains, including in the outer regions. So, while other European countries were expanding their empires by establishing new colonies, "the Netherlands had no cause . . . to look beyond those frontiers. It had quite enough blank spaces on the map within its own territory" (Locher-Scholten 2004, p. 266). The thirty-year Aceh War (1873–1904) was perhaps the final phase of this consolidation of Dutch authority in the archipelago and was an especially violent one, during which it secured lucrative natural resources, including black pepper, and eventually defeated resistance from the Acehnese sultanate (Reid 2005).

Introduced to Java in 1830 by the new governor-general, Johannes van den Bosch, the Cultivation System, or Exploitation System (van Baardewijk 1994, p. 151), was one of the main bureaucratic tools employed to achieve new levels of control. The system required villages to set aside one-fifth of their cultivable land and labor for the production of export crops. These crops, which were to include rubber, sugar, palm oil, and coffee, were to be delivered to the government as land rent. Exploitation of land and labor was nothing new for the colonial regime, but the introduction of the Cultivation System in Java represented the first systemic regime of exploitation. For the colonial ruler, the system was a success; for the peasants forced to plant the export crops, it initially meant concessions and losses in terms of land and labor, but, over time, they found ways to integrate the concessions and losses into their own patterns of production. By the late 1800s, this brought opportunities for private investment, with a particular interest in the plantation economy. On the east coast of Sumatra, tobacco, rubber, palm oil, and tea plantations flourished, opening up new agricultural tracts and necessitating the importation of large numbers of coolie laborers into these previously unsettled areas (Stoler 1995).

Morality and Colonialism

As the nineteenth century progressed, moral discomfort grew, both in Holland and in the Dutch East Indies, with Holland's colonial policies and the overt exploitation of the Cultivation System. In 1901, the Ethical Policy was put in place in response to moral protest from within the Dutch middle classes (*ethici*), which included writers, journalists, lawyers, and government officials in Java (Gelman Taylor 2003, p. 283). It was closely linked with the Association Principle, "which envisaged an assimilation of the Indonesian elite to modern Western secular civilisation and an eventual partnership in the tasks of government" (Cribb 1994, p. 5). The policy prioritized making education more available to Indies subjects and improving public health programs and infrastructure development in irrigation and agriculture. The policy imposed a welfare task that was intended, above all else, to "uplift" the natives, but not to provide a passage to self-sufficiency (Cribb 1994, p. 8). It was criticized then and has been since as highly paternalistic, overlooking the desire of Indonesians who hoped to achieve "self-rule through Indonesian leadership and Indonesian solutions" (Gelman Taylor 2003, p. 284). Historians agree that these programs were vastly inadequate to sustain the emerging aspirations of the colony's growing population (by 1930 just over 60 million) and failed to provide a pathway toward some form of decolonization. Nonetheless, access to education and new technologies equipped Indonesians with the tools to begin to assemble a vision and a movement for national independence.

Before the implementation of the Ethical Policy, few Indonesians had access to Western-style education and, therefore, few were able to join the public service, for which knowledge of the Dutch language was required. Reform of the education system to create a class of civil servants to administer the colony was a part of the Ethical Policy. Entry to Dutch-language schools had formerly been open only to members of the local aristocracy. With the educational reforms, the Dutch language was taught in the "First Class" schools open to the indigenous middle classes; once those students completed primary school, they were also eligible to attend the newly opened Training School for Native Officials (Opleiding School voor Inlandsche Ambtenaren [OSVIA]) and the School for Training Native Doctors (School tot Opleiding voor Indische Artsen [STOVIA]). The "Second Class" of government schools were separate institutions attended by lower-class Indonesians, Chinese, and Arabs, whose existence perpetuated established classifications of race and class and "a sense of difference between people of indigenous and foreign ancestry" (Gelman Taylor 2003, p. 287). A small number of elite women (mostly from the aristocracy) managed to gain a Western-style primary-school education but were unable to progress to the senior schools. One of these, Raden Ajeng Kartini (1879–1904), the daughter of an aristocrat from Jepara, became a symbol for women's emancipation in Indonesia and, later, a national hero, for her protest against the restrictions on women's access to post-primary education. A brilliant young girl, Kartini was prevented from continuing her studies after she had completed her years at a European primary school. Her struggle and frustration is documented in her letters to her friends as a teenager and young woman, published shortly after her early death at age twenty-five, following childbirth. Kartini is recognized for giving voice to early nationalist aspirations and for female emancipation (Zainu'ddin 1980).

Except for a small indigenous elite, "Dutch schooling was outside the daily existence of ordinary Indonesians" (Gelman Taylor 2003, p. 290). In 1930, only 0.14 percent of the total population was enrolled in Dutch-language schools and only a further 2.8 percent was in the state-run vernacular schools that were open to the masses. Extremely small numbers were enrolled in the small number of tertiary education institutions. Although not counted in the census, a range of private schools was operated by Christian missionaries and educational associations such as Taman Siswa, as well as Islamic schools, offering Western-style curricula alongside religious teaching. For those in the nongovernment, Second Class, and vernacular schools, the education reforms in the early 1900s had very little positive impact. Their real impact was seen in the small band of educated elites, people who did not emerge simply as loyal and capable colonial servants but became "a tiny and disaffected elite" (Ricklefs 2001, p. 203) who would go on to lead the anticolonial movement.

In the late 1800s and early 1900s, the Dutch also embarked upon significant modernization and urbanization projects in the colony, building railways and tramways and developing cities with cultural institutions and centers. Although these, too, were not within the reach of the ordinary Indonesian and did little in Java to alleviate the pressure of overpopulation and poor public health systems, they were examples of modernity that, encountered even peripherally, broadened horizons of thought and imagining about how Indonesians might shape their future (Colombijn and Coté 2014).

Birth of Nationalism

From 1908 on, new organizations among educated elites across the archipelago proliferated, as did trade unions, religious organizations, and other groups that linked villages and elites. Among these were a number with an increasingly nationalist frame and ideology based on various streams of political thinking, such as Islamic modernism, socialism, and Western-style modernity. Established in 1908, Budi Utomo is arguably Indonesia's first modern political nationalist association (although it was largely Java-centric in outlook). It emerged from the student cohorts at OSVIA and STOVIA and included members of the lower aristocracy (*priyayi*), who were not students, to promote their interests, principally within the colonial structure. In 1911, Budi Utomo was followed by the much larger mass-based and more radical Sarekat Islam (Islamic Union), which started as a cooperative movement to support Muslim batik traders in countering Chinese business dominance of their industry. In 1912, the more moderate and reform-minded Muhammadiyah was formed, and in 1926, the Nahdlatul Ulama (NU), which remain the largest Islamic organizations in Indonesia today (Ricklefs 2001; Tagliacozzo (ed.) *Southeast Asia and the Middle East* 2009).

Through the late 1920s and early 1930s, although there was agreement on the goal of independence, there was variety in the nationalist groups and streams of political thought about how independence could be achieved. Some elements within Sarekat Islam backed an armed revolution, which erupted and was quickly suppressed, as were rebellions launched by the Indonesian Communist Party (Partai Komunis Indonesia [PKI]) in 1926–1927. The Dutch responded harshly to the PKI rebellions, exiling over 1,000 of its members and stepping up police surveillance of all nationalist groups, but they were at a loss to develop an effective strategy to curb or co-opt the growing and popular opposition to their rule.

Established by the colonial government in 1917 as a means to control the spread of information, Balai Pustaka (Office of Literature) was a publishing house that published newspapers and facilitated the growth of a modern Malay literature. Over the next twenty years its activities allowed for a sense of unity to spread across the archipelago, which had not been possible previously. In 1918, there were forty newspapers, mostly in the Indonesian language; by 1938, this number had grown to 400 (Ricklefs 2001, p. 232).

Political reforms were also attempted in order to satisfy the growing aspirations of the Indonesians, stimulated partly by improvements in education brought by the Ethical Policy and by modernization more generally. The most significant of these was the introduction of the Volksraad (People's Council) in 1918 with European and Indonesian representatives, as well as representatives of other races, including the Chinese and Arabs. Established as an advisory body only, with some oversight of financial and budgetary matters, it initially had nineteen elected members, of whom ten were Indonesian, and nineteen appointed members, of whom five were Indonesian. Over the years the Council assumed greater responsibility for oversight of budget and legislation and was able to introduce new legislation. Its elected members were chosen by an electorate of a few thousand, most of whom were representatives of local councils. Appointed members were chosen by the governor-general, who at that time encouraged Indonesian involvement and critical contribution. Governor-General van Limburg Stirum appointed two Sarekat Islam leaders, Tjipto Mangunkusumo and Tjokroaminoto, hoping to curb their radicalism by bringing them into the cooperative frame of the Volksraad. In the three decades of its existence, the Volksraad was indeed critical of the colonial administration and exerted some pressure, but in the end, it was little more than a gesture on the government's part toward popular involvement, as the governor-general was under no obligation to follow any of its recommendations.

Given the token status of the Volksraad, the nationalists accepted that the impetus for change must come from outside the council, which is where the emerging leaders of the nationalist movement would be found. Many of them were already deemed dissidents by the Dutch and experienced periods of exile and detention. Generally, these leaders came from the left wing of the middle class and had been educated in the Dutch language in First Class schools but had chosen not to work for the government and gained the support of the masses in airing their significant grievances.

An Emerging Class of Nationalist Leaders

With the burgeoning of political organizations in the 1920s and 1930s, a new class of leaders emerged, mostly from members of the Dutch-educated elite who had resisted the path of colonial service, seeking instead to forge their own path as Indonesians. Among them was Sukarno, with a schoolteacher father from East Java and a Balinese mother. He was studying architecture at the elite Bandung Institute of Technology, where he established a study club in 1927. The club became the Partai Nasional Indonesia (Indonesian National Party [PNI]), which promoted an inclusive vision for an Indonesia based on the colonial territory, embracing the idea of creating unity out of its ethnic diversity, and based on secularism. Following the Youth Congress in Batavia in 1928, at which the slogan "One people, one language, one homeland: Indonesia" was adopted, there was a wave of popular opposition to Dutch rule, with several figures emerging as leaders representing various streams of political thought.

Sukarno was a highly charismatic and proficient orator who soon attracted the attention of the colonial authorities and was tried for crimes against the state and political order in 1930, and thereafter exiled. Because he was so popular, the Dutch ended his term of exile early, seeking to co-opt him by appointing him to the Volksraad. This did not have the desired effect, as he continued to speak about and publish his nationalist intentions and was exiled again in 1934, first to the island of Flores in eastern Indonesia and later on Bengkulu, off the west coast of Sumatra, where he remained until 1939.

Sukarno's fellow nationalist leaders, including Sutan Sjahrir and Mohammad Hatta, were also exiled during this time. Sjahrir and Hatta were both Sumatrans who sought to counter the Javanese contribution to the nationalist discourse, represented by Sukarno. Having received their tertiary education in the Netherlands, they represented Indonesian men (and some women) whose nationalism had developed while they were overseas. Hatta and Sjahrir were exiled by the Dutch to Boven Digul in West New Guinea and then to Banda Neira in eastern Indonesia for eight years, from 1934 to 1942 (Alwi 2008).

By the 1930s, it was apparent to the Dutch that the aim of their Ethical Policy to provide a level of emancipation, but not independence, to the Indonesians was backfiring because of the growth of secular nationalism and its class of educated political leaders. In the 1930s, a shift to conservatism was apparent within the colonial administration with the appointment of Governor-General de Jonge (1931–1936). De Jonge clamped down on the nationalist leaders, having them arrested, put on trial, and exiled. With political organization all but impossible throughout this period of repression, secular and Islamic nationalists alike turned to other forms of organization, such as study clubs, schools, and welfare services, which the Dutch also sought to curb. In 1932, de Jonge issued the Wild Schools Ordinance, which required government authorization to establish private schools. The ordinance was defeated because of opposition from the nationalists and from within the Volksraad. However, it signaled that the Dutch had started to understand how serious the potential for a united push against them had become. Indeed, without its leaders and under constant harassment from authorities, nationalism as a political movement was sufficiently repressed. In December 1935, several groups, including Budi Utomo and Persatuan Bangsa Indonesia, formed Parindra (Partai Indonesia Raya [Great Indonesia Party]), a party that backed independence through cooperation with the Dutch. Nonetheless, like those in the Volksraad who had initially believed that cooperation might lead to independence, by the mid- to late 1930s, these groups had also become disillusioned and convinced that the Dutch had no intention at all of proceeding toward decolonization.

As the global Great Depression took hold in the 1930s, severe economic crisis and suffering hit the colony as the prices received for its exports of sugar, rubber, and coffee dropped dramatically as demand from its traditional markets in Europe and North America decreased. In the Dutch East Indies, unemployment increased as plantations laid off workers and the civil service froze recruitment and reduced salaries. Imports from Europe also dried up, giving way to the importation of Japanese goods into the colony, which by 1934 accounted for 32.5 percent of all imports. This displeased the Dutch, who fought to reduce Japanese access to Indonesian markets. Just a few years later, Japanese interest in the resources of the archipelago would bring about yet another shift in the archipelago's history, involving external rulers but ultimately leading to independence for Indonesia.

Decolonization

War and Occupation, 1939–1945

When Hitler invaded the Netherlands in May 1940, martial law was immediately imposed in the Dutch East Indies and all public meetings were banned. Once again, war in Europe would have drastic consequences for the peoples of the Indonesian archipelago. However, unlike the Napoleonic Wars, the entry of an Asian power into what grew into a world war and the shift to the Pacific as a locus of contestation and conflict meant the Dutch East Indies was no longer simply a chattel or resource to be conquered for the war effort; it had become of new and critical strategic importance in a global conflict.

The Japanese attack on Pearl Harbor on December 7, 1941, followed two years of a US embargo on Japanese trade, imposed in 1939 in anticipation of Japan's formalizing an alliance with Germany and Italy in September 1940. The embargo left Japan in dire need of resources as it built its machinery of war, so it looked to its trade with Indonesia, as it had done in the past, to fill that gap. The Dutch pushed back by freezing Indonesian exports to Japan and Japanese assets in Indonesia in June 1941, but following the attack on Pearl Harbor a few months later, the Netherlands was at war with Japan. It was not long before the Japanese, with Indonesia's resources in its sights, invaded the archipelago, first entering South Sumatra in February 1942, before landing on Java on March 1, after defeating the Dutch and their allies in the Battle of the Java Sea. The nearby British colony, Singapore, also fell to the Japanese in February 1942.

Historians consider the period of Japanese colonial rule over the archipelago as one of the most crucial chapters in Indonesia's history. Before the Japanese occupation the Dutch had suppressed the nationalist movement, removing its leaders and threatening organizations that had nationalist ideologies. After three and a half years of Japanese rule, the nationalist movement flourished, backed by a large population of diverse ethnic groups and languages united in their desire for a revolutionary struggle for independence.

Initially, Indonesians welcomed the Japanese as usurpers of the Dutch colonizers and because of positive sentiment arising from their experiences with Japanese traders and business in the difficult 1930s. The Japanese allowed the red-and-white Indonesian flag to be flown and the national anthem, "Indonesia Raya," to be sung. They also garnered support by immediately removing Dutch and other Europeans from senior administrative positions and elevating Indonesian public servants in their place. However, positive sentiment toward the Japanese, particularly among the lower classes, but also generally across society, was not to last long, as Japanese demands on the Indonesian economy and disruption of its social structures set in. Any goodwill toward the Japanese evaporated within twelve months. Like the Dutch, the Japanese were intent on running the colony for their own benefit, particularly as a source of vital resources for their World War II effort, such as oil, rubber, and tin, in the short term, and to fulfill their larger goal of creating the Greater East Asia Co-Prosperity Sphere, comprising Japan, Manchukuo, China, and parts of Southeast Asia and free from Western imperialism.

During the first year of the occupation, Europeans, including Dutch and allied military and civilians (mostly women and children), were interned in camps where they endured extremely poor conditions and frequent violence, including the rape of women forced into sexual slavery as "comfort women" for Japanese troops. Once the European administrators were interned, the Japanese placed Indonesians in civil administrative positions, previously only the purview of Dutch or Dutch-trained staffers, in such services as postal and telegraph services, waste and water management, and public transportation. The occupation brought significant disruption to social structures in the cities and at the village level.

The Japanese turned Indonesia's economy toward its war effort, resorting to such measures as compulsory requisitioning of food, including rice, and the use of forced labor, which led to famine. The extremes of the use of forced labor were apparent in the creation of a cadre of laborers (*romusha*) who were sent across the archipelago and overseas to work for the Japanese war effort. This extreme measure had a profoundly severe effect at the village level, causing villages to decline as food and labor became scarce and villagers migrated to the cities.

The Dutch and English languages previously used in schools were replaced by Japanese, making higher education for Indonesians impossible. The Japanese calendar was used for official purposes, streets were renamed, and Batavia was renamed Jakarta. The Japanese set in place a campaign of anti-Western propaganda to get Indonesians behind the notion that they were united with the Japanese in the struggle for a new order in Asia. Although the anti-Western element of the propaganda resonated with the Indonesians, the Japanese underestimated the strength of the nationalist movement and the strategies developed by its leaders, including Sukarno, to take advantage of the platform that the Japanese had now given them. Moreover, the cruelty of the Japanese and the suffering caused by food shortages and forced labor very quickly undermined the overarching goal of gathering support for the Japanese empire and its Greater East Asia Co-Prosperity Sphere from the people of Indonesia, who, indeed, increasingly turned against what they saw as simply another colonial ruler.

A crucial aspect of the Japanese effort to motivate the people to get behind their greater goal was the establishment of mass mobilization organizations to spread their propaganda to the populace. Their first attempt, the Triple A Movement promoting "Japan, the leader of Asia;

Japan, the Protector of Asia; Japan, the light of Asia" failed. They realized that they would need to engage established local political leaders to help them in this effort. As time passed and the tide turned against Japanese military fortune in the region, the nationalist leaders soon assumed the upper hand and used the Japanese propaganda devices to promulgate their own message of independence and freedom from colonial rule of any sort.

Exiles Return

The Dutch had returned Sjahrir and Hatta from exile just before the occupation. When the Japanese called on their assistance, the two men decided that Hatta would cooperate with the Japanese while Sjahrir would establish an underground movement of mostly young, educated nationalists and establish contact with the Allies. Sukarno was returned to Jakarta by the Japanese in July 1942 and joined Hatta in cooperating with the Japanese. From the outset, Hatta and Sukarno saw the opportunity presented by Japan's anti-Western colonywide propaganda campaign to spread nationalism. Before entering into any agreement, the Indonesians demanded that the Japanese allow concrete steps toward independence to convince the Indonesian people that they were serious and, thereby, "fire the Indonesian people to make the sacrifices the Japanese demanded" (Anderson 1961, p. 9). As Sukarno explained it later, "To gain political concessions in terms of military training and administrative jobs for our people, we must make an appearance of collaboration" (Sukarno 1965, p. 173).

Although the two leaders had differed in their approaches in the past, they now set them aside in pursuit of the common goal—independence. In March 1943, encouraged by the Indonesian leaders, Putera (Pusat Tenaga Rakyat [Center of People's Power]) was established under the leadership of Sukarno, Hatta, Ki Hadjar Dewantoro, and from the Islamic organizations, Kiai H. M. Mansur. In October 1943, the volunteer army, Peta (Pembela Tanah Air [Defenders of the Fatherland]), was set up as an elite auxiliary guerrilla force in case of invasion. Other paramilitary bodies, including Heiho, were also established across the archipelago and trained by the Japanese, often using wooden rifles and bamboo spears in place of real arms. These infantry units would eventually become the backbone of the Indonesian army. In January 1944, Putera was disbanded and replaced by Jawa Hokokai (Javanese Service Association), with Sukarno and Hatta in senior roles. Deferring to the demands of Islamic organizations, the leaders established the Partai Majelis Syuro Muslimin Indonesia (Council of Indonesian Muslim Associations [Masyumi]).

The nationalists capitalized on the opportunity to speak to the masses through these communication channels, which reached right down to the village level. Sukarno used speaking tours that were broadcast by the radio service to promote the idea of a united Indonesia and to raise his own profile. He gave speeches to Peta battalions and members of the paramilitary groups on anti-imperialism, which his audiences took to encompass anti-Japanese imperialism. As Hatta and Sjahrir devised it, having always intended to activate a double strategy of apparent collaboration and underground resistance, these military and paramilitary units were simultaneously infiltrated by underground propaganda units, which rendered them overwhelmingly nationalist, anti-Japanese, anti-Dutch, and pro-Allies. The underground groups, including those led by Sjahrir, Amir Sjarifuddin, and others, had an important role in gathering intelligence from and disseminating pro-nationalist messages to the groups' members and down to the village level through a network of cooperatives coordinated by another close confidant, Dr. Sudarsono.

In their efforts to suppress what they saw as potentially disruptive and rebellious groups, the Japanese followed a similar pattern of co-opting opposition elements. To flush out and control the actions of increasingly rebellious youth groups, the Japanese established Angkatan Muda (Youth Association) in mid-1944. In doing so they hoped to thwart the efforts of increasingly hostile elements working underground (including some under Sjahrir's leadership) in spreading the nationalist message through mass organizations such as Peta. Anti-Japanese sentiment among young people, such as those at STOVIA, arose from such ordinances as a directive to cut their hair short, with failure to comply resulting in the students' imprisonment and expulsion from STOVIA. Political scientist George Kahin described the impact of the Japanese approach:

> Probably the deepest imprint of the Japanese occupation was left on the Indonesian youth, in particular those between fifteen and twenty-five years of age. Especially among those who received little previous education, and that was the large majority, the sustained intense Japanese propaganda left its mark. It narrowed and intensified their nationalist sentiments . . . many developed an extremely militant nationalism with a strong, emotional anti-Western bias. (Kahin 1952, p. 130)

Japanese concern about rebellion was very real. In February 1945, an attack by a Peta detachment on a Japanese armory in Blitar, East Java, resulted in fatalities on both sides. The Japanese began to fear that they were losing control of the military forces they had formed. Important here was the role of youth groups, both those associated with the elite military corps, Peta, and the paramilitary groups such as Heiho. These groups have been identified as forming "the vanguard of revolutionary nationalism" by early 1945 (Anderson 1961, p. 47) and were bringing others along with them, including student groups in urban centers working both openly and underground.

By March 1945, as it grew more apparent that they would lose the war, the Japanese were changing their attitude toward the nationalist movement. In October of the previous year, Japanese prime minister Kuniaki Koiso had announced that Indonesia would get independence in the near future. Concrete changes to Japan's policy quickly unfolded. On March 1 the Japanese established the Investigating Body for the Preparation of Indonesian Independence. At its first meeting in Jakarta on June 1, 1945, Sukarno laid down the ideological foundation for the Republic of Indonesia with his Pancasila (Pantja Sila, in the original spelling) declaration of five principles for the nation, what he called his "five precious pearls": "Nationalism . . . Internationalism . . . Government by Consensus . . . Social Justice . . . and Belief in God" (Sukarno 1965, p. 197). These principles were encapsulated in the notion of *gotong royong* (mutual/communal decisionmaking and cooperation). Islamic groups intervened subsequently to revise the first principle by including seven words known as the Piagam Jakarta (Jakarta Charter) to provide for adherents to Islam—"*dengan kewajiban menjalankan syariat Islam bagi pemeluk-pemeluknya* [with obligation for adherents of Islam to carry out Islamic law]," but it was soon clear to Muslims and non-Muslims alike that including such a provision could undermine the principle of equality for all citizens. When the constitution was announced on August 18, 1945, the Jakarta Charter was not included.

Thereafter, external events took over Indonesia's path to independence. The day after the United States bombed Hiroshima on August 6, 1945, the Japanese established the Panitia Persiapan Kemerdekaan Indonesia (Preparatory Committee for Indonesian Independence). On August 11, two days after US forces dropped a second bomb, this time on Nagasaki, Sukarno and Hatta flew to Saigon to meet the Japanese regional command, which assured them that Indonesia would be handed its independence on August 24. Events overtook this promise, however, and Japan surrendered to the Allied forces the day after Sukarno and Hatta returned to Indonesia, leaving the Indonesian leaders in political limbo; the Allies had not yet arrived to take control from the Japanese and to prepare for Indonesia's return to its previous colonizers. As Sukarno and Hatta carefully deliberated their next step, the younger generation quickly grew impatient for a declaration of independence.

On August 16, a group of *pemuda* (youth) kidnapped Sukarno and Hatta, taking them to Tasikmalaya in West Java, where the two leaders declared Indonesia's independence on August 17, 1945, in a short and simple statement that they both signed on behalf of the Indonesian people: "We the people of Indonesia hereby declare Indonesia's independence. Matters concerning the transfer of power and other matters will be executed in an orderly manner and in the shortest possible time" (Hatta 1951). The following day, at a meeting of the Preparatory Committee, the constitution was drawn up and the committee was reconstituted as the provisional national parliament, electing Sukarno as president and Hatta as vice president. The new unitary state was to have eight provinces, none of which corresponded with a particular ethnic group. Although the proclamation of the constitution did not occur until the next day and the *pemuda*'s actions had caught Sukarno and Hatta by surprise, they were nevertheless very well prepared. The Preparatory Committee for Independence was in place and the constitution had been drafted and redrafted in the month before the Japanese defeat. Indeed, it was the culmination of a campaign waged over several decades. The nationalists felt vindicated in declaring independence by the fact that the Dutch had made no attempt to oppose the Japanese but had merely acquiesced. They had neglected their obligation to protect the colony, thereby forfeiting any future claim to it.

Establishing a Nation-State

On August 18, 1945, the Republican government was established, and building on the drafts already prepared for the Preparatory Committee, the constitution was finalized within a week. As already mentioned, it did not include the Jakarta Charter, which was withdrawn in the final hours following debate about protecting the principle of equality for all citizens. Nonetheless, the issue raised by the charter would persist through the 1950s as Indonesia deliberated its permanent constitution, with clear lines drawn between those Islamic and non-Islamic parties. The first cabinet was announced, with the new ministers taking over the departments established by the Japanese and replacing the heads of government. Governors were appointed and provincial committees established for each of the eight provinces—West Java, Central Java, East Java, Sumatra, Kalimantan, Sulawesi, Maluku, and Sunda-Kecil (Lesser Sundas). Sukarno was appointed president; Hatta, vice president; and Sutan Sjahrir, prime minister.

On August 29, an army was fashioned out of the Peta units and other youth organizations, based in Jakarta with territorial units across the archipelago. It was named Tentara Keamanan Rakyat (People's Security Army [TKR]) and it seized government buildings from the Japanese. By late September, fighting between Japanese and Indonesian troops reached its most violent, just as British troops landed. The Allied forces commander in chief in Southeast Asia, Lord Mountbatten, had responsibility for accepting the Japanese surrender, releasing prisoners of war, disarming and deporting the Japanese, and establishing and maintaining law and order until the Dutch colonial administration could return. Mountbatten had very little, if any, knowledge and understanding of the situation in Indonesia, including what had transpired since the Japanese surrender two months earlier. The Allied forces' planning was out of step with what was unfolding across the archipelago, so they were utterly unprepared for what they faced when they landed. The British would be impressed by the efficiencies of the Indonesian nationalist administrative system and by many other things.

In the hiatus between the Japanese surrender and the Allied forces' assumption of control in Indonesia, Indonesia's new political leaders were content to wait and see, but the youth groups and military units forged under the Japanese in Java were more assertive, affirming their readiness by launching a campaign, known as Bersiap (Be Ready), against the returning Dutch within two weeks of the Japanese surrender. The terms of surrender required the Japanese occupying forces to lay down their arms and maintain order in Indonesia until the Allied Southeast Asia Command (SEAC) arrived. As Sukarno and Hatta had perhaps foreseen and hoped to avoid, following the declaration of Indonesia's independence on August 17, 1945, the Japanese called for Peta and Heiho units and other organizations to be disbanded. However, many of the Peta units retained their arms and disarmed the Japanese, sometimes violently and sometimes peacefully. Flying the Indonesian flag was also forbidden— an order that Sukarno overruled.

In October 1945, although Sukarno and Hatta had warned the Allied command that a backlash against Dutch troops was likely, they began returning to Indonesia under cover of the Allied forces. Dutch patrols began to appear in Indonesian towns and cities, attacking civilians in a manner commonly described as "trigger-happy." Very soon the Bersiap armed units launched attacks against the Dutch and Allied patrols and against unarmed Dutch civilians, including Indos (those of mixed European and indigenous descent), women, children, and ethnic Chinese minorities (Hewett 2016). The Allied forces' use of Japanese troops to restore law and order and reclaim cities held by Republican forces incited even more fervent attacks and clashes in Java, Sumatra, and Bali in the last months of 1945. In eastern Indonesia, where support for the Republic was less coordinated and weaker, Australian troops encountered little resistance as they accepted the Japanese surrender, took control of the territories, and handed them back to the Dutch (*Diplomasi* 1994, p. x). On the whole, the Allied forces in the Asia Pacific, led by the British and Americans, were underinformed and unprepared for what they encountered in Indonesia. Although reestablishing their rule in Indonesia was most certainly a priority for the Dutch, it was not a priority for the Americans and British and, as time wore on and the Republicans dug in their heels, the Allies' commitment to helping the Dutch restore their authority waned.

A crucial moment in the Republicans' campaign came in November 1945, when fighting broke out in Surabaya between a *pemuda*-formed wildcat army and SEAC troops, among whom were many Gurkhas from British India. An assault on Republican forces commenced on November 10 after the British commander, Brigadier A. W. S. Mallaby, was killed on October 30. British retaliation by air and sea and on the ground was uncompromising and resulted in heavy Republican losses, which galvanized local and international support for Indonesian independence. The Tenth of November continues to be commemorated in Indonesia each year as National Heroes Day. Following the Battle of Surabaya, the British encouraged the Dutch and Republicans to seek a peaceful compromise, and diplomatic negotiations between the Dutch and Indonesians commenced. The starting positions of both sides were, however, diametrically opposed, as the Dutch simply could not accept the Indonesian declaration of independence and remained adamant that they had not renounced sovereignty over the Dutch East Indies.

Politics in the Early Years of the Republic

In 1945, the Republic of Indonesia established its multiparty government in Yogyakarta, where a succession of revolutionary cabinets sought to govern in the middle of war and became increasingly isolated from the rest of the archipelago as they did so. Moreover, significant divisions threatened the Republic before it could achieve true independence, with cleavages transcending party lines. The nationalist leaders—Hatta, Sjahrir, and Sukarno—dominated the early cabinets but faced internal opposition from other elites, such as national-communist Tan Malaka. The most significant incident of this internal opposition, the Madiun Affair in late 1948, arose as a result of accusations that the nationalist leaders were making too many concessions in negotiations with the Dutch. Indonesia scholar Herb

Feith described the affair as an intra-elite conflict that is explained by the roles of two particular skill groups that were complementary but also in conflict. He characterized one group as the "administrators" and the other as the "solidarity makers," but both of them were the well-educated products of Western or Muslim institutions. This division was manifest in political parties, the military, and the bureaucracy; as Feith (1962, p. 26) noted, "In every case the question to be decided was whether power and status should go to men with modern-type skills or to men with political qualifications." Among the nationalist leadership, Hatta represented the administrators and Sukarno the solidarity makers.

Negotiations commenced in Batavia on February 10, 1946, chaired by British special envoy to Indonesia, Sir Archibald Clark Kerr, between Sjahrir, prime minister in the second and fourth Republican cabinets, and the acting governor-general, Netherlands Indies-born H. J. van Mook. In November 1946, the Allied troops departed, by which time the Dutch had an estimated 55,000 troops in Java, and the Netherlands Indies Civil Administration had been reestablished in Java's major centers and in the outer islands, with the notable exception of Aceh. The status of the remaining Dutch-controlled regions remained under negotiation. The Dutch convened a meeting of delegates from Dutch-controlled regions of eastern Indonesia in the Sulawesi town of Malino in July 1946, to which no representatives of the new Republic were invited. The Malino meeting was followed in December 1946 by the Denpasar Conference, at which the State of the Great East was established and soon after renamed the State of East Indonesia. It comprised the Groote Oost, which was one of three governments in the outer islands formed in 1938, the other two being Sumatra and Borneo. The Republican state, together with the three outer island states of Borneo, Sumatra, and Groote Oost, would come under the umbrella of the United States of Indonesia, as an independent self-governing member of the Kingdom of the Netherlands. By the conclusion of the negotiations, the Dutch had accepted the Republic's de facto authority in Java, Madura, and Sumatra, along with the precept that those areas occupied by Allied or Dutch forces would gradually come under Republican control. These arrangements were confirmed in the Linggajati Agreement on November 15, 1946, which the Dutch House of Representatives ratified in a modified version on March 25, 1947.

Negotiations on the Brink of War

The Linggajati Agreement did not grant Indonesian Republicans what they wanted—independence as a nation-state. Nor were the Dutch happy with it, so they planned military action focused particularly on bringing plantations, essential for rebuilding the Dutch colonial economy, under their control (Frakking 2012, p. 339). On July 20, 1947, the Dutch crossed demarcation lines in what became known as the First Police Action, taking over Republican territory, including parts of Java, East Sumatra, and Palembang, which were key strategic centers for ports, oil reserves, and plantations. The Dutch planters returned to their plantations in Java and Sumatra, but not without considerable resistance. Under the command of Colonel A. H. Nasution, the Republican Army engaged in guerrilla tactics against the planters in isolated locations, but with significant strategic impact as they disrupted a vital element within the Dutch economy. Within a few months, the planters became increasingly fearful and called for greater protection, which simply could not be provided by the limited Dutch military and policy resources. The Republic's Tentara Nasional Indonesia (Indonesian National Army [TNI]), made up mostly of irregular soldiers, was estimated to number 170,000, as against Dutch forces of around 100,000 troops.

In this police action, the Dutch underestimated the strength of nationalist sentiment among Indonesians and their military capacity. They had also failed to gauge world opinion, which was expressed in demonstrations against the First Police Action in Australia and Britain and at the United Nations (UN), which in August 1947, with the support of the United States, formed its Committee of Good Offices (GOC), and later the United Nations Commission on Indonesia (UNCI). Taking a mediating role in the Dutch-Indonesian conflict, the United Nations Security Council gave the Netherlands government no alternative but to negotiate with Sukarno, Hatta, and their emissaries. The United Nations ordered a cease-fire on August 4, 1947, and invited Sjahrir to present the Republic's case in New York City, an action that would legitimize the Republic as an equal partner in the dispute. The newly established GOC, chaired by the United States and on which Belgium represented the Netherlands and Australia represented the Republic, sent cease-fire observers to Indonesia so that another round of negotiations could commence. Meetings were held on board the *USS Renville,* anchored in Jakarta Bay, resulting in the Renville Agreement of January 17, 1948, which recognized a cease-fire along the "van Mook Line" of the most advanced Dutch positions in Indonesia. This gesture of compromise from the Republicans won them the goodwill of the Americans, but it led to the fall of yet another Republican cabinet, that led by Amir Sjarifuddin, who was accused of going too far in compromising with the Dutch. By this time the Dutch-held areas in Java,

Sumatra, and East Indonesia had succeeded in blockading Republican-held areas, so the Dutch forged ahead with their plans to create a federated United States of Indonesia, with or without the Republicans' agreement. Within the states held by the Dutch, pro-Republic support built steadily among both the elites and the masses.

Frustration and anger over the territorial concessions made to the Dutch in the Renville Agreement grew at the same time that Cold War tensions were reaching their height around the world (Swift 1989). Disquiet within the Republican camp following the Renville Agreement included sidelining left-wing politicians under Hatta's nonparliamentary government and coincided with the return in August 1948 of the Indonesian Communist Party (PKI) leader Musso, from lengthy exile in the Soviet Union. The PKI made a significant attempt to wrest power, which brought the party into violent conflict with the Republican army, reaching a climax in the town of Madiun in late September. As pro-PKI forces were pushed back by government units, they targeted Masyumi and Partai Nasional Indonesia leaders. PKI leaders were tracked down and killed or captured, and the PKI was removed as a threat to the Republican leadership. The Madiun Affair in the closing months of 1948 established a legacy of hostility between the army and the PKI that lasted for decades. Moreover, by their retaliatory actions the Republicans had shown that they were anti-communist at a moment in history when the Cold War was beginning to have an impact on world order, and thus they secured US support for their negotiations with the Dutch.

Another aspect of the Renville Agreement that was to have a lasting effect on the new Republic was the ceding of West Java to the Dutch. Radical Muslims led by S. M. Kartosuwirjo responded to this by establishing the Darul Islam (Islamic Armed Forces of Indonesia) resistance movement in May 1948 and by declaring in August 1949 the Indonesian Islamic State (Negara Islam Indonesia [NII]). This response lay behind a series of regional struggles against the Republic over the next decades in other regions, including in Central Java, South Sulawesi, South Kalimantan, and Aceh (Solahudin 2013a; Crouch 2014, p. 59).

Second Dutch Police Action

Faced with growing international opposition to their presence in Indonesia and intractable negotiations, the Dutch felt they had little choice other than to launch unilateral military action. In December 1948, in their Second Police Action, the Dutch successfully took Yogyakarta, the seat of the Republican government, and arrested Sukarno, Hatta, and other leaders. They cut supplies of food and other necessities to Republican areas, but, once again, underestimated guerrilla resistance and the extent of civilian noncooperation. Moreover, leaders of some of the federated states, including Premier Anak Agung Gde Agung of East Indonesia, opposed the Second Police Action. The Dutch failed to comprehend that the Republican leaders had allowed their capture in anticipation of the international condemnation that it would attract. Ultimately, it was international pressure, particularly from the United States, and political failures domestically, that forced the Dutch back to the negotiating table and to relinquish their claims in the archipelago.

At the Dutch-Indonesian Round Table Conference held in The Hague from August 28 to November 2, 1949, terms were agreed for the transfer of sovereignty to a Republic of the United States of Indonesia (RUSI), which was to include the Republican and federated states. The transfer document was signed by the Dutch queen Juliana on December 27, 1949. In the following months, resistance and revolt by remnants of the Dutch army shifted opinion within the federated states in the Republic's favor, and by the end of March, most of them had joined the Republic. Ongoing resistance in East Indonesia, mostly from Ambonese pro-federalist politicians and *adat* (traditional) leaders, with soldiers in the Dutch colonial army, proclaimed the Republic of South Maluku in Ambon on April 25, 1950. The resistance was eventually crushed, and the single unified state was established across the archipelago. Nonetheless, there were many challenges ahead for the new Republic.

After five years of conflict, the economy and infrastructure of Indonesia were devastated. Its peasant-based population lacked the education and skills needed to rebuild them, and factions and bitterness between and within political groups would rise again to the surface. The form of government adopted in the independent nation-state—parliamentary democracy—was a Western model that was not necessarily suited to the cultural, political, ethnic, and geographic diversity of Indonesia, and its suitability would be debated for many years. Given the complex political structure of the Republic and the many federal states, the experiences of the revolution varied, as did ambitions and hopes for the new state (Kahin 1985). For many in the Republic, what had bound the peoples of Indonesia through five years of revolution was the revolution itself; they had been united against a single foe. What remained to be seen was what would emerge once the pressure of an external foe was no longer there to bind the nation and "divisions within Indonesian society began to reassert themselves" (Zainu'ddin 1980, p. 241).

Sukarno's unifying vision of a state based on the Pancasila and the principle of *gotong royong* would ideally encompass the main streams of thought and traditions in Indonesia—Javanese, Muslim, and Western traditions. Nevertheless, as Sukarno admitted,

> Challenges overwhelmed us on all sides. With industry completely undeveloped, with insufficient foodstuffs and insufficient confidence, with a people scarred by feudalism, colonialism and fascism, most of whom couldn't read or write—we still had to pick ourselves up and make order out of the chaos (Sukarno 1965, p. 264).

3

The Slide into Authoritarianism

THE SUKARNO ERA OF INDONESIA'S HISTORY WAS A PERIOD OF economic and political instability as the new nation-state attempted to find its feet, addressing internal divisions, establishing new systems of governance, controlling and regulating the economy, and making its first forays into representing itself on the international stage. The government's first nation-building tasks were, on the one hand, practical and technical, involving education and infrastructure projects, drafting of laws, and establishing peace and security. On the other hand, it faced the task of building a nation of peoples with a unified and common outlook, purpose, and vision for a future that embraced modernity and an all-Indonesian culture that abandoned old divisions.

The Sukarno Era

Liberal Democracy, 1950–1957

In 1950, the Indonesian population was largely illiterate. Newly independent Indonesia made education a priority. By 1961, literacy had risen to 46.7 percent of the population, up from the 7.4 percent recorded in the 1930 census. The population continued to grow rapidly, rising from an estimated 77.2 million in 1950 to 97 million in 1961, with urban centers growing particularly fast—Jakarta's population exceeded 2 million by 1961.

As a condition of the November 1949 Round Table Conference Agreement, the Dutch were to continue to operate their businesses, including those in agriculture, shipping, and banking. The economy was slow to recover from the war against the Dutch; demand for goods was high as the population grew and domestic development restricted export earnings from oil and other resources. Moreover, the continued dominance of key industries, such as the oil industry, shipping, and banking, by foreign-owned businesses meant that Indonesia was not economically independent. Between 1950 and 1957, inflation and the cost of living increased by 100 percent. Independence had not brought the prosperity Indonesians might have hoped for, but, for Sukarno and other national leaders, the development of social ideals came before economic progress; economic prosperity would follow national stability and the primacy of nationalism. Throughout the early 1950s, demand for goods outstripped supply and, with little foreign aid to fill the gap, inflationary pressures were strong. The cash-flow problem meant that critical infrastructure projects, such as the maintenance of major roads and irrigation systems, were not carried out.

Political leaders set about filling the gaps in the 1945 constitution to produce a "resolutely democratic constitution" heralding the rule of multiparty democracy and "free political life" for the decade ahead (Bourchier 2008, p. 100). The 1950 constitution brought into being the unitary Republic of Indonesia on August 17, 1950. Throughout a necessary period of transition, the nation faced many challenges as it sought to unify its various regions and political groups. Until the first national parliamentary election was held in 1955, the political system was adopted when the Dutch handed over sovereignty prevailed, whereby the president appointed the prime minister, who then formed a cabinet.

The political vehicle for the newly formed nation-state was democracy, but as Feith and others have detailed, democracy and constitutional democracy were understood and interpreted across the political parties and within the populace in very different ways, and even perceived at times as aspirational. A symbiosis of democracy and modernity lay beneath the forward-looking orientation of the early Indonesian state. As Feith (1962, p. 42) put it,

> Sometimes democracy was an abstract symbol of future aspirations. At other times it was thought of as a legitimizing principle and an educational and nation-building force, and then it was usually linked with parliament and parties, cabinet responsibility, and elections. But it was only very rarely associated with such features of the constitutional system being adopted as individual rights, majority rule and minority rights and the institutionalized opposition.

Indonesians had little experience of participation in constitutional politics or the workings of parliamentary institutions; only a few could draw from their limited involvement with Dutch parliamentary politics and the prewar Volksraad. At the time that the Round Table Conference Agreement was signed in November 1949, it was "expedient for Indonesia to adopt Western constitutional forms" (Feith 1962, p. 43).

In the early years of independence, the multiparty system was highly unstable; there were five cabinets between December 1949 and the national elections in September 1955. Politicians and observers hoped for stability once the people had had the opportunity to elect their own representatives in government. Meanwhile, the army continued as a significant center of power in Indonesian society, with its moral authority bound up in its role as a revolutionary army that had fought for and won Indonesia's independence. Concerned about losing power, regional commanders resisted Colonel Nasution's efforts to professionalize the armed forces by reducing their numbers and overhauling their command structures. At the same time, the inherent instability of the 1950s required military action to deal with such disturbances as the separatist/Islamic rebellions in Ambon, Aceh, and South Sulawesi; the persistence of the Darul Islam movement in West Java; and the unresolved question of West Irian's inclusion in the Republic. Against this backdrop of unrest, politicians and bureaucrats sought to build institutions and establish their own centers of power.

Bandung Conference. In the midst of these significant domestic concerns and preparations for the September 1955 national elections, President Sukarno and Prime Minister Ali Sastroamidjojo launched the fledgling Republic into international politics. The Indonesians led the first conference of leaders from Asian and African nations, held in Bandung, West Java, on April 18–24, 1955. It followed a meeting in Colombo, Sri Lanka, a year earlier of the prime ministers of these newly decolonized and independent states: Ceylon, Burma, Indonesia, India, and Pakistan. The Bandung Conference was attended by representatives from twenty-nine countries, most of them newly decolonized nations, but also from the People's Republic of China and other Asian states (Mackie 2005). Held at a time when international relations were becoming increasingly polarized along Cold War lines, the Bandung Conference was a major international event. Observers at the conference were fulsome in their praise for the impressive multilingual Sukarno and Prime Minister Ali. It was considered a great success, launching the beginnings of the Non-Aligned Movement of nations, although it remains essentially a one-off event with no lasting institutional legacy. For Indonesia and other newly decolonized states in attendance, the conference was a platform for anticolonialism and anti-imperialism and for calls for peaceful coexistence between nations (Finnane and McDougall 2010). In effect, it reinforced the earlier proclamation by then minister for foreign affairs, Mohammad Hatta, of Indonesia's "free and active" foreign policy, which heralded nonalignment with either US or Soviet interests: "Her independent policy keeps her from enmity with either party, preserves her from the damage to her own interests that would follow from taking sides, and permits her to be friends with all nations on a basis of mutual respect" (Hatta 1953). Jamie Mackie described the conference as the "landmark success story of Sukarno's commitment to non-alignment," entrenching nonalignment as central to Indonesia's foreign policy position for the next decade (Mackie 2010, p. 20). In domestic politics, it soon became clear that the success of the conference and Ali's leadership of it gave his party, Partai Nasional Indonesia, a well-timed boost so close to the elections.

Elections. After more than two years of preparations and public education programs, the first democratic elections were held on September 29, 1955, with more than twenty parties contesting seats in the national parliament. In addition to the large national parties, such as the Islamic parties (Nahdlatul Ulama [NU] and Masyumi), the Communist Party (Partai Komunis Indonesia [PKI]), the Socialist Party (Partai Sosialis Indonesia [PSI]), and the Indonesian National Party (PNI), there were also regionally and ethnically based parties. More than 39 million Indonesians voted—a 90 percent turnout (Feith 1962, pp. 434–435)—in elections that were peaceful, with only traces of intimidation by some parties, mostly in villages where local and religious leaders put pressure on people to vote along certain lines. By October, the vote count had delivered some surprises for the political elite. Four major parties of significantly different ideological positions emerged with relatively equal political power. PNI won 22.3 percent of the vote, Masyumi 20.9 percent, NU 18.4 percent, and PKI 16.4 percent, which together made up 78 percent of the vote. It was not entirely unforeseen that the "big four" would win so many votes, but the very poor showing of some parties, such as PSI, with only 2 percent of the vote, and the Partai Indonesia Raya (Great Indonesia Party [Parindra]), which had played major roles in revolutionary and early Republican cabinets, surprised observers (Feith 1962, p. 436).

Following the 1955 elections, the number of parties with representatives in the parliament rose from twenty to twenty-eight. None of the big four had won enough of the vote to govern outright, so the political situation remained unchanged, as a coalition needed to be formed to govern. The parties were riddled with corruption and, with the exception of the

PKI, were ill disciplined and poorly organized. The elections reinforced regional divisions between Java and the outer islands as each of the big four, except for Masyumi, had won over 85 percent of its votes in densely populated Java, which was then home to two-thirds of Indonesia's population. The election results hardened the three dominant streams of political thinking—nationalism, religion (Islam), and socialism. As they had before the 1955 elections, parliamentary cabinets continued to fall as coalitions crumbled. Stepping away from his constitutional role, President Sukarno became increasingly outspoken and critical of parliamentary democracy, describing it as based upon inherent conflict rather than on the Indonesian concept of harmony.

Guided Democracy, 1957–1965

"Guided democracy" was explicitly authoritarian, bringing about a period of political repression and curbing of the freedom of the media and the judiciary in Indonesia. The same set of identities and players remained in place, but they played their roles within a changed set of rules and institutions. Above it all was Sukarno, with his exclusive ideological goals, around which the two largest holders of power, the armed forces and the PKI, vied for his attention, influence, and ultimately, power.

In March 1957, under pressure from the army, the second Ali Sastroamidjojo cabinet resigned. Martial law was declared, and the legally elected parliament was disbanded. In its place Sukarno appointed a Dewan Nasional (National Council) of forty-one representatives of functional groups, which he chaired, and a Kabinet Karya (Working Cabinet) headed by a nonparty independent, Djuanda Kartawidjaja. Sukarno argued for a system of government that was more authentically Indonesian. On July 5, 1959, the 1945 constitution was reimposed and reinterpreted to enable Sukarno to be installed as both head of state and head of the government, giving him back the power to appoint and dismiss cabinet members (Bourchier 2008, p. 100), which the 1950 revision of the constitution had removed.

Opposition to the president grew on various fronts at home and overseas throughout 1957. On November 30, Sukarno survived an assassination attempt as he was leaving his children's school, in what came to be known as the Tjikini Affair. Blame for the attack was leveled at a military faction sympathetic to rebellious officers in the Sumatran regional command with links to the Masyumi Party, although this was never proven (Kahin and Kahin 1995, p. 234). In the US Embassy in Jakarta and the US State Department, concern was growing about Sukarno's closeness to the strengthening PKI (Kahin and Kahin 1995, pp. 117–118), and at the United Nations, Indonesia's claims over West Irian were met with opposition, as two-thirds of the General Assembly voted against a motion to support Indonesia's request that the Dutch negotiate over the territory. The campaign for West Irian has been described as "peculiarly Sukarno's" (Lev 1966, p. 48). Sukarno had warned there would be consequences if the United Nations rejected Indonesia's claim. Within days of the vote in the United Nations in November 1957, the army began to seize Dutch businesses across the country, thereby assuming control of major economic interests and adding to its own power base. In early December, the government issued an order expelling 46,000 Dutch nationals (Lev 1966, p. 49). The takeovers resulted in a further decline in Indonesia's economy, but Sukarno and his supporters defended them as necessary to establish a truly independent nation and economy.

The resource-rich regions of Sumatra and Sulawesi had become increasingly restive during this period. They did not trust Sukarno and wanted greater autonomy over their economies at a time of growing inflation and general economic depression brought on by the poor economic policies of the so-called Guided Economy (Thee 2009, pp. 53–54). In February 1958, leaders from Masyumi and PSI established the Revolutionary Government of the Republic of Indonesia (Pemerintah Revolusioner Republik Indonesia [PRRI]) in Padang, West Sumatra, with Sjafruddin Prawiranegara as prime minister and a cabinet that included leading politicians and former ministers. They hoped to call Sukarno's bluff and force an ultimatum that he dissolve the Kabinet Karya and install a new cabinet led by Hatta and the sultan of Yogyakarta until elections could be held; they also wanted to get Sukarno to return to the presidential powers as defined in the 1950 constitution (Kahin 1999). They were not mounting a rebellion to break up or break away from the Republic but wanted to force change at its center and turn it away from authoritarianism (Elson 2008, pp. 195–196). Armed struggle continued for three years, until the PRRI leaders and soldiers gradually surrendered between April and September 1961. At about the same time, there was a rebellion, known as Permesta (Piagam Perjuangan Semesta [Universal Struggle Charter]), in South Sulawesi, which, like the Sumatra rebellion, had the support of local military commanders. The central government reacted emphatically against Permesta, too, launching attacks on Padang and Manado in quick succession and crushing Permesta by June 1958.

Both the PRRI and Permesta groups received support from the United States through covert Central Intelligence Agency (CIA) operations that provided military support, arms, and supplies (Kahin and Kahin 1995). As the Cold War intensified, the United States became concerned about the increasingly autocratic nature of Sukarno's Guided Democracy, especially about the increasing role within it of the Indonesian Communist Party (Doeppers 1972). Sukarno's uncompromising efforts to introduce a traditional and harmonious vision of Indonesia at the expense of tolerating difference and democracy meant that those offering alternative understandings of Indonesia, whether they be Islamists, separatists, or regional dissidents, were left with few options other than "to go outside the cauldron of parliamentary politics and adopt confrontationist or violent efforts to achieve their goals" and face the state's uncompromising response, which often took the form of violent retribution (Elson 2008, p. 197).

Over the next few years, Sukarno became more and more autocratic as he increasingly saw himself at the center of the nation. In 1959, he dissolved the Konstituante (Constitutional Assembly), thereby ending any last semblance of parliamentary democracy in Indonesia. Because of their part in the rebellions, both Masyumi and PSI were banned in August 1960, and many of their members fled into exile, thus ending any debate about whether the foundation of the nation should be Pancasila or Islam. In April 1961, all but ten political parties were dissolved by presidential order; those remaining were PNI, NU, PKI, Murba, Partai Syarikat Islam Indonesia (Islamic Union Party [PSII]), Persatuan Tarbiyah Islamiyah (Perti), Partai Ikatan Pendukung Kemerdekaan Indonesia (IPKI), Partai Indonesia (Partindo), and two Christian parties. The army supported Sukarno and Guided Democracy because it eliminated elections, thus reducing the opportunity for the PKI to make further gains, although Sukarno continued to engage the PKI to counterbalance the army's power (Crouch 1978). For those groups, as Feith (1964) put it, "the triangle changes shape"; the army had the guns and the PKI could mobilize the masses, and both looked to Sukarno for support in the hope of becoming his successor. Meanwhile, Sukarno continued to balance these two forces until he eventually proved too weak to hold the balance any longer. Led by Army Chief of Staff General Nasution, Guided Democracy also marked the beginning of the participation of military officers in civilian government, which led to the later implementation of the *dwifungsi* (dual-function) doctrine. Martial law remained in place for six years, from 1959 to 1965, during which time political activity was limited and the army became entrenched at the center of the nation's power.

On Independence Day, August 17, 1959, having dissolved the Konstituante, Sukarno announced to the nation the ideology behind Guided

Democracy and declared it the path toward the "rediscovery of our revolution." His speech was elevated into the Manipol USDEK (Political Manifesto of the Republic), which encompassed the 1945 constitution, Indonesian socialism, Guided Democracy, Guided Economy, and Indonesian identity. Government, schools, and the media were required to adopt the ideology, and some media organizations that failed to do so were subjected to bans. In a further example of his use of symbols and acronyms, Sukarno introduced the doctrine of NASAKOM (Nasionalisme, Agama, Komunisme) in an effort to establish an alliance of communist, Muslim, and nationalist parties and organizations to counterbalance the military. In this doctrine, Sukarno was in part reviving an argument he had written about as a student in the 1920s—that parties based on religious belief, nationalism, and communism were not incompatible (McIntyre 2005, p. 72). Commentators have remarked that the requirement to use the vocabulary of this doctrine did more to raise the level of political uncertainty and anxiety than to convince Indonesians of a truce between these groups (Cribb 1999, p. 32).

As the nation drifted into radicalism in 1959, hyperinflation was almost permanent. In the late 1950s and early 1960s, there was widespread hunger and malnutrition across the country, largely because of a shortage in rice and other food supplies, which Pierre van der Eng (2012) attributed to a complex mix of factors, including drought, but principally to mismanagement of the logistical agencies. Nationalization of foreign firms and protectionist policies ruined the export and manufacturing industries upon which Indonesia relied heavily (Thee 2009, pp. 51–52). The economic crisis deepened and the rupiah was devalued by 75 percent in late August 1959 (Crouch 1978). Foreign-owned businesses, which were at first forced to concede operations by trade union groups with links to the PKI, were soon brought under the control of the military, seemingly following a pattern of economic and administrative engagement by the military that had begun in the wake of the regional rebellions. As the takeover and nationalization of Dutch-owned companies continued, the government, led by elements within the army, also turned its focus to ethnic Chinese, who commonly played the role of middleman in the economy, particularly in the rural areas. The army was empowered by General Nasution's instruction on May 12, 1959, for regional commanders to impose controls over the residence and movement of foreigners. As the army expanded its business interests, it sought to dislodge Chinese and Arab interests. In November 1959, a presidential ruling, Persatuan Presiden 10 (PP10), was introduced to ban retail trading by "aliens" in rural areas, requiring ethnic Chinese to move to urban centers, sometimes forced to do so by the army (Purdey 2006, p. 11). Consequently, relations between China and Indonesia weakened, and the Chinese government sent ships to Indonesia to repatriate those who wished to leave, an offer accepted by an estimated 199,000 Chinese Indonesians (Coppel 1983).

By 1961, with the PRRI and Permesta rebellions suppressed, the army was freed up to deal more intensively with another rebellion causing irritation to the central government—the Darul Islam movement in West Java. In late 1962, the army captured and executed its leader, Karto-suwirjo, and effectively ended the movement. Meanwhile, Sukarno drew military support into his campaign to complete the process of decolonization by including West Irian in the Indonesian nation. In his Trikora (Tri Komando Rakyat [Peoples' Triple Command]) speech on December 19, 1961, Sukarno announced the escalation of Indonesia's claims on Papua, into which there had already been military incursions for some time. Investment in its military campaigns and in nation-building infrastructure projects at a time of severe economic crisis meant that Indonesia was deeply indebted to foreign lenders, especially to the Soviet Union and the socialist nations of Eastern Europe (Thee 2009, p. 52).[1] Although Australia, the United States, and the United Kingdom backed the Netherlands' claims to West New Guinea, they stopped short of providing military support to the Dutch. The United States, hoping to gain concessions from Sukarno on its anti-communist position, pressured the Dutch to negotiate a settlement. At the same time, in an effort to balance the scales and aware of Indonesia's strategic importance, the United States provided aid and military training even through the most difficult periods of its diplomatic relations with Indonesia. On August 15, 1962, the New York Agreement between Indonesia and the Netherlands, regarding the administration of West New Guinea, was signed at the United Nations. The territory was transferred to Indonesia through a process of temporary UN administration. President John F. Kennedy, who was closely involved in the negotiations, agreed to immediately upgrade US economic and military aid (US Department of State 1995, p. 294).

Despite his many successes from 1957 into the early 1960s and his acquisition of all the formal powers of a dictator, Sukarno still did not have control over the military. Indonesia's military leaders were largely anti-communist and, because of their memory of the 1948 Madiun Affair, continued to consider the PKI dangerous and untrustworthy (Roosa 2006).

The rise of the PKI. The PKI grew steadily as it maintained its support for Sukarno and Guided Democracy. After winning 6 million votes (16.4 percent of the vote) in the 1955 national and 1957 provincial elections, the PKI emerged as a significant and powerful party. Its support was particularly strong in Java, but it extended its base across the archipelago through membership drives and literacy, education, and publishing programs. Its rapid growth was also attributable to the active recruitment of women members through its organizations and education programs and through associated organizations, such as Barisan Tani Indonesia (Indonesian Peasants Front [BTI]), Sentral Organisasi Buruh Seluruh Indonesia (Central Labor Organization of the Republic of Indonesia [SOBSI]), Pemuda Rakyat (People's Youth), Gerakan Wanita Indonesia (Indonesian Women's Movement [Gerwani]), and Lembaga Kebudayaan Rakyat (Institute for the People's Culture [Lekra]). By the end of 1962, the PKI claimed it had over 2 million members (Hindley 1964, p. 101). Sukarno kept the PKI at a slight distance, appointing party leaders Njoto and Aidit as advisory ministers without portfolio and outside the inner cabinet in March 1962.

Driven by the dynamics of the Cold War, the Americans and Australians became increasingly concerned about the PKI's strengthening position in Indonesian politics; it had become the third-largest communist party in the world, after the Chinese and the Soviet parties. As the United States and Soviet Union competed to expand their spheres of influence, both took great interest in Indonesia because of its abundant natural resources and its maritime strategic importance. As mentioned briefly, following negotiations brokered by the Americans, including President Kennedy's brother Robert, the Dutch agreed on August 15, 1962, to transfer West Irian to an interim UN administration on October 1, in preparation for handing it over to Indonesia by May 1, 1963. This was on condition that a popular plebiscite be held before the end of 1969 to determine whether the inhabitants of West Irian would remain in Indonesia or seek self-determination.

Even though the negotiations about West Irian's future were fruitful, Sukarno managed to isolate Indonesia from both the United States and the Soviet Union as they proceeded. The United States had been highly concerned from the early 1960s about Indonesia's strengthening relations with the Soviet Union. While he went along with the American-led negotiations, Sukarno at the same time accepted Soviet military and operational support for the Indonesian offensive in West Irian from 1960 to 1962 (Easter 2015). Sukarno made no secret of his "playing of both sides" but rather "played on Washington's anxieties about the developing relationship between Indonesia and the USSR" by encouraging American engagement in negotiations to persuade the Dutch to leave West Irian (Easter 2015, p. 216).

In 1963, with the West Irian question seemingly settled and Darul Islam crushed, Sukarno had risen to the status of a "god king" within Indonesia, despite spiraling inflation and economic crisis bringing persistent food shortages and starvation in some parts of the country (Coppel 1983). Perhaps emboldened by his successes and by the adulation of his people, but also because he needed to keep the momentum of popular mobilization generated by the West Irian campaign going, Sukarno took a further radical turn in his foreign policy. He responded to the formation of Malaysia in September 1963 by criticizing the new federation for allowing Britain to retain its military bases and announced the Ganyang Malaysia (Crush Malaysia) campaign on September 23. He described the confrontation with Malaysia as part of the broad conflict between new emerging forces and the forces of colonialism, neocolonialism, and imperialism (Nekolim). Diplomatic relations between Malaysia and Indonesia had been suspended on September 19, and the British Embassy in Jakarta and other diplomatic buildings were set alight by crowds of rioters (Mackie 1975).

This radical foreign policy shift coincided with Indonesia's rejection of an offer of aid from the United States that was conditional on the exclusion of PKI from government. This rejection was made in the middle of an economic crisis aggravated by a poor rice harvest and out-of-control inflation that grew to 134 percent by 1964. Support for the Konfrontasi with Malaysia was strong among the PKI, who saw advantage in keeping the army preoccupied elsewhere, while the army was similarly aware of the need to be watchful within Indonesia. Thus, Sukarno's anti-imperialist policy had the effect of strengthening the participation of the left-wing party in domestic politics.

In 1963, the PKI commenced unilateral action to enact land reforms, seizing land in ways that led to violent conflict with landlords, among whom were devout Muslims, PNI supporters, civil servants, and army and NU members. Land was seized in West Java and in East Java, where the NU youth wing, Gerakan Pemuda Ansor, became heavily involved in retaliatory measures against the PKI. At the same time, the Indonesian armed forces were largely unsuccessful in the undeclared border war with Malaysian, British, and Australian troops. Meanwhile, on the advice of the Chinese, with whom the PKI had become increasingly close, the PKI backed the establishment of an auxiliary militia for which civilians, mostly members of PKI organizations, were trained. By 1964–1965, the careful balance that Sukarno had achieved between the PKI and the army in the early 1960s had given way to a polarization between the army and anti-communist forces on one side and Sukarno, the PKI, and other progressive forces on the other. The discourses of Sukarno and the PKI had become so alike that it had become difficult to trace the origin of ideas (Mortimer 1974, p. 91).

In January 1964, President Kennedy made a final attempt to broker an end to the Malaysia-Indonesia confrontation but failed, with Sukarno telling the Americans to "go to hell" with their aid offer and its conditions relating to the PKI. The United States, by this time deeply engaged in the Vietnam conflict, withdrew from negotiations. Sukarno's radical provocations during Konfrontasi had drawn the wrath of both the United States and the Soviet Union and, in January 1965, when Malaysia was elected as a nonpermanent member of the UN Security Council, Indonesia withdrew from the United Nations. Relations with the United States deteriorated further as Indonesia opposed its military operations in North Vietnam.

By 1965, Indonesia had shifted its alignment toward communist China. Formally announced as the "anti-imperialist" Jakarta-Beijing axis by Sukarno in his speech to the nation on August 17, 1965, the alliance has been described as "one of the most daring challenges to global superpower bipolarity during the Cold War" (Schaefer and War-daya 2013, p. 6). Indonesia's increasing isolation in the late 1950s to the mid-1960s had a profound impact on how the West responded, and on the Soviet Union's lack of response, to events to come in the years ahead. In his August 17, 1965, speech, entitled "Reach to the Stars! A Year of Self-Reliance," Sukarno belied the reality of the state of the national economy, which continued to suffer with a decline in export earnings as prices for Indonesian products stayed low because of increased competition from palm oil and coffee producers elsewhere in Asia and in Africa. The cost of living increased by 170 percent in 1962, 119 percent in 1963, 134 percent in 1964, and again by a further 50 percent from January to August 1965 (Survey 1965, p. 6).

The attempted coup and anti-communist purge. In August 1965, at the age of sixty-four, Sukarno fell ill while on a public outing, heightening constant speculation about his health and about a possible successor. Ahead of the mass gathering of troops in Jakarta for Armed Forces Day on October 5, rumors of a military coup spread through the capital and beyond, against a backdrop of ongoing economic crisis and the violence and paranoia between communists and anti-communists.

It has since been revealed that despite the distance between the United States and Sukarno, the Americans had been working closely with the Indonesian army throughout 1965 to find a way to defeat the

PKI (National Security Archive 2017; Schaefer and Wardaya 2013; Hamilton-Hart 2012; Simpson 2008; Bevins 2017). The army needed a pretext to launch an offensive against the PKI. In September 1965, American covert operations helped mount a propaganda campaign to spread rumors about the possibility of an army coup, hoping to draw the PKI into making the first move (Roosa 2006). Supported by the army's information outlets, including its newspapers, the campaign was effective. At the end of September, an inner circle of PKI leaders, headed by Secretary-General Aidit with Kamaruzaman Sjam, came together and made contact with pro-PKI military men to plan a preemptive strike. Three military officers were involved—Colonel Latief of the Jakarta Army Command, Lieutenant Colonel Untung of the Presidential Guard, and Major Soejono of the Indonesian Air Force. They had only a relatively small number of troops at their command, so some auxiliary PKI militia with basic military training were brought in. Sjam acted as mediator between the military men and the PKI Special Bureau, and together they became the Thirtieth of September Movement (hereafter, the Movement). In the early hours of October 1, the Movement's troops set out to abduct seven military leaders, including six generals, among them General Nasution, and one high-ranking army officer. In what John Roosa (2006, p. 218) has described as a "botched operation," three were shot and killed when they attempted to resist arrest. Nasution was the only one of the seven who managed to get away, but his daughter was shot and later died, and his aide was later found murdered alongside the three others who had been detained. Seven bodies were discovered a few days later in a well at Halim Airbase. The army alleged that they had been mutilated, although this has never been proven (Pohlman 2015). The Movement took over the national broadcaster Radio Republik Indonesia on the morning of October 1 and issued a statement that it had abducted the military leaders in an effort to protect Sukarno from a coup attempt by the army generals. Later that day, however, in an entirely contradictory statement, the Movement announced the decommissioning of Sukarno's government and transfer of power to the forty-five-member Revolutionary Council. PKI leader Aidit fled to Central Java to garner further support.

Historian Roosa (2006) has concluded that the divergence from the first statement arose because of a breakdown in the tripartite structure of the groups involved. The military members were on one side, the political grouping on the other, with Sjam as negotiator in between. When Sukarno heard of the abduction and killing of the generals on the morning of October 1, he sent word to those involved that they should desist. However, because of their disjointed alliance, it appears that by afternoon the political side had decided that it would resist Sukarno's directive, while the military side capitulated.

The head of Kostrad (Komando Strategis Angkatan Darat [Army Strategic Command]), Major General Suharto, stepped in as interim commander of the armed forces, replacing the slain General Yani, and launched a counterattack. It is possible that Suharto knew of the plans of his old friend Latief, Untung, and his fellow officers but chose not to intervene to stop them. Roosa (2006) concluded that there is, however, no evidence that Suharto had any hand in instigating the Movement. Within twenty-four hours, the armed forces had put down the Movement in Jakarta, and a few days later, in Central Java.

In the wake of the Movement, the anti-communist elements within the army had the pretext they needed to launch an assault on the communists and their sympathizers, and ultimately on Sukarno. Assisted by American and British covert operations that had been under way for almost a year, on October 2 the army closed down pro-PKI and pro-Sukarno newspapers and embarked on a propaganda campaign using its own newspapers and issuing threats to other news outlets to warn them against publishing any stories critical of the anti-PKI campaign as these would be taken as evidence that they too were communists (Roosa 2006, p. 38; McGregor 2007). An anti-PKI movement was mobilized very rapidly that moved to shut down the PKI and its affiliated organizations, driving the PKI leadership underground. Meanwhile, Sukarno devolved powers to Suharto, who refused to step down from the position he had assumed on General Yani's death in spite of Sukarno's directive to do so. Soon after October 1, violence ensued in some parts of Indonesia, spreading to other parts months later, which indicated that it was not the spontaneous violence of enraged mobs but the result of a systematic spread involving the police and military. Anti-communist groups helped these forces round up suspected Communists, putting them in prison and detention camps. A pattern of significant periods in detention, which included torture, starvation, and forced labor, followed, before executions that were usually secret and late at night. Not until the end of authoritarian rule three decades later in 1998 were the mass graves of those executed discovered and their stories told by eyewitnesses.

An estimated 500,000 to 1 million people were killed between late 1965 and 1967 in what scholars and legal experts argue amounts to genocide (McGregor, Melvin, and Pohlman 2018, p. 12). Western governments, including the United States, United Kingdom, and Australia, knew a great deal about the killings and, through their silence and sometimes their actions, in effect supported them. American historian Bradley Simpson (2013, p. 51) claims that "the US responded enthusiastically to the mass murders in Indonesia." Some historians argue that the scale of the killings was in large part due to external factors, such as Indonesia's desire to win the support of the United States and other Western powers, including Australia, by proving that Indonesian leaders were truly anti-communist and, therefore, worthy of promised and prized American aid and investment (Simpson 2008).

Throughout this period, the military and police, often with the help of civilian militia, arrested suspected Communists for direct or indirect involvement in the attempted coup. The military described this as an "annihilation operation," the purpose of which was to seize state power and eliminate its political rival, the PKI (Melvin 2018, pp. 51–52). Among those arrested were teachers who were members of the PKI-aligned teachers union, women who were members of Gerwani, BTI members, students, academics, and artists, none of whom had any knowledge of the PKI's political operations or of the attempted coup. In Bali, North Sumatra, East Indonesia, and Central Java, the detention and disappearance of suspects were carried out in a campaign of fear and terror mounted by the army's propaganda machine, which made up stories about the coup, including about the mutilation and torture of the generals by Gerwani and Pemuda Rakyat members. The stories, as Annie Pohlman (2015, p. 7) writes, were taken as evidence of PKI's "immorality, savagery and godlessness." The army, police, and co-opted civilians created fabricated reports of death lists and graves dug in readiness, which fed the image of the PKI as a dangerous enemy. A particularly strong theme within this propaganda was the involvement of Gerwani in the violence at Lubang Buaya, including acts of sexual violence on the generals (Wieringa 1998). Most of the arrests and killings occurred between October 1965 and March 1966, in Bali, Central and East Java, and North Sumatra and Aceh; there were also some in other parts of Indonesia, including East Nusa Tenggara. Arrests and detention without trial continued into the 1970s. Crimes against humanity committed in this period include murder, sexual assault, torture, disappearances, and forced labor. An estimated 600,000–750,000 political prisoners were detained for periods of up to fourteen years, many of them on the prison island, Buru, where they were kept as slaves for the duration of their imprisonment (Hedman 2008, p. 14; Kahin 2015, p. 461).

The legitimacy of the New Order government, formally installed in March 1967 when Suharto replaced Sukarno as acting president, was based upon the mass killings and purges and the stigmatization of the left across all facets of Indonesian politics and culture (Heryanto 2006). Historians and anthropologists argue that the existence of the regime was in large part predicated on perpetuating the threat of a communist resurgence in Indonesia, however unlikely it might have been. To ensure this, the official narrative of the Thirtieth of September Movement was written into Indonesian history books, and any alternative narrative was prohibited for the duration of the New Order and beyond (McGregor 2007).

By February 1966, it was clear that the removal of the PKI from the political constellation shifted the balance of power in the army's favor. In a last-ditch effort to cling to his power and Guided Democracy in February 1966, Sukarno reshuffled his cabinet, removing Nasution as defense minister. Nasution, who was close to Suharto, was defiant. Meanwhile, the army-backed student organization Kesatuan Aksi Mahasiswa Indonesia (KAMI), and later Kesatuan Aksi Pelajar Pemuda Indonesia (KAPPI), held mass demonstrations calling for Sukarno to face trial alongside the Thirtieth of September Movement members and step down. On March 11, 1966, as demonstrators threatened to close in on the presidential palace, Sukarno was forced to flee Jakarta. Then, Sukarno followed his carefully constructed plan and handed over full authority for Indonesia's government and security to Suharto, through an executive order known as Supersemar (Surat Perintah Sebelas Maret [Order of the Eleventh of March]). Sukarno was stripped of his "President for Life" title, the PKI was banned, as was the Indonesian Chinese party, Badan Permusjawaratan Kewarganegaraan Indonesia (Indonesian Citizenship Consultative Council [Baperki]), and Marxism, and the government was purged of those loyal to Sukarno. A new cabinet was installed led by Suharto, with Sultan Hamengkubuwana IX as minister for economic affairs and Adam Malik as minister for foreign affairs. Diplomatic relations with China were suspended as Indonesia sought to realign its foreign policy to the West, so that it could attract desperately needed emergency credit and aid. The new anti-communist New Order regime was immediately more attractive to the United States and Japan, and aid quickly followed. In April 1966, Indonesia rejoined the United Nations. Confrontation with Malaysia was brought to an end, with Suharto sending a goodwill delegation to Malaysia in May. On August 8, 1967, Indonesia established the Association of Southeast Asian Nations (ASEAN) with Malaysia, Singapore, Thailand, and the Philippines, establishing its secretariat in Jakarta, promoting economic development through regional integration, and agreeing not to intervene in the domestic affairs of other members.

Indonesia accepted Western demands to implement economic reform measures in exchange for a gradual debt repayment plan. The economy reopened to foreign investment, allowing British and Americans to return and reclaim companies seized from them. Thus, the government intervened in the economy more actively, doing such things as removing subsidies on gasoline, which led to a steep price increase, and clamping down on monopolies held by private enterprises, especially in rice milling, in which ethnic Chinese business was prominent. Legislation was also introduced in 1966 banning the use of Chinese characters and language and promoting measures that required Chinese names be changed to Indonesian ones (Coppel 1983). On March 12, 1967, the Majelis Permusyawaratan Rakyat Sementara (Provisional People's Consultative Assembly [MPRS]) stripped Sukarno of all his powers and titles and appointed Suharto as acting president. Pancasila was declared the only state ideology. Sukarno remained under de facto house arrest until his death in June 1970.

Suharto's New Order, 1966–1998

On March 27, 1968, Suharto was officially sworn in as Indonesia's second president. In June he established his first Development Cabinet, making it clear that he would initially concentrate his efforts as leader on developing Indonesia. Suharto was very different from Sukarno. He had no education beyond high school and had been raised in a traditional Javanese household. His priority was to achieve stability, politically by dismantling the left and economically through reforms that targeted growth. Among his key advisers were economists who had studied in American institutions, known as the Berkeley Mafia, but exiles of the PRRI rebellion were also in the first cabinet, including Sumitro Djojohadikusumo, principal interlocutor with the Americans during the PRRI insurgency, who returned from exile to become minister of trade. This team of economists put together the first Five Year Plan, which was issued in 1969 and was intended to improve agricultural production and provide cheap food. With the help of foreign aid from the United States and Japan, the government also engaged in rapid infrastructure development, the effects of which were noticeable as soon as 1970. It encompassed significant investment in boosting rice self-sufficiency for Indonesia, through what has been called the Green Revolution, which involved the use of fertilizers and pesticides. Suharto also reached out to ethnic Chinese businessmen, including Bob Hasan and others, known as *cukong*, who worked closely with his government to build their business interests in a deeply symbiotic process of personal enrichment, but which contributed to a pillar of the regime's legitimacy—economic development. It was not long before an anti-corruption team, led by former prime minister Wilopo and including Hatta, reported that corruption was rife throughout the military and bureaucracy. The president's own family was suspected of corruption, as investigations of the business activities of Suharto's wife, Ibu Tien Suharto, had raised suspicions. The team's report elicited no response from the government.

As well as courting ethnic Chinese business conglomerates for assistance with his economic agenda, Suharto's government had what it called a "Chinese Problem." Indonesia's relationship with China was fraught because of the government's strong anti-communist stance and because of China's response to the mass killings and suspected genocide of ethnic Chinese. The Indonesian government was torn on this issue but eventually implemented a raft of discriminatory laws against ethnic Chinese, which forced a program of assimilation and erasure of their ethnicity while also highlighting their difference and keeping this group of economic middlemen structurally vulnerable and dependent on the regime (Heryanto, 2006; Purdey 2006, pp. 20–21).

When he assumed power, Suharto had promised elections in 1968, but these were delayed in the interests of ensuring political stability as the economic programs were rolled out. Indonesia's second general elections were held on July 3, 1971, in what was a watershed occasion for the future of Suharto's regime. With these elections, the New Order regime "abandoned the rhetoric of popular democracy" once and for all (Cribb and Kahin 2004, p. 298), after which the strong role of the military and political repression were cemented within a patrimonial system. Before the election, the government mandated that all government employees, including the military, must be fully loyal to the government and have no affiliations with any political party. They were strongly encouraged to join Golkar (Golongan Karya [Functional Groups]), formed in October 1964 by army leaders as a coordinating body that became a federation of anti-communist social organizations. In 1967, the government announced that Golkar would become the regime's parliamentary party (Cribb and Kahin 2004, p. 1616) and thus would "serve as the electoral vehicle of the authoritarian regime" (Tomsa 2007, p. 77).

The outcome of the 1971 election reflected the political repression following the decimation of the PKI and pro-Sukarno parties. Golkar won 65.6 percent of the seats in parliament, NU 18.7 percent, and PNI only 6.9 percent (Ward 1974). The government took these results as confirmation of its plan to do away with the old parties altogether and restricted the number of parties to three, forcing all Islamic parties to amalgamate within the Partai Persatuan Pembangunan (Development Unity Party [PPP]) and all nationalist, secular, and Christian parties in Partai Demokrasi Indonesia (Indonesian Democratic Party [PDI]). Golkar was the third party and would remain the largest party throughout the New Order, winning every general election between 1977 and 1997.

Over the next decade, the Suharto government continued to restrict political freedoms and silence its critics as it progressed through its development agenda. The oil boom of the early 1970s, precipitated by the Arab-Israeli war of October 1973, saw the oil price jump 430 percent between 1972 and 1974, causing the percentage of oil in the total value of Indonesia's exports to increase from 30 percent in 1966 to 74 percent in 1974. The boom in the oil price was timely, as public concern about the growth in foreign investment, particularly among indigenous (*pribumi*) businesses, grew. The oil boom meant that the government no longer needed to rely so much on foreign investment to fund its second Five Year Development Plan (1974–1979) and to implement programs to assist *pribumi* entrepreneurs, subsidies, and social programs.

Total foreign investment approved between 1967 and 1972 was just over $2 billion, with a significant percentage of this coming in the last two years of this period. Compared with neighboring countries, this level of foreign direct investment was not particularly high, but the speed with which it was appearing, particularly in Jakarta, was noted by analysts at the time; Jakarta was "taking on the appearance of a transformed city. Multistory hotels are reaching into the sky, new markets and wider roads are being built" (Survey 1972).

In January 1974, a visit by Prime Minister Kakuei Tanaka of Japan incited large demonstrations dubbed Malapetaka Januari (January Disaster). Led mostly by students, the demonstrators were protesting the dominance of foreign investment in the Indonesian economy, but more generally, they were also against corruption within the bureaucracy, the military, and the government. The government responded with mass arrests and a further crackdown on freedoms of speech, the press, and association as it shut down media organizations and detained their editors and the student leaders of the protests. The effect of the crackdown was to reduce critical comment in the publications that survived to its lowest level since Sukarno's last years.

Deepening Authoritarianism

In April 1974, the left-wing Movimento das Forcas Armadas (Portuguese Armed Forces Movement [MFA]) in the Portuguese army launched a military coup against the Estado Novo government, placing power in the hands of a military junta that announced Portugal's intention to withdraw from its possessions in Africa and Asia, including East Timor. The eastern half of the island of Timor had become Portuguese in 1859 following the signing of the Treaty of Lisbon by Portugal and the Netherlands. From 1942 to 1945, East Timor was occupied by the Japanese but was returned to Portuguese authority at the end of World War II. After the coup d'état in Lisbon, East Timor declared its independence from Portugal on November 28, 1975, as the Democratic Republic of East Timor. Consistent with its anti-communist stance and wanting to suppress the leftist Fretilin Party (Frente Revolucionária de Timor-Leste Independente [Revolutionary Front for an Independent East Timor]) from leading the fledgling republic and to quell potential secessionist movements in its own separatist provinces, Indonesia sent its army to invade East Timor on December 7, 1975, annexing it as the twenty-seventh province of the Republic of Indonesia. Twenty-four years of military occupation followed, during which East Timorese resistance groups fought a guerrilla war in which they were vastly outnumbered and underresourced. Deaths related to the conflict have been estimated at between 102,800 and 200,000 during the Indonesian occupation. In addition to murder, other crimes committed by the Indonesian armed forces against pro-independence activists and their suspected supporters were torture, sexual violence, and disappearances (van der Wolf, Tofan, and de Ruiter 2011).

Every year, the Indonesian occupation of East Timor was raised at the United Nations, as advocates for its independence fought to keep it on the agenda. The United States and Australia, along with other states, sided with the Indonesians. Australia was the only Western country to recognize Indonesia's annexation of East Timor, formally in 1978 by the government of Malcolm Fraser, following the support in 1974 and 1975 of the Gough Whitlam government. Australia's position was in keeping with the foreign policy stance it took on Papua in 1961 and consistent with its view that it was undesirable to support small unviable states close to its borders (Chauvel 2015). Australia's decision to support Indonesia's annexation of East Timor persisted throughout its negotiations with Indonesia over seabed boundaries in the Timor Sea and potential oil reserves within them (McGrath 2016; Stepan 1990), which culminated in the signing of the Timor Gap Treaty between Australia and Indonesia on December 11, 1989.

For two decades of New Order rule, political and human rights and freedoms were repressed while Indonesia remained in the grip of military control. Secessionist movements in Aceh, West Papua, and East Timor were violently put down and access to these regions was severely restricted. In late 1979, 10,000 political prisoners were released but continued to be stigmatized; many of them were unable to work, and they and their family members were kept out of government jobs. Some PKI members were not executed until August 1985 (Setiawan 2004).

Underpinning the authoritarian regime were relatively steady economic growth and government social programs linking citizenship with loyalty to the New Order through an indoctrination process that promoted Pancasila as the state's political ideology (Morfit 1981). Nevertheless, resistance to the regime persisted, often with dire consequences for those involved. In 1980, the Petition of Fifty, a significant statement of opposition to New Order Indonesia signed by fifty retired generals, former politicians, intellectuals, lawyers, and students, brought together several streams of dissent (Bourchier 1987). Dissent had built throughout the 1970s as Suharto sought to further strengthen the army's role in politics and demonstrated no intention of easing restrictions on political freedoms imposed after 1965. The press was banned from reporting on the petition and, despite their high profile, its signatories were subjected to harassment, including death threats, bashings, and close surveillance.

Dissenters whose voices were suppressed inside Indonesia frequently sought channels outside the country to broadcast their protest. Revelations of the Suharto family's extensive fortune by *Sydney Morning Herald* journalist David Jenkins in April 1986 caused a major crisis in Australia-Indonesia relations but allowed knowledge of their corruption, known within Indonesia for some time, to spread to the outside world (Hill 2007, p. 154). Like other foreigners critical of the government, including many academics and journalists, Jenkins was blacklisted from entering Indonesia. Indonesian dissent, whether from students, urban poor, Muslims, labor activists, or environmentalists, was met with threats and violence. On November 11, 1991, at least 250 East Timorese were killed by Indonesian military at Dili's Santa Cruz cemetery. Coverage of the killings by foreign journalists and of the death of a foreigner in the shooting reached a worldwide audience, resulting in significant international pressure on the Indonesian government. In 1993, under growing international pressure because of Indonesia's military occupation of East Timor and human rights abuse in general (identified in UN Human Rights Commission Resolution 1993/97), Suharto established the Komisi Nasional Hak Asasi Manusia (National Commission on Human Rights [Komnas HAM]) in Presidential Decree No. 50 of 1993.

Fall of the New Order

Late in 1997, the Asian economic crisis deepened, precipitating a considerable fall in the value of the rupiah and sharp rises in food and fuel prices in Indonesia. Food riots and other violence broke out across the archipelago in early 1998 as opposition to the government mounted. The crisis struck at the very heart of the New Order's legitimacy—its ability to sustain economic growth. As the time approached for Suharto to renew his presidency for another five-year term to start on March 20, 1998, opposition groups became increasingly vocal in calling for his resignation. In February, students and activists from universities and labor unions were kidnapped and held without charge by the Indonesian Army Special Forces Command (Kopassus), led by Lieutenant General Prabowo Subianto, Suharto's son-in-law and son of Sumitro Djojohadikusumo. Many of them disappeared without trace. Meanwhile, the government sought to divert responsibility for the economic crisis to the ethnic Chinese minority, which for a long time had been the middlemen in the economy. As the government's campaign to make them the scapegoats for the crisis took hold at the end of 1997 into early 1998, the businesses of ethnic Chinese were attacked in local food riots, especially in Java (Purdey 2006).

Successful in his efforts to shut down any opposition to his power, Suharto was reappointed president for a sixth five-year term. It appeared that Suharto would keep his iron grip on power and the resilience of his authoritarian regime would persist for the foreseeable future (Crouch 2010, p. 4). Nonetheless, although few had predicted it in the preceding months, by May 1998, a combination of an internal fracturing of the regime led by the elite, the effects of the Asian economic crisis, and violent social unrest had brought about the fall of Suharto. Fractures and tensions among the elite within the corridors of power had been brewing for some time and came to a head in the chaotic events on the streets of Jakarta and other Indonesian cities in the middle of May. Action was eventually taken to remove the president, whose dictatorship had left little room for anyone else to express power, by a growing number of people who were fearful for their own survival and also of the nation's survival (Aspinall 2005a, p. 4; Crouch 2010, p. 4).

By early May 1998, members of the growing opposition movement, made up largely of student groups and elements of civil society, were protesting regularly on campuses across the country. The student protesters soon began to leave their campuses and took to the streets, where they faced heavy-handed police action and frequent violence that reached fever pitch on May 13, when Jakarta police opened fire on unarmed students at Trisakti University, killing four and injuring dozens more as they retreated.

In the days that followed, students occupied the national parliament buildings in the nation's capital. Other major cities, including Jakarta Solo, Surabaya, and Medan, were rocked by rioting that claimed an estimated thousand lives in violence that included unprecedented levels of gang rape and sexual assault (Purdey 2006). For more than two days, the military and police were strangely absent from the streets of these cities, as crowds of men, some of whom the government's investigation later described as military-like in appearance and behavior, ran riot, targeting in particular the property, homes, cars, and businesses of ethnic Chinese Indonesians. Of the 100 victims of sexual assault, including gang rape, ethnic Chinese women were a large percentage. The riots shocked the nation and the international community alike, and independent investigations later concluded that they were a systematic effort by the government and military forces to destabilize the country and use the resultant instability as a pretext for tightening its grip and quelling dissent. A decisive and critical split within elite political circles eventually convinced Suharto that he had to step down. He resigned as president on May 21, 1998, appointing his minister for technology and protégé, B. J. Habibie, in his place. Although Suharto and a few others had handed over their power, there was little change in who held power, and, in the absence of a cohesive opposition movement to step up and bring real change, the new Habibie government carried over much from the previous regime (Crouch 2010, p. 4).

For more than three decades of New Order rule, Indonesia had had a politically authoritarian government supported by military repression of any opposition and dissent. There had been significant economic growth, with an annual rate of 7 percent recorded, which had supported an expansion of the middle class, urbanization, and improvements in education and health. Yet cronyism and nepotism in government and business led to deeper corruption, patronage, and a system of sultanistic oligarchies with the Suharto family at its center (Winters 2011; Hadiz 2003). The networks of patrimonialism and corruption reached deep into the armed forces, the police, and all levels of the civil service. Because much of the New Order regime remained intact after the fall of Suharto on May 21, 1998, meeting the expectations and hopes of the pro-democracy protesters who took to the streets and celebrated his resignation euphorically that day would not be straightforward.

Note

1. By the end of 1965, Indonesia's foreign debt had reached almost US$2.4 billion (around 25 percent of its GDP), 60 percent of which was owed to socialist countries, including US$990 million to the Soviet Union (Thee 2009, p. 52).

4

Political Reforms
After 1998

WHEN PRESIDENT SUHARTO WAS FORCED TO RESIGN IN MAY 1998 in the face of escalating popular protests and the desertion of key allies, few of the dictator's closest associates went with him. Upon his resignation, Suharto handed power to his trusted protégé, Vice President B. J. Habibie, next in line for the presidency under the Indonesian constitution. Habibie retained twenty-two of Suharto's thirty-nine cabinet ministers, seventeen of them in the same positions they had occupied prior to Suharto's resignation. The armed forces commander also remained in place. Beyond the executive arm of government, the national legislature—the People's Representative Assembly (Dewan Perwakilan Rakyat [DPR])—was untouched, with four-fifths of the seats in the 500-member body controlled either by the Suharto regime party Golkar (325 seats) or occupied by military appointees (seventy-five seats). Outside of formal politics, the large-scale business interests, having become enriched through their close connections to power under Suharto, also managed to reconstitute themselves anew in the democratic era. The protest movement that had precipitated Suharto's fall thus found itself largely excluded from the design of democratic reforms, which would instead be steered by leaders drawn from the authoritarian regime (Malley 2009, p. 137; Horowitz 2013).

Such continuities should not distract us from the fundamental transformation of Indonesia's polity after Suharto's fall from centralized authoritarian to decentralized democratic governance, a transformation that commenced almost as soon as Suharto's decades of dictatorial rule ended, ushering in the so-called Reform era or *reformasi*. Over the course of Habibie's eighteen months in power, his government passed

61

fifty laws, almost half as many as had been enacted across the preceding three decades of authoritarian rule (Anwar 2010a; Crouch 2010). In particular, Habibie's government established competitive elections and a democratic party system, initiated decentralization reforms to reverse the extreme centralization of power under Suharto, and began the process of establishing civilian supremacy over the military, which had dominated the Suharto regime. Far-reaching constitutional change to entrench these reforms in the nation's most fundamental source of law commenced immediately upon the end of Habibie's time as president.

This seeming paradox—a fundamental transformation of the institutions of Indonesia's political system despite the carryover of many authoritarian-era personnel—continues to shape Indonesian politics as of 2019. It has seen Indonesia tread a middle path between the aspirations of some activists for comprehensive liberal democratic reform and the ambitions of some of these Suharto-era holdovers to engineer a reversion to authoritarianism.

Early Continuities and Rapid Reforms

Suharto's surrender of power to B. J. Habibie gained sufficient public legitimacy to succeed because of an absence of viable alternatives. The transfer of power to the new Habibie government nevertheless split the anti-Suharto protest movement, which demobilized rapidly. A section of the student protest movement that had precipitated Suharto's fall remained implacably opposed to Habibie as an authoritarian holdover, but this diffuse protest movement had not agreed upon either a workable alternative form of government or an obvious alternative leadership candidate. Under such circumstances, the movement split, with many opting to wait and see how Habibie would perform as president.

Also important, the protest movement lacked the support of the "semi-oppositional" figures of the New Order era who would go on to occupy the chief posts of democratic politics. Their interests lay in an orderly transition to the competitive electoral politics that they were poised to dominate, rather than more revolutionary political change. Aspinall (2005a, pp. 6–7) dubs these figures the "semi-opposition" because they worked within the authoritarian regime's formal structures, embracing compromise and using "regime language and ideological formulas to argue for political change." Their ranks included Abdurrahman Wahid and Megawati Sukarnoputri, the next two presidents to follow Habibie. Wahid, president from 1999 until his impeachment in 2001, headed Indonesia's largest Islamic organization, Nahdlatul Ulama, from

1984 until 1999. As chairperson, he allowed the regime party Golkar to corral votes from NU for the 1997 elections, and in 1998 publicly called for an end to protests in the final days of Suharto's rule, although he had privately advised the dictator to resign (Aspinall 2005a, p. 234). Megawati Sukarnoputri, daughter of founding president Sukarno, served as vice president to Wahid, replacing him upon his impeachment in 2001 and holding office until her defeat in Indonesia's first direct presidential election in 2004. She became a broader symbol of opposition to Suharto after his regime arranged her ousting from the PDI chairmanship in 1996, but she maintained caution and provided no clear direction to her supporters, even as they grew more numerous and vocal. It would not be until the election of Joko Widodo as president in 2014 that Indonesia would be governed by a figure drawn from outside the Suharto regime establishment or its semi-opposition.

Contemporary observers note that many Indonesians saw Habibie only as an interim president. Reflecting this mood, some government officials opted merely to paper over "vice" on their previous official portrait of Habibie as vice president, Adrian Vickers (2013, p. 212) recounts, rather than purchasing a new official photograph. Habibie, however, aspired to rule for much longer. He thus immediately set about implementing previously antithetical political reforms, in the hope of carving out a modicum of democratic legitimacy (Crouch 2010). Although his government's reforms were "drastic policy reversals" compared to previous governance arrangements (Crouch 2010, p. 334), Habibie's personal commitment to democratic reforms was partial. Habibie's reforms were not a "gift from an enlightened leader"; his government initially proposed to reserve almost one-third of the seats in a new People's Consultative Assembly (Majelis Permusyawaratan Rakyat [MPR]) for appointed loyalists, which would have effectively guaranteed his reelection as president (Robison and Hadiz 2004, p. 176). He also resisted calls to prosecute his predecessor, Suharto, which is indicative of his continuing personal loyalty to the former president (Anwar 2010a).

Nevertheless, in the first weeks of his presidency, Habibie revoked several of the most visible pillars of authoritarianism (Crouch 2010, p. 27). Among other measures, he began the release of political prisoners, announced that restrictions on a free press would soon be relaxed, permitted banned publications to return to print, and foreshadowed amendment of the antisubversion law, a key tool of repression. The next key milestone in his program of reform was a November 1998 special session of the MPR, which set a timetable for fresh elections in June 1999 and for a staged drawdown of military representation in the legislature. This session also established a two-term limit for the president and vice president, cleared the way for constitutional change without the need for a referendum, and foreshadowed decentralization of the political system, which was subsequently achieved through regional autonomy legislation in 1999 (Anwar 2010a; Robison and Hadiz 2004, p. 181). These areas of reform are seen as the key enduring achievements of the Habibie government. So, too—at least outside Indonesia—is the Habibie government's referendum for East Timor in 1999, in which the territory opted for independence. Each area of reform is covered in greater detail below. Despite the major political reforms that his government introduced, Habibie's personal ambitions to retain the presidency were to be dashed. He lost the support of his party during the October 1999 MPR session that would elect a new president, and he eventually withdrew from the race (Crouch 2000, p. 119).

Ultimately, the Habibie presidency was ambiguous in its impact. His administration undoubtedly laid the initial foundations for a more competitive democratic polity (Crouch 2010). But his government's accommodation of old interests also set the stage for their enduring influence throughout the democratic era (Robison and Hadiz 2004, p. 256).

Key Early Reforms:
Elections, Decentralization, Civil-Military Relations

The three most important areas of reform initiated under the Habibie government are discussed below. The separation of East Timor, also initiated under Habibie but finalized under his successor, Abdurrahman Wahid, is discussed later in the chapter in the context of a set of large-scale intercommunal and ethnonationalist conflicts that accompanied Indonesia's democratic transition.

Elections and the Party System

The Indonesian national legislature that served during the Habibie period had been elected in 1997 under the Suharto regime's highly undemocratic restrictions on political activities. Only three regime-approved parties were able to contest elections, and the two opposition parties faced vetting of their candidates and prohibitions on village-level political activity, among other controls. The regime's own electoral vehicle, Golkar, thus dominated the national and most local legislatures, alongside military appointees. The fresh elections held on June 7, 1999, swept away this system. Forty-eight parties qualified to contest the elections, out of around 200 that initially registered, twenty-one of which gained seats in the DPR. Golkar and the military had controlled 400 of 500 seats in the 1997 DPR, but now they held just 158 seats following the election (King 2000; National Democratic Institute for International Affairs [NDI] 1999). International observers concluded that the voting had been fairly conducted, with only a post-hoc change to seat allocation rules that saw a handful of seats switch between parties attracting significant criticism (NDI 1999). Along with 135 regional representatives chosen by provincial parliaments and sixty-five functional group representatives chosen by the electoral commission, these newly elected members then convened in November 1999 to elect a new president, choosing Abdurrahman Wahid, the head of Nahdlatul Ulama.

New laws on political parties, elections, and the composition of the DPR and MPR were drafted, debated, and finalized over the course of just five months ahead of these 1999 elections (King 2000, p. 90). Unsurprisingly, in light of this haste, Indonesia has continued to tinker with its electoral system ahead of each subsequent election. Nevertheless, the 1999 election established several features of the party system that persist as of this writing.

First, the elections produced a national legislature not dominated by any single party. Ostensibly, reformers within the government wished to avoid this outcome, guided by the experience of the 1955 elections, which had produced a fractious parliament divided among twenty-eight parties (King 2000, p. 92). But proposals that might have produced a more consolidated legislature—a high electoral threshold to compete in subsequent elections, and plurality-based district electorates for most DPR seats—were rejected (King 2000, pp. 92, 101–103). In the event, Megawati Sukarnoputri's Partai Demokrasi Indonesia Perjuangan (Indonesian Democratic Struggle Party [PDI-P]) won the highest share of the vote in 1999, at 34 percent, a figure no party has approached since. The DPR has indeed become more fragmented over time. PDI-P again won a plurality in the 2014 elections, with just 19 percent of the vote, as one of ten parties to gain seats. In 2019, the party gained its third plurality, with just over 19 per cent of the vote, in a nine party legislature. The fragmented composition of the DPR has led every president to amalgamate an almost incoherently broad range of interests within his or her government, in what are called rainbow coalitions (Diamond 2009; Sherlock 2009). Indeed, this practice has become so commonplace that it could be argued to reflect a norm of broad inclusion that resonates both with elites and with voters.

Second, all parties in the 1999 elections were national parties. In 1999, parties were required to have offices in one-third of provinces and one-half of the districts and municipalities in those provinces (King 2000, p. 91), in measures designed to exclude local or ethnic parties and thus decrease the risk of national disintegration. Although early fears about Indonesia's viability as a unitary political entity proved to be misplaced, a requirement for national representation remains in place.[1] Similarly, Indonesia's directly elected president must obtain a majority of the vote nationally, and at least 20 percent in one-half of Indonesia's provinces, otherwise a second-round runoff is held.

Third, much as the newly competitive party and electoral system fractured Golkar's dominance, the three authoritarian-era parties remained key players. Golkar, the PDI-P, and the Partai Persatuan Pembangunan (Development Unity Party [PPP]) garnered a remarkable 67 percent of the vote in the 1999 elections. These three parties continue to win a significant if decreasing share of votes, capturing 36 percent among them in 2019. Golkar's overall share of the vote may have dropped precipitously in 1999 to 22 percent, but this still gave the regime party the second-highest vote tally by a considerable distance, with no other party exceeding 13 percent. PDI-P and Golkar have in fact ranked first and second in three of the five postauthoritarian elections, and have both been among the top three parties for all of these elections, underlining the advantage they have derived from their long-standing lineage. The thirty-eight military appointees in the 1999 national legislature (reduced by one-half from seventy-five in 1997) were another continuity with the authoritarian era. The military bloc was abolished altogether in the national legislature in 2004, and in local legislatures starting in 2009.

Fourth, Islamic parties received only minority support, even though Muslims compose almost 90 percent of the population in Indonesia. Islamic parties received 38 percent of the vote in 1999, a figure they equaled in 2004 but have not exceeded as of 2019. The ideological position of these parties varies regarding Islam, as will be covered in Chapter 5.

Decentralization

Suharto's regime was highly centralized. The national government controlled most government revenue, and the primary role of local governments was to implement policy decisions taken in Jakarta, for which they received earmarked funds. The central government also retained final say in the selection of local heads of government, many of whom were active military officers stationed in the outer islands. With the end of authoritarianism, the regions immediately pushed for a greater say in their own affairs. Indeed, the early stage of democratization took place against a backdrop of anxiety about the possibility of regions seeking to split off as small independent nations, leading to a Balkanization of Indonesia of the sort seen in Yugoslavia in the 1990s (Mietzner 2014).

In response to such pressures, center-periphery relations were reconfigured under Habibie in a manner no less drastic than the changes to the party and electoral system. Far-reaching decentralization legislation that was passed in May 1999 reserved just six core areas of governance as the exclusive domain of the central government, namely, foreign affairs, defense, security, religion, finance, and judicial affairs.[2] Primary responsibility for other government functions was devolved to Indonesia's third tier of government—districts and municipalities. This devolution thus skipped the provinces, as it was feared they could form large enough autonomous political units to challenge the authority of the central government. Districts and provincial legislators were granted authority to elect mayors and governors, respectively, without central government interference. District governments would also no longer serve as representative offices of the central government; regional offices of central ministries were either closed or transformed to become local government offices, along with their staff. Alongside these political changes, fiscal devolution legislation that was passed at the same time gave local governments a much greater share of revenue, both through block grants from the central government and as a greater share of their own resources and other locally generated revenues. Consequently, when these laws came into force in 2001, as Michael Malley (2009, p. 140) has observed, local governments' share of overall government spending doubled from 15 percent to 30 percent within the first year.

Whereas the package of political laws that was passed under Habibie to enable early elections was the subject of prolonged debate and compromise, the two new decentralization laws passed almost without amendment (Malley 2009; Smith 2008). Indeed, Malley (2009, p. 138) recounted, the team of academics that drafted the bills took on the task at their own initiative, after completing work on the aforementioned package of political laws. As the laws did not directly impinge on legislators' own short-term prospects and may even have been predicted to increase their electability as reformers, these far-reaching bills were largely waved through (Smith 2008). As will be discussed in detail in Chapter 5, after the full impact of this early decentralization project became clear, the central government and DPR worked to wind back various aspects of these bills.

Civil-Military Relations

Military reform posed a formidable challenge to the Habibie government. The military had formed the backbone of Suharto's authoritarian
regime, during which time it was accountable only to the president,
who was himself an army general (Crouch 2010). Numerous institutional arrangements gave the military the power to resist civilian control. The *dwifungsi* (dual-function) doctrine mandated the military to
maintain domestic political stability and promote national development, in addition to having defense and security roles (Sebastian and
Gindarsah 2013, p. 31). The *dwifungsi* doctrine underpinned the military's territorial command structure, under which it deployed troops in
parallel to the civilian administration throughout the archipelago, as
well as its *kekaryaan* (nonmilitary function) principle, under which the
military placed active and retired officers within the civilian government, bureaucracy, and legislatures (Crouch 2010; Sebastian and Gindarsah 2013). The military also had substantial financial autonomy
from the civilian government, funded by a network of legal and illegal
businesses throughout the archipelago. Adding to the challenge for the
Habibie government, as Harold Crouch observes (2010, p. 130), the
military's senior command came through the transition intact and
regarded the new civilian president Habibie with little of the respect it
had afforded his predecessor. Beyond his civilian status, Habibie had
antagonized the military as a Suharto-era minister with his perceived
meddling in procurement, committing the armed forces to buying aging
East German warships.

Under such circumstances, various scholars have observed, the
civilian government could not impose reform upon the military, even if
such reforms were a crucial element of democratization (Crouch 2010,
p. 128; Sebastian and Gindarsah 2013). Nevertheless, the military's
position was not without weaknesses. David Bourchier (1999) outlines
three factors that temporarily set the military back during the transition.
The transition exposed the military to intense public criticism, for its
failure to maintain order in the final weeks of the Suharto regime,
because of its *dwifungsi* doctrine, and as the newly free media carried
extensive reports on past atrocities. The financial crisis that had precipitated the Suharto regime's demise also severely circumscribed the military's ability to raise funds independently of its budget allocation,
which was demoralizing for local commands. Finally, the military was
riven by factionalism, most notably between armed forces commander
Wiranto and his rival Prabowo Subianto, son-in-law of Suharto. Facing

such pressures, a small group of officers within the military garnered sufficient internal support to institute internal reforms.[3]

The landmark moment in this push for reform was the formulation of a "new Paradigm" at a military seminar in Bandung in September 1998 (Crouch 2010, p. 132; Sebastian and Gindarsah 2013, p. 33).[4] Under this paradigm, the military committed to withdraw from a formal political role, abandoning the *dwifungsi* doctrine, dissolving its Social and Political Affairs Branch, and requiring military officers seconded to civilian roles to relinquish their positions or retire from the military. It also committed to relinquish its appointed bloc in the national and local legislatures (albeit more gradually than civilian politicians ultimately determined) and to sever ties with the Suharto regime party, Golkar. The police were separated from the military in 1999, although for the remainder of the year continued to report to armed forces commander Wiranto in his role as minister of defense (McKenzie 2018, p. 215). The military renamed itself Tentara Nasional Indonesia (TNI [Indonesian National Army]), setting aside its previous designation as the Indonesian Armed Forces (Angkatan Bersenjata Republik Indonesia [ABRI]).

Much as these changes amount to a significant reconfiguration of civil-military relations, the arrangements left some key sources of military power untouched. Indeed, Jun Honna (2013, p. 186) characterizes the new equilibrium as a "grand bargain" under which the "TNI supports transition to civilian-led democracy and promises military disengagement from politics while civilian leaders respect TNI's institutional autonomy and overlook its lack of accountability." Crouch (2010, cited in Honna 2013, p. 197) highlights four untouched areas of military unaccountability following the Habibie-era reforms: the military's continuing role in internal security, despite the separation of the police; its maintenance of the territorial command, which if anything has expanded over subsequent decades (Institute for Policy Analysis of Conflict 2016, p. 8); the issue of military finances, with off-budget funds addressed only partially after a new TNI law was passed in 2004 (Sebastian and Gindarsah 2013, p. 35) and budget allocations to the military consistently below what defense planners estimate is required to develop a minimum essential force; and accountability for past human rights violations, with ad hoc courts set up to try military officers for past abuses not securing a single conviction (McGregor and Setiawan 2019). To these might be added the military's incomplete accountability to a civilian Ministry of Defense. Not until the government of Abdurrahman Wahid was the position of defense minister allocated to a civilian (under President Joko Widodo the defense minister has reverted to a retired military officer), and within the ministry, active generals continue to occupy key strategist posts (Honna 2013, p. 185; Sebastian and Gindarsah 2013, p. 35). Civilian politicians in the post-Habibie period would push only inconsistently for further reform on these fronts, when it suited their political interests to do so (Crouch 2010).

Constitutional Change

Following the far-reaching political change of the Habibie period, the next task for democratic reform was to amend the constitution. In contrast to preceding reforms, constitutional change was to be undertaken by a democratically constituted MPR, formed out of the 1999 elections (Horowitz 2013, p. 1). The process of constitutional change spanned three years, with both the process and its outcomes attracting significant criticism from scholars and Indonesian civil society at the time. Nevertheless, as of 2019, in the fifteen years since it was finalized, the amended 1945 constitution has proven a robust basis for Indonesia's democratic polity, despite criticisms of the amendment process being incomplete.

At the end of authoritarian rule, Indonesia's legal system was underpinned by its founding 1945 constitution, drafted in haste to support a declaration of independence before colonial rule could be reinstituted following the defeat of the Japanese. Although its drafters explicitly intended the document to be temporary and had drafted its provisions to provide maximum possible flexibility (Ellis 2002, pp. 117–118), Sukarno and Suharto's authoritarian regimes had sought to imbue the document with an almost sacred legitimacy as a symbol of the independence struggle (Ellis 2002, pp. 123–124; Crouch 2010, p. 46). Nevertheless, the document was entirely unsuited as a basis for democracy. It did not provide for either a parliamentary or a presidential system—the two basic forms of democratic governance. Nor did it provide any guarantees of individual rights, reflecting the integralist state ideology of its founders (Ellis 2002; Lindsey 2002, p. 253). Despite these deficiencies, it was decided Indonesia's democratic constitution would be drafted as a series of amendments to the 1945 document rather than starting afresh. This decision reflected the document's continuing legitimacy, compared to international cases where constitutions had been drafted by a discredited regime (Ellis 2002), as well as fears that starting anew would result in deadlock, based on an attempt to draft a replacement constitution in the 1950s (Horowitz 2013, p. 24).

Donald Horowitz highlights three aspects of Indonesia's constitutional amendment process as unusual. First, he characterized this process as unusually nonparticipatory, including when compared to other recent and contemporaneous democratic transitions in Indonesia's region (Horowitz

2013, p. 14). The MPR chose to handle the constitutional amendment process itself, with little public involvement, rather than delegating the process to a specially formed constitutional commission (Horowitz 2013, p. 261). Efforts to engage public attention on the amendment process—if not to directly involve the public—also largely failed (Ellis 2002). Horowitz (2013, pp. 3–4, 89) also highlights the risk that the MPR may have rejected an externally produced document, whereas its consensual drafting among Indonesia's main political forces facilitated its broad acceptance. He points to the fractured nature of Indonesia's opposition upon democratization as partly explaining the nonparticipatory model Indonesia adopted, particularly given that Indonesia lacked a cohesive opposition coalition that could claim the process of constitutional reform for itself. Such a drafting process exposed the constitution to extensive political compromise (Lindsey 2002, p. 275), but this may have been a necessary cost to facilitate its broad acceptance by Indonesia's main political forces (Horowitz 2013, pp. 3–4, 89).

The sequence of Indonesia's constitutional reform is a second anomaly, with postauthoritarian elections in Indonesia preceding the amendment process rather than signaling the endpoint of the democratic transition (Horowitz 2013, p. 2). Fresh elections were required to confer sufficient legitimacy on the MPR to undertake the task of constitutional change, Horowitz argues, which could not have been commanded by the authoritarian holdover legislature. Even then, as with the overall reform process, authoritarian-era figures played a greater role than the broader reform movement; for example, the man chairing the ad hoc MPR committee that led the amendment process was Jakob Tobing, who had served as a DPR member for Golkar from 1972 to 1992 (Tomsa 2008).

Third, Donald Horowitz characterizes Indonesia's process of constitutional change as unusually gradual, achieved as it was via four annual amendments. It then took at least two more years to enact legislation to spell out the details of these amendments. Both Ellis and Horowitz argue this incremental approach counterintuitively enabled more far-reaching changes than might otherwise have been possible. Partial amendments were agreed to without their full implications being widely understood, Andrew Ellis (2005) argues, and Horowitz (2013, pp. 3–5) observes that the gradual approach gave conservatives time to become comfortable with amendments they might otherwise have rejected.

The first of the four amendments, formulated prior to a comprehensive process of constitutional review, was passed at the same MPR session in 1999 that elected Abdurrahman Wahid as president. In the main, this initial amendment clarified and strengthened the role of the newly elected DPR vis-à-vis the president (Ellis 2002, p. 126). This amendment placed the legislature on a more level footing with the government in the drafting of legislation, with laws to be jointly agreed on with the president, rather than submitted for the legislature's approval. It also required the president to consult with the legislature on ambassadorial appointments and the granting of amnesty, and it confirmed the two-term limit for the president, stipulated in 1998 by MPR decree (Ellis 2002, p. 126; Lindsey 2002, p. 249).

The three subsequent amendments, negotiated in each of the next three annual MPR sessions, drew upon a comprehensive review of the constitution undertaken by an ad hoc MPR committee following this first amendment. The committee of representatives of all political parties and groups appointed in the MPR proposed an amended constitution comprising twenty-one chapters, six of which were entirely new (Ellis 2002, p. 128). Issues that were more likely to be agreed upon swiftly were prioritized, on the understanding that issues resolved in each amendment would not be revisited in subsequent rounds. The pace of constitutional debate was also guided by the understanding that an amended document needed to be completed by 2002, so that the 2004 elections could proceed smoothly (Ellis 2002, p. 136).

The most significant amendments concluded in 2000 concerned defense and security, the composition of the legislature, regional autonomy, and human rights (Ellis 2002, pp. 131–133; Lindsey 2002, pp. 250–256; Horowitz 2013, p. 98). On defense and security, the constitution specified differing, if overlapping, roles for the police and the military, granting the DPR the power to legislate to determine the details. This amendment also determined that the DPR would be elected in its entirety and further strengthened the DPR's legislative role by determining that bills agreed to by the DPR would pass into law after thirty days, even if the president failed to sign.[5] A constitutional basis was added for regional autonomy—already legislated in 2000—along with the requirement that mayors and governors be "democratically elected."[6] Although explicit wording requiring direct elections was rejected during this constitutional debate, the DPR subsequently legislated to this effect in 2004. Finally, this amendment introduced a new chapter on human rights to the constitution, for the most part closely modeled on the Universal Declaration of Human Rights. The MPR thus overturned the aforementioned integralist ideological underpinnings of the 1945 constitution. These changes were contained within just seven of the proposed chapters of the constitution, however, leaving many of the most fundamental questions regarding Indonesia's political system unresolved (Ellis 2002, p. 131).

The third set of amendments passed in 2001 are generally high-lighted as the most significant, although Ellis (2002, p. 140) notes that their importance was largely missed within Indonesia at the time. Indeed, as Tim Lindsey (2002, pp. 265–266) observes, the perception that the MPR was unfavorably deadlocked led to fresh calls in 2001 for an independent constitutional commission, although this proposal ulti-mately did not gain support. Negotiated in the wake of the MPR's impeachment of President Abdurrahman Wahid in July 2001, this set of amendments established Indonesia as a presidential system, substan-tially increasing the president's autonomy from the MPR (Ellis 2002, pp. 140–143; Lindsey 2002, pp. 259–265; Horowitz 2013, pp. 115–116). This amendment determined that the president and vice president would henceforth be elected directly and be free to set their govern-ment's policy direction, as the MPR's power to set broad outlines of state policy in the State Policy Guidelines (Garis-garis Besar Haluan Negara [GBHN]) and to remove the president for not adhering to them were abolished. Impeachment would now require misconduct on the part of the president and involve the adjudication of a newly created consti-tutional court. This amendment also established the directly elected Regional Representative Assembly (Dewan Perwakilan Daerah [DPD]), and an independent State Audit Board and Judicial Commission, and provided for judicial independence, albeit only in a "nominal [manner] at best" (Lindsey 2002, p. 264).

Three core unresolved issues were then finalized in the fourth set of amendments in 2002 (Ellis 2005; Lindsey 2002, pp. 267–271). It was decided a second-round runoff for the presidential election, if required, would also be a direct election, and not an indirect election via the MPR. This amendment also determined that the MPR would be fully elected after the 2004 elections, with the military and functional group appointees abolished, with the result that the MPR would thereafter consist of the DPR and the DPD. This was one of the few provisions that required a vote to resolve (Ellis 2005). Finally, repeating a decision made during the drafting of the original 1945 constitution six decades earlier, and avoiding the risk of a fundamental schism over the relationship between Islam and the state, the MPR determined that the amended constitution would not contain the so-called Jakarta Charter, which would make adherence to Islamic law compulsory for Muslims. Recognizing the significance of the moment, Ellis (2005) recounts, the members marked the closing of this MPR session with a rendition of the national anthem.

Although the fourth amendment concluded the changes to the text of the constitution, Horowitz (2013, p. 2) observes that Indonesia's process of constitutional change might more accurately be thought of as extending until 2008 or beyond, encompassing the period of legislative change and the elections that brought the newly defined executive and legislative branches of the government into being. At least thirteen laws were required to spell out the details of the constitutional amendments (Lindsey 2002, pp. 271–272); with some exceptions, most were passed in 2003 and 2004.

Not everyone saw the fourth amendment as the end of Indonesia's constitutional amendment process; both activists and scholars called for further change. In response to civil society pressure, the MPR formed a constitutional commission after the conclusion of this amendment. This commission proposed that there be a fifth amendment in 2004, but it was not adopted (Lindsey 2002, p. 272; Horowitz 2013, pp. 158–159). Lindsey (2002, p. 275) characterized the amended constitution as urgently requiring further "significant and effective constitutional reform." Despite its imperfections, however, the amended 1945 constitution has proven a robust basis for the democratic polity for the past seventeen years, and pressure for further democratizing reforms in its formulation has receded. If anything, from the mid-2010s on, more concerted efforts have been made to wind back the reforms of the amended constitution than to extend its provisions. Prabowo Subianto's presidential campaign platform in 2014 included a promise to return to the original 1945 constitution, for example, and he called during the campaign for an end to direct elections for the president (McRae 2014a). There have also been calls from the MPR during the first Jokowi administration to restore the broad outlines of State Policy Guidelines. It is unclear how such a restoration could be compatible with a system in which the president is directly elected.

Violent Transition

For most Indonesians, the reforms set out so far in this chapter entailed a period of increasing civil liberties and democratic participation after four decades of authoritarian rule in Indonesia. In stark contrast to this general pattern, however, eight provinces in Indonesia encompassing 7 percent of the population (Aspinall 2008a) experienced large-scale violent conflict, as mostly new communal conflicts erupted and long-standing secessionist insurgencies intensified. Small-scale conflicts, riots of short duration, and crime-like social violence were more widespread and in some cases caused very significant casualties. Around 1,000 people are estimated to have died in rioting in Jakarta the week before Suharto resigned, for example. Overall, the large-scale conflicts are estimated to have caused around 21,000 deaths during the transition period (Barron, Jaffrey, and Varshney 2016, p. 194), a figure that excludes deaths in Papua. Such experience of violence means that Indonesia's democratic transition cannot be described as peaceful, even if large-scale violence was confined to specific localities and the number of fatalities was far lower than during the regime transition of 1965–1966. Equally, however, these conflicts were transitional. Levels of violence had diminished significantly by 2002 in most of these areas and receded further still in 2005, when a peace deal ended the war between separatists and the central government in Aceh.

Although the contexts of the large-scale communal conflicts and the intensification of the secessionist insurgencies are clearly related, each is discussed separately below.

Communal Violence

Scholarly consensus has emerged regarding the enabling factors for the large-scale communal conflicts, constructed in the main by three authors who compare the conflicts as a set (Bertrand 2004; Sidel 2006; van Klinken 2007).[7] These enabling factors span both the overall national context and the particularities of each of the five sites of violence.

At the national level, the uncertainty of the post-Suharto transition, particularly the far-reaching changes to the electoral system and the decentralization of governance, were the key factors. These changes left groups that had gained privileged access to state resources under Suharto uncertain about how they could maintain their advantage, whereas theretofore excluded groups saw an opportunity to advance

Table 4.1 Sites of Large-Scale Violence During Indonesia's Democratic Transition

Communal Violence			
Inter-religious	*Inter-ethnic*	Secessionist Conflict	Major Riots
Central Sulawesi (Poso)	West Kalimantan	Aceh	Jakarta[a]
Maluku	Central Kalimantan	Papua	Medan
North Maluku		East Timor[b]	Solo

Notes: a. Many other towns and cities also experienced riots; Jakarta, Medan, and Solo are highlighted because of the scale of violence and because each is a major Indonesian city.
b. East Timor voted to secede from Indonesia in 1999 and is now Timor-Leste.

their position (Bertrand 2004; Sidel 2006; van Klinken 2007). Exacerbating the risk of conflict, the state's coercive capacity was also temporarily weakened just as these changes were taking place, as set out in the discussion of civil-military relations above. Once the conflicts began, their simultaneous occurrence further impaired the security forces' capacity to respond, as they experienced troop shortages (Kammen 2003; Crouch 2010, p. 249).

Such uncertainty, though, was experienced nationally, whereas large-scale communal conflict happened only in five provinces, and in some of these provinces, only in a certain district or districts. To explain this localized incidence of violence, scholars highlight several features of the local social structure and economy common to each location. In demographic terms, each province where violence occurred had a significant religious minority. As John Sidel (2006, p. 190) observes, the Muslim population of each fell within the admittedly broad range of 30–85 percent. (Nationally, in 2000, the percentage of Muslims in Indonesia was 88 percent, according to census data, whereas the percentage of Muslims in eastern Indonesia, where these conflicts occurred, was 72 percent.)[8] Regarding the local economy, contestation over state resources was disproportionately important to the local economy in each site of violence, which lacked major industry or an otherwise developed private sector that could have created nonagricultural jobs not linked to the local government (van Klinken 2007). The stakes were thus unusually high in local competition for control of the government between rival patronage networks, many of which were formed along ethnic and religious lines.

Under such common circumstances, five large-scale communal conflicts erupted. Each conflict differed markedly in duration and intensity, the forms of violence, and the actors responsible. First was West Kalimantan (1997 and 1999), which, along with Central Kalimantan (2001), was one of two cases of violence that took place along ethnic lines, with each episode of violence lasting only a few weeks. In each of these episodes, groups claiming indigenous status murdered hundreds of Madurese migrants and forcibly evicted many more (Davidson 2008; van Klinken 2007). Uniquely among these conflicts, the first episode of violence in West Kalimantan preceded Suharto's fall, leading Jamie Davidson (2008) to trace its occurrence to a local history or to recurrent rioting between Dayak and Madura ethnic groups, triggered in the first instance by competition between these two groups to occupy lands left behind by departing ethnic Chinese in the 1960s, themselves displaced by military counterinsurgency operations.

Two sites—Poso (1998–2007) and Maluku (1999–2005)—experienced Christian-Muslim religious conflicts that lasted many years. Both differed in scale and intensity, however. At the peak of the fighting, the Maluku conflict was far more intense than that in Poso, causing thousands rather than hundreds of deaths. As the Maluku conflict engulfed the provincial capital, the damage to public infrastructure was also much more severe than in Poso, a regional town even within the isolated province where it is located. This comparison was reversed during the longer phase of sporadic violence that followed the peak of fighting in each location, during which approximately twice as many people were killed in Poso as in Maluku. The North Maluku conflict (1999–2000) was different again; the worst fighting was between Christians and Muslims, but the conflict also included episodes of interethnic fighting and even clashes between different Muslim factions. Fighting there was especially intense; the conflict had all but concluded within a year but resulted in as many deaths as did the conflict in Maluku (Wilson 2008). Fighting in North Maluku also engulfed that province's main urban center on the island of Ternate, but the worst violence was on the nearby island of Halmahera.

By 2002—and even earlier in West Kalimantan, Central Kalimantan, and North Maluku—the scale of violence in each of these conflicts had diminished significantly or stopped altogether. Heavy deployments of security forces contributed, as did partially effective peace agreements brokered by the central government in Poso and Maluku. In several of these conflicts, fighting diminished when conflict reached a new equilibrium or stalemate and communities questioned whether there was more to gain from further large-scale fighting (McRae 2013a; Wilson 2008; Barron, Jaffrey, and Varshney 2016). Sporadic violence continued—in the case of Poso for many years thereafter—but Patrick Barron, Sanu Jaffrey, and Ashutosh Varshney (2016, p. 201), comparing annual deaths for the periods 1998–2003 and 2004–2012, observe a 79 percent reduction in fatalities in the provinces where there had been large-scale communal violence.

Separatist Violence

At the same time that these communal conflagrations were breaking out, Indonesia faced concerted challenges to its national unity in three provinces at opposite ends of the archipelago—East Timor, Papua, and Aceh. In each of these provinces, armed separatist movements had challenged Indonesian rule during the authoritarian era, and in each there was renewed agitation for independence soon after Suharto fell, with starkly different outcomes. East Timor was offered a referendum in 1999 and exited the republic the same year. Aceh gained far-reaching special autonomy as part of a 2005 peace deal between insurgents and the central government, after earlier autonomy deals had failed to terminate the conflict. The Papua conflict remained unresolved in 2019, with its own special autonomy deal apparently having done little to diminish support for independence among indigenous communities (Chauvel 2005).

Aceh, East Timor, and Papua each have differing, if troubled, histories of incorporation into Indonesia. Aceh was seen as a nationalist stronghold during Indonesia's struggle for independence in the 1940s but had become the site of an Islamist rebellion by the 1950s. That initial rebellion was not secessionist; this political direction only emerged with Gerakan Aceh Merdeka (Free Aceh Movement [GAM]) in the 1970s. GAM was quickly defeated militarily but reemerged in the late 1980s and remained the most powerful pro-independence force in the province (Aspinall and Berger 2002; McGibbon 2004). Like Aceh, Papua was also part of the Netherlands-administered East Indies, but the Dutch refused to hand over the territory when Indonesia gained independence in 1949, spurring a prolonged struggle by Indonesian nationalists to gain control of the territory. A 1962 agreement between Indonesia and the Netherlands established UN administration in Papua in anticipation of its handover to Indonesia, with Indonesian rule confirmed in a so-called Act of Free Choice (Penentuan Pendapat Rakyat [PEPERA]) in 1969, when around 1,000 handpicked delegates opted for incorporation with Indonesia. Throughout the authoritarian era, a small insurgency resisted Indonesian rule, calling itself the Organisasi Papua Merdeka (Free Papua Movement [OPM]) (Aspinall and Berger 2002, pp. 1013–1015; Bertrand 2004, pp. 144–153). East Timor, by contrast, was never part of the Dutch colony; instead, Portugal controlled this territory until the colonial power's departure in 1974. A brief civil war ensued, won by pro-independence party Fretilin, before Indonesia invaded in December 1975. As it was never part of the Dutch colony, the United Nations never recognized East Timor as part of Indonesia, although Western nations such as Australia and the United States acquiesced to Indonesia's military intervention at the time, and Australia subsequently recognized Indonesian sovereignty. Fretilin conducted a guerrilla war against Indonesian control until East Timor won its independence (Aspinall and Berger 2002, pp. 1010–1013; Bertrand 2004, pp. 136–142).

Nevertheless, scholars identify commonalities in each territory's experience of Suharto's authoritarian rule that fueled their demands to secede (Aspinall and Berger 2002; Bertrand 2007; McGibbon 2004). The Indonesian military waged a heavy campaign of repression during the New Order, targeting both the independence movement and the broader civilian population. Each was a site of large-scale natural resource extraction, with only a fraction of their resource wealth channeled back to local communities. Each territory was also subject to the New Order's rollout of uniform administrative arrangements across all of Indonesia, despite local political forces claiming distinct ethnic or religious identities. In each case, mainstream New Order discourse depicted indigenous residents of the provinces as less developed, or otherwise inferior, to other Indonesians and denigrated them as ungrateful despite receiving the state's development largesse (McRae 2002). Additionally, in comparative terms, each territory also shared characteristics, identified by Thomas Parks, Nat Colletta, and Ben Oppenheim (2013) as common to all sites of "secessionist sub-national conflict" across Asia: each was on an international territorial or maritime border, with a low share of the national population and of the nation's territory.[9]

All three provinces experienced large protests demanding independence almost immediately after Suharto resigned (Aspinall and Berger 2002, p. 1009). The central government responded first to Timor, for which Habibie decided in January 1999 to hold a referendum offering autonomy arrangements within Indonesia or independence. With the military temporarily weakened, senior generals in the Indonesian cabinet could not prevent the referendum—a state of affairs Crouch (2010, p. 26) describes as "incredible." Instead, the military formed a set of pro-autonomy militias to intimidate the civilian population into opting against independence. These militias were responsible for around 1,500 deaths before and after the referendum (Barron, Jaffrey, and Varshney 2016, p. 199) but could not dissuade 78 percent of Timorese voters from choosing independence in the August 1999 vote. Upon this result, the military and its auxiliaries destroyed most public infrastructure in Timor, and 250,000 people were displaced across the border into Indonesian West Timor in what Rod McGibbon (2004, p. 12) interprets as a warning to other provinces of the cost of secession. Nevertheless, after an international force was deployed to restore order, East Timor was placed under UN administration in October 1999 and became the fully independent nation of Timor-Leste in May 2002.

Large post-Suharto civilian protest movements in Aceh and Papua failed to gain a similar offer of a referendum from the Habibie government. Instead, Habibie's first response was to enact limited special autonomy legislation for each province, which did nothing to dampen demands for independence (McGibbon 2004, p. 11). Following the Habibie period, different actors within central authorities pursued a mix of accommodation and coercion. Habibie's successor, Abdurrahman Wahid, was personally accommodating, initially entertaining demands for a referendum in Aceh and allowing the raising of the Morning Star flag (Bintang Kejora)—a Papuan independence symbol—only to be overruled in each case by the military (McGibbon 2004; Honna 2013, p. 187). The national legislature also opted for accommodation, directing the government in 2000 to conclude more substantial autonomy arrangements and passing autonomy legislation for each province in 2001 (McGibbon 2004). Although the government bureaucracy substantially circumscribed these autonomy arrangements during the drafting stage, McGibbon (2004) and Jacques Bertrand (2007) emphasize their significance as a departure from uniform, unitary Indonesian nationalism. Unlike Habibie's 1999 decentralization legislation, these laws allowed different terms of incorporation into the nation for Aceh and Papua, at least ostensibly based on local particularities, and in Papua's case, uniquely allowing the formation of political institutions defined in ethnic terms (McGibbon 2004, pp. 22–24; Bertrand 2007, pp. 592–605).

Undercutting these measures, however, the military continued a campaign of coercion. In Aceh, it undermined a 2002 Cessation of Hostilities Agreement with GAM (McGibbon observes GAM was not blameless, either) and successfully pushed the Megawati government to enact martial law in 2003 (McGibbon 2004, pp. 43–53). In Papua, the military responded with violence to independence protests and assassinated independence leader Theys Eluay, thereby curtailing the ability of pro-independence groups to mobilize support and articulate their demands (Bertrand 2004, p. 158; McGibbon 2004, pp. 40–41; International Centre for Transitional Justice and KontraS 2011, p. 2). At the same time, the Megawati government undercut the new autonomy arrangements. It split Papua into two separate provinces in 2003, in direct violation of special autonomy legislation, and effectively suspended autonomy altogether in Aceh in 2003 with the imposition of martial law. Freed of the crisis situation that prompted the initial grant of special autonomy, McGibbon (2004, p. viii) writes, the state moved to wind back these concessions, in line with an international tendency toward reversal of autonomy arrangements.

As of 2019, Aceh and Papua's circumstances have diverged considerably. In 2005 in Aceh, where GAM established itself as a credible military adversary and fought to the point of a "hurting stalemate," an internationally brokered peace deal was concluded. The deal was enshrined in autonomy legislation in 2006 that far exceeded earlier laws in details and scope (Bertrand 2007), and GAM and its political party have since controlled the governorship and the provincial legislature. Papua, however, appears no closer to resolution. Dissatisfaction with special autonomy is widespread; sporadic violence continues between independence supporters and the Indonesian military, which maintains a heavy presence; slated dialogue between central authorities and Papua has not come about either under the current Jokowi government or its predecessors.

Conclusion

Democratization in Indonesia brought about a fundamental transformation of the nation's political institutions, despite strong continuities in its political elite between the authoritarian and democratic eras. Over time, however, political reforms have slowed or stagnated, and even regressed in some instances. To gain a full appreciation of the likely future trajectory of political change in Indonesia, we now turn to look more closely at the mechanisms underpinning the democratic polity.

Notes

1. Local parties are allowed only in Aceh, as part of the 2005 peace settlement between the Indonesian government and the Free Aceh Movement, and these parties can compete only for the provincial and district legislatures. Special autonomy legislation for Papua also included provision for local parties, but none were ever allowed to form.

2. Malley (2009) and Crouch (2010) provide good summaries of the details of the two decentralization laws passed in 1999; the remainder of this paragraph draws on their accounts.

3. Differing accounts of this dynamic are given by Crouch and by Sebastian and Gindarsah. Where Crouch (2010, p. 132) describes Wiranto entrusting reform-minded officers "with the task of re-conceptualizing the military's future role," Sebastian and Gindarsah (2013, p. 33) describe these same officers as "eventually persuad[ing] Wiranto to implement internal reforms."

4. Both Crouch (2010) and Sebastian and Gindarsah (2013) summarize well the initial reforms made by the TNI; the remainder of this paragraph draws on their accounts.

5. Despite this provision, the requirement for bills to be jointly agreed, inserted during the first amendment, provides the president with an effective right of veto, as the president can prevent the DPR from finalizing any law by refusing to discuss the legislation.

6. We use the term *mayor* to denote the heads of the two different third-tier units of government in Indonesia, namely, *kabupaten* (districts) and *kota* (municipalities). In some other works the heads of districts are called "district heads," but this distinction is not necessary for the analysis herein.

7. This scholarly consensus is set out in more detail in McRae (2013a, pp. 19–33), with a focus on Poso, upon which this summary draws.

8. The figure for "eastern Indonesia" is calculated from Suryadinata, Arifin, and Ananta (2003, pp. 104, 109–110, 138), based on all provinces outside Java and Sumatra.

9. Papua is a partial exception, as its share of Indonesian land territory is large, although far removed from the national center of power.

5

The Structures of Democratic-Era Politics

THIS CHAPTER OUTLINES FOUR OF THE KEY STRUCTURES OF democratic-era politics in Indonesia: decentralization, elections, political parties, and patronage politics. Across the board, the picture that emerges is of a political system fundamentally altered after the demise of the Suharto regime, yet still marked by significant democratic deficits.

Decentralization

Chapter 4 introduced the far-reaching decentralization legislation of 1999 that transformed Indonesia from a highly centralized polity to governance arrangements that some observers have described as "de facto federalism" (Hill 2014, p. 2). To recap, the legislation reserved sole authority for the center in only six areas of governance. Over time, it has more than doubled the share of government revenue allocated to subnational governments—more than 34 percent of government expenditure in 2018 was at the subnational level, according to government budget figures. The 1999 decentralization laws passed with very little debate or modification but reflected regional pressures for changes to Indonesia's governance arrangements preceding their enactment (Malley 2009). These arrangements for decentralization have been modified twice through new legislation—in 2004 and 2014—with a slight recentralizing effect. Nevertheless, the same arrangements as enacted in the 1999 legislation remain substantially in place.

Two impacts of decentralization on the Indonesian polity explain its resilience and persistence in largely unmodified form. First, decentralization has stabilized center-periphery relations, heading off fears of a Yugoslavia-style disintegration in Indonesia (Mietzner 2014, pp. 62–63).

Second, a constellation of powerful local interests now profits from decentralization, using control of local political posts for personal enrichment (Hadiz 2010; Choi and Fukuoka 2015). Before turning to a broader analysis of the impacts of decentralization, two aspects of decentralized politics that have been fundamental both to its effects on center-periphery relations and on local governance need to be sketched as background.

The first fundamental aspect is the direct election of governors and mayors (used here to refer to heads both of urban municipalities and nonurban districts), introduced by the first amendment to decentralization arrangements in 2004.[1] Prior to the 2004 amendment, these offices were indirectly elected by local legislatures. Indirect elections answered demands for regions to have the ultimate say over their local executives (who under Suharto had been chosen by the Ministry of Home Affairs, which often appointed Javanese or Sundanese officials to preside over ethnically distinct regions) (Malley 2009, pp. 141–142; Mietzner 2014). Indirect elections soon fell out of favor, however, because of widespread vote buying and because mayors and governors were excessively beholden to local legislatures, which could dismiss them if they rejected annual accountability reports. Under the current system of direct elections, coalitions of political parties holding at least 15 percent of the votes or seats in each local legislature nominate candidate pairs, who are directly elected. Since 2008, independent candidates have also been allowed. Until 2014, these elections were scattered across the years between each of Indonesia's five-yearly general elections; since 2015, they have been grouped into three sets, held in the first, third, and fourth years after a general election. By 2027, the government hopes to further consolidate the timing of these elections so that all of them are held on a single day.

The second feature is the immense proliferation of new districts in particular, but also of provinces, under a process known in Indonesia as *pemekaran* (blossoming). Since decentralization after Suharto's presidency, the number of districts and municipalities has grown from 314 in 1998 to 508 in 2014, and eight new provinces have been established in the same period, bringing the total number of provinces to thirty-four (Hill 2014, p. 3; Kementerian Dalam Negeri Republik 2014). A large majority of the new divisions have been made outside of Java (Booth 2011a; Chauvel 2008; Mietzner 2014). The concentration of this *pemekaran* process in the more sparsely populated outer islands has produced sharp discrepancies between the population size of subnational units in different parts of the country. Anne Booth (2011a) observes that five of the newly created provinces have populations smaller than the average district in Java. Indeed, the small size of many of the new areas being created and attendant concerns over their viability eventually prompted a moratorium on further divisions. Nevertheless, new campaigns for additional *pemekaran* divisions have continued to proliferate, driven by the desire to secure central government transfers for often marginalized areas of existing districts and provinces, as well as the opportunity for local elites to position themselves at the apex of patronage networks in newly created regions. As of mid-2017, Home Affairs Minister Tjahjo Kumolo told the press that 314 applications for further divisions had been tabled with his ministry (Rahadian 2017).

The Threat of Disintegration

Indonesia's post-Suharto decentralization legislation was enacted as secessionist movements were intensifying, and at a time when other regions were voicing secessionist rhetoric to claim a greater share of revenues derived from their natural resources. Several scholars identify these centrifugal dynamics as the key concern motivating central government policymakers to enact decentralization legislation (Aspinall 2013a; Mietzner 2014, p. 45). Aspinall (2013a, p. 129), for example, observes, "the dominant public justification was that decentralization would respond to swelling discontent in the regions and so bolster national unity."

This concern for national unity is reflected in the decision to devolve political authority mainly to Indonesia's then 300-odd districts and municipalities, rather than to its roughly thirty provinces. Bypassing the provinces prevented them from becoming political units that could challenge the center and demand secession, but that structure greatly complicated intergovernmental coordination. As fears for Indonesia's national unity have receded, each amendment to decentralization arrangements has incrementally strengthened the role of the provinces. Apart from the choice to devolve authority primarily to the district level, the requirement that national parties nominate local executives and the equalizing effect of central government transfers on inequalities between regions have also undercut secession (Mietzner 2014, p. 64).[2]

Two decades of decentralized governance have also stabilized center-periphery relations by making radical recentralization far less likely. As early as 2004, one of the chief architects of decentralization, Ryaas Rasyid (2004, p. 73), predicted that any attempt to recentralize would produce "great tension" between the central and subnational governments. Vedi Hadiz (2010, p. 179) made this argument most forcefully several years later, writing that the "interests that preside over local power are by now so well-entrenched that they cannot simply be ignored or wished away" and predicting that any concerted effort to recentralize Indonesia's polity would entail a violent, unpredictable struggle. The next section highlights the governance deficits associated with decentralization that have facilitated the local consolidation of power.

Bringing Governance Closer to the People?

It is clear that local predatory interests have thrived under decentralization, belying the good governance agenda of international institutions and donors such as the World Bank (Hadiz 2010; Choi and Fukuoka 2015). This agenda assumes a "largely mutually reinforcing relationship between decentralisation, good governance and the advancement of market economies" (Hadiz 2010, p. 23). Instead, according to Hadiz, predatory interests similar to those that oligarchists see as dominating national politics have taken control of decentralized politics and have used their control of political office for self-enrichment. The money and political experience of New Order–era bureaucrats, politicians, and businesspeople enabled them to outcompete civil society, labor, and the peasantry in direct local elections as the latter groups struggled with the legacy of authoritarian repression.

The predatory nature of much decentralized politics is clearly visible in the natural resources sector, encompassing such industries as mining, logging, and palm oil production. Under decentralization, district and provincial governments gained the authority to issue small-scale licenses for these industries, as well as an increased share of government royalties. This created a strong incentive for local actors to facilitate the expansion of these industries. Palm oil production more than tripled between 2000 and 2012, for example, although decentralization was only one of the drivers (Pichler 2015, p. 517). Rates of deforestation also increased under decentralization (Adrison 2013), although mining exploration and exploitation may actually have decreased, at least in the case of legal activities (Fox, Adhuri, and Resosudarmo 2005, p. 104; Gandataruna and Haymon 2011, p. 224). Natural resource license fees and royalties provided local governments with locally derived revenue, prized as non-earmarked funds that could be used for local discretionary spending, as well as the opportunity to raise off-budget funds through kickbacks. In addition to self-enrichment, such kickbacks and other donations by rent-seeking local businesspeople were an important source of funds for local politicians to fund expensive campaigns to win office as mayors and governors (Mietzner 2011).

So strong were the incentives to issue new licenses for resource exploitation that district, provincial, and national authorities often issued overlapping concessions to different resource companies or designated different uses for the same tract of land (for one example, see Erman 2005, p. 212). In response to these problems, the central government revoked the power of subnational government to issue forestry licenses in 2002 and sought to clarify the division of authority to issue mining permits between different levels of government in a 2009 law on mining. In the case of forestry, the central government also sought to give force to its revocation of local authority through a concerted law enforcement drive against illegal logging in 2005 (McCarthy 2011, p. 103). John McCarthy observes the irony that such law enforcement may simply have shifted rent seeking and profiteering to another industry; powerful forestry actors evaded arrest and were spurred by the new transaction costs of forestry to move to the palm oil sector.

Predatory interests, including many bureaucrats, businesspeople, party politicians, and powerful families, have also done well in local direct elections (Buehler 2013a). Undercutting the competitiveness of these elections, incumbents have also enjoyed a significant advantage, winning more than 50 percent of the vote overall by various estimates, and perhaps as many as two-thirds of contests in which there has been at least one incumbent running (McRae and Zhang 2015). Hadiz (2010) draws on such details to argue that local direct elections have facilitated, and perhaps even strengthened, control of local politics by local oligarchs. The high cost of running for office means candidates without their own reserves of capital typically become indebted to oligarchic backers. Incumbents thrown out of office are replaced by members of the same dominant social interests, rather than by genuinely new candidates. The requirement for candidates to be nominated by political parties helps the same social interests to dominate, because marginalized groups such as labor and the peasantry lack a political party to aggregate their interests.

Notwithstanding these successes, the imperative to attain electoral success places an important new constraint on the same predatory interests (Mietzner 2010). The imperative to attain electoral success requires candidates to present a pro-people image, spurring increased spending of public funds on community interests (Zhang and McRae 2015), including the rollout of local health insurance plans. In at least a few intriguingly high-profile cases, local elections have also facilitated the entry into the political system of reformist candidates who would otherwise have been unlikely to gain office. Notable examples include the former governor of Jakarta, Basuki Tjahaja Purnama (Ahok); Surabaya mayor Tri Rismaharini; former mayor of Bandung and now governor of West Java, Ridwan Kamil; and the former mayor of Solo and current president Joko Widodo.

As we write this in 2019, current president Joko Widodo merits brief separate discussion in this context. Originally a furniture trader, Widodo lacked the political connections or degree of wealth that would have been required to win office through indirect elections. When direct elections began in 2005, however, the local branch head of the Partai Demokrasi Indonesia Perjuangan (Indonesian Democratic Struggle Party [PDI-P]), a Christian, was uncertain he could win a popular vote and opted instead to position himself as Jokowi's running mate. Upon winning office, Widodo's consultative brand of politics, including seemingly impromptu visits to public spaces frequented by the lower classes, gained him local popularity and national renown (Mas'udi 2017). He gained more than 90 percent of the vote in 2010, running for a second term, and became PDI-P's candidate for the much more important Jakarta gubernatorial elections in 2012. A two-round victory over mediocre incumbent Fauzi Bowo saw Jokowi's profile increase still further, and less than two years into his term in Jakarta, he won office as president.

An apparent paradox, given their poor governance outcomes, is the popularity with voters of both decentralization and local direct elections. Indonesians consistently express satisfaction with decentralization and local public-service delivery in opinion polls. Similarly, the government was forced to backtrack on the abolition of direct local elections in 2014 in the face of a public backlash. Mietzner attributes decentralization's popularity to the space it has created for the expression of local identities, in spite of its poor governance outcomes. Blane Lewis (2014, p. 152), by contrast, attributes the popularity of decentralization to insufficient demand from citizens for a better quality of service provision from the government. Regardless, scholars across the spectrum of analysis of Indonesian politics are united in their judgment that Indonesia's polity will remain significantly decentralized for the foreseeable future.

Elections

Viewed twenty years after the end of authoritarian rule, the reforms to Indonesia's authoritarian-era electoral system now look substantial. The president, governors, and mayors are all now elected by popular

vote, whereas each was indirectly elected by legislatures under authoritarian rule. In legislative elections, voters only had a choice between
three regime-approved parties under Suharto; they can now choose
either a party or one of the party's individual candidates. These
changes were made incrementally, however, and were driven as much
by the political interests of political parties as by a broader impulse
for democratic reform.

Indonesians turned to the task of holding fresh elections in 1999
following the fall of Suharto. It was widely acknowledged that the
authoritarian-era closed-list electoral system in which seats were allocated proportionally by province offered insufficient accountability
(Ellis 2004, p. 499). Consistent with the centralized pattern of
Suharto's rule, this system allowed Jakarta-based party leaders rather
than voters to determine who represented their party in the legislature—the ballot paper listed only parties, not candidates—and the size
of electorates made members of parliament (MPs) only weakly
accountable to constituents. A team appointed by Habibie to draw up
new electoral rules for the first postauthoritarian elections in June
1999 proposed a new system composed primarily of single-member
electorates, but political parties rejected this proposal (King 2003, p.
56). Instead, these elections retained the closed-list system and continued to assign votes to parties by province. Virtually the only accommodation of concerns over accountability was to nominally assign
MPs to represent districts within each province, to establish a connection with constituents (Ellis 2004, p. 500). The electoral commission
charged with implementing the 1999 election was also subjected to
greater, if imperfect, accountability. Half of its commissioners were
government officials appointed by the president and half were representatives of political parties, producing what Dwight King (2003, p.
54) terms a semi-independent commission.[3] Despite these various
changes to the system for legislative elections, the conduct of the
1999 presidential election was consistent with authoritarian-era practice, whereby the president was elected indirectly by the MPR rather
than directly by popular vote.

Despite dissatisfaction with the conduct of the 1999 elections, further legislative change was deferred until after the completion of constitutional reforms in 2002 (Ellis 2004, pp. 504–505). In the meantime,
these constitutional reforms in themselves altered Indonesia's electoral
system. The third amendment established direct elections for the presidency, a change soon also made via legislation for the elections of
mayors and governors.[4] In both cases, these executive leaders were

required to run as a single ticket combining a candidate and a deputy. The constitution also established that the DPR and MPR would be elected in their entirety, eliminating military and other appointees. In lieu of its appointed members, the MPR would henceforth comprise the DPR and an elected regional Representative Council (DPD). The latter body comprises four non-party representatives per province, elected by direct vote on the same day as legislative elections. Because the DPD has turned out to be largely powerless in Indonesian politics, the process of its election is not discussed further in this chapter. Continuity was maintained with the past in five-year terms for the legislature and executive, although the president, governors, and mayors were all made subject to a two-term limit.

Following these constitutional changes, the new election law for the 2004 legislative elections made two key changes. First, DPR members would now be elected from multimember electorates, typically spanning one to several districts and ranging in size from three to twelve members (Ellis 2004, p. 507). Second, voters could now choose a (political party) candidate rather than just a political party, as part of a semi-open-list system. Under this system, a candidate lower on a party list would automatically be elected ahead of candidates higher on the list if they reached a certain quota of individual votes. In practice, this reform still gave political parties almost absolute control over which of their candidates would represent the party, as the quota was set so high that only two candidates achieved it (Ufen 2010, p. 282). This election was also the first to include a gender quota, requiring political parties to allocate at least 30 percent of candidate slots to women. After this quota produced only a modest increase in female representation from 9.6 percent in 1999 to 11.1 percent in 2004, the gender quota for the 2009 elections contained the additional requirement that one of every three candidates in descending order on a party list be a woman (Hillman 2017, pp. 39–40). Since this modification, the proportion of female candidates elected has risen to between 17 and 20 percent (Hillman 2017, p. 41; Ristianto 2019).

Following these 2004 elections, most significant changes to Indonesia's electoral system have been forced by constitutional court decisions rather than enacted by the government and the legislature. First, in 2008, the constitutional court loosened party control over elections by ruling the semi-open-list system unconstitutional, establishing instead that the 2009 election would use an open-list system, meaning that whoever among a party's candidates received the highest individual vote tallies in an electorate would occupy any seats that the party won regardless of their position on the party list (Ufen 2010, p. 282). As observers have widely noted, this system encourages all but the highest-ranked candidates to campaign as individuals, rather than relying on the party machinery to mobilize votes (Aspinall et al. 2017, p. 9). Subsequently, in 2014, the constitutional court also intervened to force the legislative and presidential elections to be held on the same day, starting in 2019. This was a surprising decision; writing just before the 2004 elections, Ellis (2004, p. 505) judged that the amended constitution was silent on whether elections would be held simultaneously or in staggered fashion. These simultaneous elections in 2019 were generally viewed unfavorably. Voter turnout was high, but the added complexity of holding five elections on the same day was widely seen as an excessive burden for electoral authorities.

Interests

What interests underpin the choices that have determined Indonesia's democratic-era electoral system? It is clear that political party self-interest has consistently played a strong role in most choices. Ellis (2004, p. 500) provides an illuminating example from deliberations over the 1999 election law, observing that the regime party, Golkar, rather than newly formed parties, was the chief supporter of ostensibly reformist proposals to adopt a system composed primarily of single-member electorates.[5] Golkar judged this system would be to its advantage, Ellis recounted, because it could expect to dominate smaller electorates outside Java, where state spending under Suharto had been especially important to local economies. In the same vein, for the 2004 elections, Golkar supported and PDI-P opposed a continuation of anti-Java bias in the allocation of seats in the DPR, consistent with the geographic pattern of each party's support. Disparate party interests have also ensured that Indonesia maintains only a modest parliamentary threshold, currently set at its highest level ever of 4 percent for 2019. Larger parties have typically favored a higher threshold but have compromised with minor parties worried about their parliamentary survival. Party self-interest was also an important factor in political decisions on the shift to direct elections for the presidency. PDI-P's decision to shift from opposing direct elections to supporting them is widely held to have been driven by Megawati's ultimately mistaken belief that she could win the first direct election in 2004, for example (Horowitz 2013, p. 120).

Self-interest has not been the only factor driving electoral-system decisions, however. A concern for national stability is another important

factor. For legislative elections, this concern is reflected in the requirement that election participants be national parties, and arguably also in
Indonesia's modest parliamentary threshold. On the latter point, Ellis
(2004, p. 508) argues that although Indonesia's fragmented parliament
frequently attracts criticism, a significant further reduction in the number
of parties would risk leaving important social interests unrepresented in
the national legislature. On elections for heads of government, Marcus
Mietzner (2014, p. 64) highlights the requirement for joint tickets that
include a candidate and his or her deputy in gubernatorial and mayoral
elections as a shrewd electoral design decision that encourages cooperation across ethnic and religious divisions in local elections. (The same
requirement of course applies to Indonesia's direct presidential elections.)

Implications

Several important features of Indonesian democracy result from the
choices made regarding the country's electoral system. Scholars have
traced in particular detail the effects of the open-list system for legislative elections on the nature of electoral competition and who gets elected
to the DPR. Aspinall et al. (2017, pp. 3, 9) argue that this open-list system promotes vote buying as an important part of electoral competition
(see the section on patronage below), as candidates must develop personal networks outside the party machine in order to outcompete their
party colleagues, whom they perceive as their main competitors. Sebastian Dettman, Thomas Pepinsky, and Jan Pierskalla (2017, pp. 112, 117)
also trace the advantage the system confers on incumbents and its disad-
vantageous effect for women; in a context in which they found that the
average winning candidate gained 5.45 percent of the vote in 2014,
incumbents received a share of the vote 2.67 percentage points higher
than nonincumbents, and female candidates received a 0.5 percentage
point lower share of the vote. This "penalty" for female candidates is
doubly notable, given that the open-list system partially nullified the
gender quota requirement that one in every three candidates in descending order on party lists be a woman. Ben Hillman (2017, p. 43) argues
that apart from freeing voters to choose any candidate regardless of ranking on the list, the high-cost individual-based campaigning the open-list
system promotes disadvantages female candidates, who in patriarchal
Indonesia generally have less access to business-community sponsors.

The parliamentary and presidential election thresholds also have an
important effect on Indonesia's democratic polity. Minor party interests
have arguably dominated in the case of the parliamentary threshold,

which has ranged from 2 percent in 1999 to 4 percent in 2019. This threshold has also been weakly applied; after it failed to meet the parliamentary threshold for the 1999 election, at which time the threshold determined participation in the next election, the Partai Keadilan (Justice Party [PK]) was nevertheless allowed to compete in the 2004 elections simply by altering its name slightly to the Partai Keadilan Sejahtera (Prosperous Justice Party [PKS]).

The presidential election threshold, by contrast, is set at a level that significantly constrains electoral competition, reflecting major party interests. Under this threshold, to nominate a candidate pair, political parties must form coalitions composing at least 20 percent of seats in the DPR or 25 percent of valid votes in the preceding general election.[6] Although in mathematical terms as many as five candidate pairs could contest an election, in practice no more than three candidate pairs are likely to contest an election held with this threshold. This small number of candidate pairs has produced strong, even excessive, continuity in the choices offered to voters. The first election held under this threshold in 2009 was criticized for its uninspiring set of candidates, contested as it was by the incumbent president, his first-term deputy, and the incumbent's defeated rival in the 2004 election. Despite a manifest public mood for new leadership choices, the 2014 election was then contested by only two candidates—the winner Joko Widodo and his defeated rival Prabowo Subianto. The 2019 election was a repeat of 2014, with Jokowi and Prabowo the only two candidates.

Free and Fair

Finally, do Indonesian elections reliably reflect the will of the voters? This question was understandably a major concern for Indonesians and international observers in the early democratic era, given extensive fraud in Suharto-era elections (King 2003, p. 53). Ellis (2004, p. 506) writes that concerns about fraud were a significant constraint on election-system design, effectively restricting Indonesia to systems in which votes could be counted at the voting station. Such counts often attract a crowd of local residents, with voting-booth officials holding up each ballot paper in public view before recording the vote.

Concern about fraud prompted Indonesian authorities to invite international observers to monitor its elections in 1999 and 2004.[7] Among the monitors have been the Carter Center, the National Democratic Institute, the European Union (EU), and the Asian Network for Free Elections (ANFREL). Although these groups have noted various deficiencies in the implementation of elections in Indonesia, they have declared these elections free and fair, being without systematic vote-rigging or other fraud.

Over time, concerns regarding fraud in Indonesian elections have come to focus on the so-called recapitulation process, whereby votes are tallied at progressively higher levels of administration. In the 2014 legislative elections, some candidates feared that rivals (including, or even particularly, candidates from the same party) could pay off electoral officials to inflate their individual vote tallies and thereby win a seat in the legislature. Concern about post-ballot manipulation peaked with the 2014 presidential elections, however, in which both candidates publicly claimed victory on election night. Although credible quick counts showed Joko Widodo to be the winner on election night (July 9), the official result was not announced until July 22 (Zhang 2014). A volunteer movement called Kawal Pemilu (Guard the Election) mobilized to conduct its own tabulation well ahead of the official result, however, relying on a transparency initiative undertaken by the electoral commission to post scans of all voting-station ballot forms on its website (Postill and Saputro 2017). This crowd-sourced tabulation effectively made it impossible to manipulate the count, and Jokowi was confirmed as the winner after Prabowo's challenge of the result at the constitutional court failed.

Concerns that the tabulation process would be manipulated were again raised in 2019, but this time by the Prabowo camp. Quick counts again showed Prabowo to have lost the election; he again claimed victory, regardless. Alleging cheating, Prabowo appealed to his supporters to guard the tabulation process from the ballot box upward through its various stages. Some of his principal supporters also called for "people power" if cheating occurred. Despite this pressure, the electoral commission's official count showed Joko Widodo to be the winner, in line with the election-day quick counts. Prabowo supporters launched violent protests following the announcement of the result, targeting the Electoral Supervisory Body (Bawaslu), which had rejected claims by the Prabowo camp that electoral authorities were biased, for lack of evidence. Eight people were killed in riots stretching over two nights and a day, although the circumstances of their deaths remained unclear (Pramono 2019). The Prabowo camp lodged a challenge to the election result with the constitutional court, which once again failed to change the result.

Political Parties and Political Islam

Indonesian political parties have acquired an invidious reputation, among both voters and scholars. Parties, along with the national legislature, consistently rank as the least trusted of Indonesia's public institutions in opinion polls, often with a majority of respondents expressing little or no trust in them.[8] Illustrative of the low esteem in which they are held, proposals to increase state subsidies to political parties routinely founder in public controversy, although a modest increase was achieved in 2017. For their part, various scholars criticize Indonesian parties for lacking ideological consistency and failing to effectively represent societal interests, for cartel-like collusion, and for concerning themselves primarily with profit seeking rather than programmatic policy outcomes (Tomsa 2018; Slater 2018; Hadiz 2010). Political scientist Stephen Sherlock (2012, p. 559) encapsulates much of this critique: "At the very bottom of the hierarchy of matters of interest to national party leaders stands the power of the [parliamentary] committees to make policy decisions, to review the objectives of legislation drafted by government ministries or to decide on the appropriate wording of a bill initiated by parliament." Except when a bill impinges directly upon party interests or has come to particular public attention, he writes, matters of policy are a lower priority for party leaders than occupying party leadership or cabinet positions, securing influential positions for supporters, or controlling parliamentary committees with authority over finances.

Those with a more favorable view of Indonesian political parties acknowledge many of these deficits but observe that Indonesian parties do not perform unusually poorly. Mietzner (2013, p. 218) argues that perceived deficits, such as the weak association of voters with parties, are typical of the global shift away from a mass-membership model. Overall, he judges, Indonesian parties compare favorably with their counterparts in other new democracies in East Asia, Latin America, and Eastern Europe.

These bleak assessments of Indonesian parties are a stark reversal from the euphoria that greeted the opening of the political system in 1998. For most of Suharto's New Order, only three political parties were allowed, representing the regime (Golkar), Islam (Partai Persatuan Pembangunan (Development Unity Party [PPP]), and secular nationalism and minority religions (Partai Demokrasi Indonesia (Indonesian Democratic Party [PDI]). Such had been the dissatisfaction with the constrained party system of the New Order that a protest movement had sprung up calling for voters to punch the blank white space between the party symbols on the ballot paper rather than choose any of the regime-approved parties. Voters thereby cast a so-called *golput* (*golongan putih,* or white group) vote, a satirical play on words of the name Golkar, the regime party. In the 1999 elections, with the restrictions removed, around 200 new parties registered to compete against their New Order–era forebears, of which forty-eight were approved to compete and twenty-one gained seats in the national legislature. Indicative of the enthusiasm for parties and the political process at the time, turnout in these elections was 93 percent, a percentage that has not been matched in subsequent elections. The number of political parties gaining seats in the national legislature has roughly halved in subsequent elections—sixteen parties contested the 2019 election, and nine gained seats in the national legislature[9]—as a result of Indonesia's modest electoral threshold. Nevertheless, as noted in Chapter 4, multi-party elections, with no party approaching a majority share of seats or votes, have persisted as a core feature of the political system.

What distinguishes present-day Indonesian political parties? In setting out the differences between Indonesia's current parties, Mietzner (2013, p. 219) argues that the most important ideological cleavage results from attitudes about political and social Islamization. Opponents of such Islamization include two of the New Order–era parties, PDI (rebranded as the PDI-P) and Golkar, as well as each of three so-called presidential parties (Tomsa 2018), which lack any programmatic agenda of Islamization. Formed primarily to serve as personal political vehicles for their patrons, the ideological positioning of the presidential parties is not surprising, given that two of the three are splinter parties from Golkar.[10] The fourth, Partai Demokrat (Democratic Party), describes itself as "nationalist-religious," a designation Mietzner analyzes as intended to distinguish it both from more secular parties and from explicitly Islamic parties.

Stretching toward the opposite end of the spectrum, in support of Islamization, are Indonesia's four Islamic parties.[11] Admittedly, these parties vary considerably in their commitment to Islamization. Andrée Feillard and Rémy Madinier (2011, p. 223) explain the different parties' varying commitment in terms of a divide between pluralist Islamic parties, for which Islam is an identity, and Islam-based parties, for which Islam is a programmatic project. The pluralist category includes the two parties associated with Indonesia's largest Islamic organizations—Partai Amanat Nasional (National Mandate Party [PAN], associated with the religious organization Muhammadiyah) and Partai Kebangkitan Bangsa (National Awakening Party [PKB], associated with Nahdlatul Ulama). Both are ambivalent advocates of Islamization, having the Pancasila rather than Islam as their ideological basis. By contrast, the New Order–era PPP and PKS both have Islam as their explicit ideological foundation, thus composing Feillard and Madinier's Islam-based category.

Indeed, PKS is typically considered the most explicitly Islamist of Indonesia's political parties, having arisen out of the Islamic *tarbiyah* (education) campus study group movement in the 1970s.

For these four parties, their support of a greater role for Islam in public life has brought only limited electoral success. The cumulated vote for Islamic parties in postauthoritarian Indonesia has never exceeded 39 percent, even though Muslims form an overwhelming majority in Indonesia. That percentage is lower than public support for several elements of an Islamic agenda in politics, but not decidedly so. In a 2017 survey, Diego Fossati (2017, p. 6) found that an average of 46 percent of the population supported seven elements of political Islam, ranging from 36 percent support for Islam to be Indonesia's only official religion, to 58 percent support for the importance of choosing only a Muslim as leader in elections, and 63 percent support for sterner penalties for blasphemy.

Moreover, even among voters who desire greater Islamization, Islamic political parties face challenges from both flanks. At one extreme, non-Islamic parties have adopted elements of the Islamization agenda, diminishing the electoral appeal of the Islamic parties. Tomsa (2018) notes that at the other end of the spectrum, militant organizations such as the Front Pembela Islam (Islamic Defenders Front [FPI]) have usurped even PKS as the most visible champions of Islamist causes, further eroding their appeal. Nor have Islamic parties been immune from the corrupt practices that pervade Indonesian politics, with PKS in particular mired in the lurid "Beef-gate" corruption scandal ahead of the 2014 elections. PKS used its control of the Ministry of Agriculture to manipulate beef import quotas and build an electoral war chest; senior party figures were prosecuted, and lurid details of their behavior were splashed across the pages of Indonesia's newspapers (McRae 2013b, p. 295).

Mietzner (2013, p. 181) argues that the religious cleavage just discussed is linked to a second dividing line among various Indonesian parties, based on their differing views on center-periphery relations. In broad terms, he posits that more Islamic parties are more supportive of regional autonomy, whereas nationalist opponents of Islamization, such as PDI-P (as well as traditionalist Islamic parties such as PKB), support strong central control. This divide reflects a historical association between Islamism and regional rebellion, a correlation Fossati (2017) has sought to demonstrate at the societal level through public opinion polling; in his 2017 survey, Fossati finds a correlation between political Islamism and support for local governments to have the power to enact heterogeneous local laws.

It is worth noting that the divide between opponents and supporters of Islamization should not be seen as absolute. As mentioned above, non-Islamic parties have at times embraced an Islamizing agenda. Michael Buehler (2013b), for example, observes that Golkar politicians have often been the driving force behind adoption of local *syariah* (Islamic law) by-laws in several of Indonesia's districts and provinces, as opposed to politicians from Islamic parties. These by-laws range from prohibitions of vice to regulation of Islamic education, finance, and alms to various other doctrinal matters (Pisani and Buehler 2017, p. 739).

The 2017 Jakarta gubernatorial election also demonstrates both the salience and the blurred lines of this cleavage. In this election, the incumbent Christian Chinese-ethnic governor Basuki Tjahaja Purnama (Ahok) lost over two rounds to former Islamic university rector Anies Baswedan, despite preelection polling indicating high approval ratings for Ahok's performance as governor. Two months before the election, a doctored video of a speech by Ahok circulated in which he appeared to say that voters were being deceived by a verse of the Quran into voting against him, providing the pretext for hard-line Islamic groups to mobilize huge protests against him under the banner of "Defending Islam." The protests secured Ahok's prosecution for blasphemy, for which he received a two-year prison sentence soon after his electoral defeat (Hadiz 2017a; Mietzner and Muhtadi 2017; Wilson 2017).

Regarding the salience of party ideological divides, on the one hand, the coalition of parties that nominated Ahok were all opponents of Islamization, exposing him to Islamist attacks. On the other hand, the presidential party Gerindra, led by Prabowo Subianto, joined with the Islamist PKS to back a candidate who openly supported the notion that only a Muslim could legitimately lead Jakarta. Indeed, although Gerindra as a party does not have a programmatic emphasis on Islam, party leader Prabowo has long cultivated links with hard-line Islamic groups for political advantage.[12] Overall, in determining coalition-forming behavior, ideological divides work only at the extremes. It is almost unforeseeable for PDI-P and PKS to enter into a coalition in the national legislature, for example. Beyond this example, we do not generally see ideologically coherent coalitions, either to nominate presidential candidates or in government.

A brief digression is in order here to consider the influence on political outcomes of extra-parliamentary groups such as the FPI and Hizbut Tahrir Indonesia (HTI). Although their shared involvement in the massive mobilization against Ahok in late 2016 has seen the two groups lumped together, the two organizations differ markedly in overall goals and methods. FPI operates openly as a vigilante group concerned with "a socially conservative 'anti-vice' and 'anti-apostasy' agenda" rather than with the "radical transformation" of the Indonesian state to become an Islamic state (Wilson 2014, p. 248). With a membership of around 150,000 and clear links to the security forces, leading scholar of the FPI Ian Wilson (2014, pp. 264–265) writes that the group "has sought to occupy an ambiguous middle-ground between Islamic organization, assistant to the authorities and also 'radicals' prepared to take violent direct action." HTI differs in that it has as its explicit goal the establishment of an Islamic state in Indonesia that would become part of a global caliphate; it also rejects violence as a means to reach this political end. It existed as a clandestine organization during the Suharto era and has retained some of this secrecy under democratic rule; although it operates openly, it reveals neither the identity of its leadership nor the size of its membership. A further contrast with FPI is HTI's international dimension. Hizbut Tahrir is a transnational organization operating (and banned) in many countries across the globe (Ward 2009, pp. 150–151). Also in contrast to FPI, it has maintained a program of infiltration of government agencies to serve its political goals (Institute for Policy Analysis of Conflict 2018, p. 18).

Such groups are presented with the opportunity to position themselves credibly as representatives of Indonesia's Muslims, Hadiz (2014, p. 44) argues, because of the failure of Islamic political parties in Indonesia to mount a credible challenge to achieve control of the state. Indeed, FPI prizes attacks on targets that have also attracted the opprobrium of the mainstream Muslim community, so as to overcome the disdain of other Muslim groups for its methods and its general whiff of gangsterism (Wilson 2014, p. 258). Such targets have included the Indonesian version of *Playboy* magazine and advocacy for anti-pornography legislation, the Ahmadi sect of Muslims, and perhaps most famously, Ahok. The modus vivendi of these often violent protests, Wilson writes, is to gain visibility for the organization that extends beyond its modest membership numbers, while avoiding well-connected targets or levels of violence that would spur decisive state action against it. Whether FPI transgressed these boundaries in its actions against Ahok remains an open question. Following Ahok's conviction for blasphemy, police announced an investigation into FPI leader Rizieq Shihab on pornography charges pertaining to leaked screenshots of salacious Whatsapp exchanges with a female follower, spurring Rizieq to go into self-imposed exile. He remained overseas for the entirety of the 2019 elections.

HTI has attracted an even sterner response to its involvement in the anti-Ahok protests. The Indonesian government enacted emergency legislation in 2017, giving it broad powers to proscribe "anti-Pancasila" organizations, which it promptly applied to ban HTI. This move stood in stark contrast to previous government tolerance of the group, which Ward (2009, p. 162) had judged likely to continue for as long as the group maintained its nonviolent approach. The Jakarta-based Institute for Policy Analysis of Conflict (IPAC) attributes this shift in attitude to changed political circumstances. Banning HTI in the wake of the anti-Ahok campaign enabled the government both to directly weaken the protest movement and to court favor with traditionalist Islamic mass organization Nahdlatul Ulama, for which HTI was a despised competitor for influence among its membership (IPAC 2018, pp. 18–19).

The anti-Ahok protests may thus constitute the high-water mark for the influence of extra-parliamentary advocates of political Islam, at least in the short term. With no sign of Islamic parties expanding beyond their supporting role in the party system, however, such groups will continue to enjoy the opportunity to present themselves as the authentic champions of an Islamic agenda.

Patronage, Corruption, and Dynasties

Democratic Indonesia inherited a highly corrupt system of government from Suharto's authoritarian regime. At all levels of government, public officials and bureaucrats allocated state resources to clients and cronies, and kickbacks were required to solicit favorable government decisions or even receive routine government services. Suharto exercised highly centralized control over what the economist Ross McLeod (2000, p. 101) describes as a "franchise" system, in which Suharto enjoyed the power to privately tax economic activity, with subordinates at lower levels of government as franchisees able to act in the same way. In return, Suharto received loyalty and either direct payments or favorable business terms for himself and his closest cronies. Over time, as Vedi Hadiz and Richard Robison (2013) observe, various of these franchisees also expanded beyond the mere taxing of economic activity to become businesspeople in their own right, with the illegal businesses of senior military officers a notable example. Nevertheless, under this system, no rival emerged to credibly challenge Suharto's control. In the words of the political scientist Jeffrey Winters (2013, pp. 105), "No matter how big or rich you became, Suharto could break you." When Suharto fell, his control of the system was removed, but most of those who had profited under his rule were nevertheless able to preserve their wealth (Hadiz and Robison 2013; Winters 2013, pp. 106–107; Aspinall 2013b, p. 34). Under democratic rule, therefore, a more diffuse system of patrons competing for influence and control of resources emerged to replace Suharto's highly personalized and centralized patronage network.

Money Politics

Howard Dick and Jeremy Mulholland (2011, p. 66) describe the Indonesian democratic state as a political marketplace where monetary payments "become an explicit part of negotiations over political outcomes within the state itself, as well as between state actors and the rest of society." Examples abound to illustrate the resultant pervasive nature of such illicit payments and broader corruption. Much as no single case can illustrate the full extent of such practices, the following example is perhaps emblematic of the pervasiveness of the political marketplace. In 2017, the Riau provincial prosecutor's office brought charges against eighteen individuals for suspected graft in the construction of an anticorruption monument in the provincial capital, Pekanbaru (Reuters 2017)!

Corrupt practices are endemic in most Indonesian law enforcement and judicial institutions (McRae 2013b). Bribes to police, prosecutors, and judges are routine, and all such institutions are periodically the focus of major public scandals. Perhaps the highest-profile law enforcement scandal of the Jokowi government has been the cancellation of President Jokowi's nomination of a new national police chief in 2015, because the respected Komisi Pemberantasan Korupsi (Corruption Eradication Commission [KPK]) promptly named the nominee as a corruption suspect. Indeed, it was indicative of the checkered track record of many prominent political figures that when President Jokowi asked the KPK to vet an initial shortlist of cabinet appointees for his first administration, the commission assigned black marks to several prospective ministers and rejected them.

Beyond law enforcement and the judiciary, numerous ministers, governors, and mayors around Indonesia have been arrested for corruption, often while in office, as have equally large numbers of MPs. Political parties use their control of ministries to amass electoral war chests, partly because of the low level of state funding they receive, compared with their counterparts in less corrupt jurisdictions (Mietzner 2015). Bribes and kickbacks are rife within Indonesia's national and local legislatures, determining budgetary allocations, the appointment of public officials, the issuing of licenses, and even the content of legislation (Dick and Mulholland 2011, pp. 79–83). Vote buying by candidates is widespread in legislative elections, encouraged by an electoral system in which candidates must compete not only against other parties but also to surpass the individual vote tallies of their own party's other candidates.

Newer institutions formed under democratic rule, such as the constitutional court, were initially seen as relatively clean, owing to their at least partial detachment from entrenched patronage practices. Since 2010, however, the constitutional court has also been repeatedly rocked by corruption scandals. Its chief justice was sentenced in 2014 to life imprisonment for corruption and money laundering pertaining to an electoral dispute. Another judge at the court, former justice minister Patrialis Akbar, was imprisoned in 2017 for bribery, and still another judge resigned in 2011.

Although illicit payments are ever-present in the operation of Indonesian democracy, it would be wrong to think of the Indonesian polity as a system where political outcomes are simply auctioned to the highest bidder. As Dick and Mulholland (2011, p. 66) emphasize, "monetary payments . . . are only part of the transaction" in a political marketplace. Many patronage networks are structured at least loosely along long-standing religious, ideological, and ethnic divisions in Indonesian society (Aspinall 2013b). Such divisions thus continue to play a role in determining access to resources. For instance, anthropologist Lorraine Aragon (2007, pp. 41–42) highlights the practice of "unequal opportunity buying," whereby bureaucrats may help other members of their ethnic group obtain jobs without themselves receiving any direct material benefit. In another example, a fine-grained study of vote buying in Central Java in the 2014 elections found that monetary payments by candidates to voters functioned as an "entry ticket," "akin to the price of entry paid by candidates, who are then assessed by voters on other grounds" (Aspinall et al. 2017, p. 21). Aspinall and his associates found candidates were most successful if they had strong personal networks of loyalists, in addition to the ability to pay this entry ticket.

Powerful political families are another feature of Indonesian patronage politics that ensures that the spoils do not simply accrue to the highest bidder. A feature of political landscapes across Southeast Asia, such families are present in Indonesia at both the national and local levels (Purdey 2016a). Two key examples in national politics are the Sukarno family, of which both Indonesia's founding president Sukarno (1945–1966) and its fifth president, Megawati (2001–2004), were members (Mietzner 2016), as well as the Djojohadikusomo family, notable in contemporary politics on account of Prabowo Subianto's frequent forays into presidential elections (Purdey 2016b). Former president Susilo Bambang Yudhoyono appears to be attempting to forge multigenerational influence, with one of his sons currently an MP for the Partai Demokrat, and another son running unsuccessfully for the post of Jakarta governor in 2017.

Typically, the reach of such families extends beyond formal elected office into other positions of political agency, such as media, political parties, state institutions, and business, often in rent-seeking industries (Purdey 2016a, p. 323). Interestingly, though, despite the broad patronage resources such networks place within their control, in the Indonesian case such families have struggled to maintain control of electoral office. For example, Megawati Sukarnoputri was roundly defeated as an incumbent candidate by Yudhoyono in Indonesia's first direct presidential election in 2004, and again defeated by Yudhoyono in 2009, and none of her children are considered realistic presidential candidates, although many suspect that her daughter Puan aspires to the role. Prabowo Subianto was Megawati's running mate in their unsuccessful 2009 campaign, then losing to Jokowi in 2014 and 2019. Agus Yudhoyono, son of Susilo Bambang Yudhoyono, turned out to be the lowest ranked of the three candidates in the 2017 Jakarta gubernatorial campaign. At the local level, too, powerful local families have struggled to monopolize political office, as the structure of the economy does not make poor voters dependent en masse on local elites, nor does it enable local elites to rig electoral rules to their advantage or bring local security and judicial institutions under their direct control (Buehler 2018). Consistent with such a conclusion, in case studies of attempts at dynastic succession at district level in Central Kalimantan Province, Aspinall and Uhaib As'ad (2016, pp. 421–422) found that outgoing district heads who had completed their two-term limit typically tried to install a family member as their successor, but that the anointed successor in most cases failed to win office.

Combating Corruption

Of the various efforts the Indonesian government and nonstate reformers have undertaken to combat corruption and patronage politics, the establishment in 2003 of Indonesia's Corruption Eradication Commission, the KPK, stands as the most important. Before its establishment, most high-profile corruption cases had not resulted in conviction. A long cast of powerful figures, including former president Suharto and DPR speaker Akbar Tanjung, were able to use their political connections and financial resources to have the legal cases against them thrown out (Juwono 2016). Reflecting this track record, the legislation establishing the KPK empowered it both to take over stalled cases from police and prosecutors and did not permit the KPK to drop a case prior to court trial once it had established an individual as a suspect. Since its formation, the KPK has consistently tackled high-profile cases. According to the commission's own statistics, between 2004 and 2017, it prosecuted twenty-five government ministers or heads of state agencies, 144 national or local MPs, eighteen provincial governors, seventeen judges, seven prosecutors, and two police officials, among others (KPK 2017). During President Yudhoyono's administration, the KPK prosecuted a close relative of the president and the chairperson and treasurer of Yudhoyono's political party. As mentioned above, the KPK forced President Jokowi to cancel his nomination of a new police chief, and it has also arrested the speaker of the national legislature, Setya Novanto, whom many viewed as untouchable. Its persistent pursuit of such high-profile cases has established the KPK as one of the most trusted and popular institutions in present-day Indonesia. Illustrative of its popularity, Joko Widodo courted then KPK chairperson Abraham Samad as his running mate in 2014, although the partnership ultimately did not proceed.

Its pursuit of such high-profile figures has, nevertheless, exposed the KPK to repeated attacks. Three confrontations with the police, in 2009, 2012, and 2015 in particular, have taken a heavy toll on the commission. Each of the confrontations was triggered by the KPK's investigation or prosecution of a senior police official, and in each case the police retaliated by bringing trumped-up charges against KPK commissioners. Although all but one of these cases were ultimately dropped, the KPK received only belated support from the president in each instance, effectively illustrating the limits of its reach. Additionally, legislators have repeatedly sought to remove the KPK's powers to wiretap without a court warrant and to handle its own prosecutors, as well as to defund or disband the institution. Any such moves are deeply unpopular, and as of 2019, all have foundered.

Although public support for the KPK is clear, some scholars have questioned its effect on levels of corruption within Indonesia, which remain consistently high. In 2017, Indonesia ranked ninety-sixth of 180 in the Transparency International Corruption Perceptions Index, alongside Peru, Brazil, and Thailand and below Timor-Leste, the Solomon Islands, and Kuwait. Dick and Mulholland (2016), for example, criticize the KPK's capacity to have impact as amounting to "cutting off the heads of a hydra." Within Indonesia, such criticisms have manifested in pressure on the KPK to focus more on prevention rather than prosecution—pressure that has at times appeared to be motivated less by a concern to reduce levels of corruption than to reduce the number of prosecutions brought by the commission.

Conclusion

Close examination of the mechanisms of Indonesian politics makes clear both the new spaces where the public might exert pressure on political and business elites, and the manifold successes of entrenched interests in insulating themselves from new accountability processes. Discussion in the following chapters will further explore the impacts of such democratic deficits on various dimensions of Indonesian politics and society. The next chapter, for example, concentrates on the relationship between business interests and politics, as manifested in money politics, corruption, and patronage, and the brakes this puts on efforts to improve social indicators.

Notes

1. This choice is made for simplicity, as the analysis in this chapter does not rely on a distinction between urban municipalities (*kota*) and nonurban districts (*kabupaten*). In other accounts, the latter are sometimes called "district heads."

2. The province of Aceh is an exception to the requirement for national parties to nominate local executives, as local parties are allowed in the province under the 2005 peace deal with GAM.

3. In the event, the electoral commission was considered to have performed poorly in 1999 and was replaced by an independent commission soon afterward (Ellis 2004, p. 504).

4. The constitutional provision on these elections for local heads of government was ambiguous, saying only that they must be "democratically elected."

5. King (2003, pp. 60–63) recounts that Golkar also proposed using electorates based on districts rather than provinces, but this proposal was also rejected on the basis that it would advantage the regime party because of its penetration of the civil service.

6. The first direct presidential election in 2004 employed a lower threshold of 15 percent of DPR seats or 20 percent of valid votes.

7. One of the authors, Dave McRae, was a member of the Carter Center observation team for the presidential election in 2004.

8. In 2016, for example, only 39 percent of Indonesians expressed trust in political parties and 49 percent in the national legislature, compared to 79 percent expressing trust in the presidency and 80 percent in Indonesia's anticorruption commission (Indikator 2016, p. 11).

9. In addition to these national parties, several local parties contested the 2014 and 2019 elections for the provincial and district legislatures in Aceh province in an exception granted to Aceh as part of the 2005 Helsinki peace agreement. The most successful of these was the Aceh Party, associated with the former Free Aceh Movement (GAM) independence movement.

10. The patrons of these two parties were formerly senior Golkar politicians: former general Prabowo and his Partai Gerakan Indonesia Raya (Great Indonesia Movement Party [Gerindra]); and business and media mogul Surya Paloh and his Partai Nasional Demokrat (National Democratic Party [Nasdem]). Another presidential party, Hanura, held seats in the national paliament from 2009–2019. Its initial patron was retired general, Wiranto.

11. A fifth Islamic party, Partai Bulan Bintang (PBB: Crescent Star Party), also contested the 2014 elections but did not meet the electoral threshold.

12. As part of a so-called green Islamic faction within the military, Prabowo established contact with hard-line Islamic groups during the late authoritarian period (Feillard and Madinier 2011, pp. 57–60); he would later found Gerindra, along with Fadli Zon, the leader of one of these groups.

6

Persistent Inequality: Health, Education, and Work

THIS CHAPTER SHEDS LIGHT ON SEVERAL INTERRELATED ASPECTS of the fabric of Indonesian society—demography, health, education, employment, and poverty—in order to identify factors and drivers of inequality across the nation. It starts with a rough overview of Indonesia's demographic growth and population distribution and proceeds to a number of basic facts on health and health care. Given that people under the age of twenty constitute the largest cohort of Indonesians, their concerns, particularly education and employment, are emphasized. Finally, the chapter directs attention to poverty and persistent inequality. A study by the World Bank (2016) found that "Indonesia is at risk of leaving its poor and vulnerable behind." While poverty reduction is stagnating, income inequality is rapidly rising. According to a study by Oxfam International (2017), the gap between the richest and the poorest has grown faster in Indonesia than in any other Southeast Asian country in the twenty-first century. Not only are there more millionaires and billionaires than ever before, but the four richest Indonesians have accumulated more wealth than the poorest 100 million people. Generally speaking, inequality is impeding poverty reduction, suppressing economic growth, and threatening social cohesion. However, given Indonesia's regional disparities, there are significant local differences.

Demography

Since becoming independent in 1945, the population of Indonesia has more than tripled, rising from 72 million people to more than 263 million in 2017. Between 1970 and the late 1990s, the infant mortality rate declined dramatically, reaching an estimated rate in 2016 of 23.5 deaths per 1,000 live births, and life expectancy increased by almost twenty years (Maralani 2008, p. 696). The average life expectancy for Indonesian men is now 68.53 years and for women it is 73.69 years. Children make up the largest cohort of the population, with 29 percent of the population being under fifteen years in 2013 and only 8 percent over sixty, resulting in a median age of about twenty-seven years for both sexes. It is expected that by 2035, there will be 71 million old people (14 percent of the population), most of whom will be women (Thristiawati et al. 2015). Lower birth rates, longer life expectancies, and better health care are having an effect on the statistics of aging in Indonesia, but compared to its Southeast Asian neighbors, the population of Indonesia is still aging much more slowly (McDonald 2014, p. 40). While urban populations age more slowly, in part because of the constant flow of young arrivals to the cities, populations in rural areas are aging rapidly. The consequences of these imbalances will only be fully understood in a decade or two, when the impacts on agricultural productivity become more apparent. Across both urban and rural populations, less than 16 percent of Indonesians are covered by old-age pension plans, thus the increase in life expectancy will result in higher poverty among old people (Thristiawati et al. 2015).

Generally speaking, the distribution of Indonesia's population is extremely unbalanced. More than 130 million people live on the island of Java, which has a population density of 2,903 people per square mile, whereas Kalimantan, four times the size of Java, has only 15 million inhabitants and a population density of seventy-six people per square mile. Nevertheless, Kalimantan, which has had an economic boom, is now one of the fastest-growing regions in the archipelago. Although the dynamics of urbanization have been powerful since the 1970s, just over one-half of Indonesia's population lives in urban areas at present. Urban economic development and growth have been concentrated in Java's largest cities (McDonald 2014, p. 45), making Jakarta, Surabaya, and Bandung the nation's largest cities by far.

With more than 263 million inhabitants in 2017, Indonesia's population makes up 3.5 percent of the world's population; nevertheless, Indonesia ranks as the world's fourth most populous country. It is predicted that Indonesia's population will reach 323 million people by 2050 (McDonald 2014, p. 40), or 380 million if the fertility rate stays at its current level (Hull 2012, p. 208), which would make Indonesia the world's third-most-populous country. Because such estimates are based on statistics of fertility and mortality that may often be flawed or not comprehensive owing to inconsistent data collection, it is advisable to apply a healthy skepticism to their interpretation.

Fear of a population explosion has been common for many decades, and that fear of overpopulation is at risk of politicization by populist politicians. Marriage and parenthood remain crucial aspirations in the lives of Indonesians. Because it was assumed that lower fertility rates would help raise the standard of living, reducing the high fertility rate has been a concern for Indonesia since the 1960s. Through a state-sponsored family planning program, the Indonesian government promoted a "two children are enough" (*dua anak cukup*) policy. Through this program, not only were contraceptives distributed but education about family planning, reproductive health, and other advantages of postponing marriage was also delivered to change societal norms of fertility preferences and family size. Since the family planning program's early days, Muslim clerics have questioned the government's interventions in birth control, criticizing in particular the use of intrauterine devices, condoms, and abortion (Hull 2012). However, with the depoliticization of Islam under Suharto, many clerics became more supportive of the family planning policy, not least because their compliance gave them access to government funding for prayer and Quran reading sessions in their local communities (Hull 2012, pp. 201–202).

Although the fertility rate declined dramatically from the 1970s until the early 1990s, from 5.6 to 2.9 children per woman (Maralani 2008, p. 697), the decline has since stalled, and the fertility rate has even increased slightly (Hull 2012; McDonald 2014), resulting in continued rapid growth in the Indonesian population. Some academics have suggested that more conservative (Islamic) views became more widely accepted during the reform era or *reformasi* and once again stimulated higher birth rates (Hull 2012), but this view is countered by the fact that fertility has declined sharply in almost all other Islamic countries (McDonald 2014). Moreover, in 2010, the highest fertility rates tended to be in Indonesia's eastern provinces, where there are greater numbers of Christians and higher levels of poverty. Others have argued that decentralization has had a negative impact on the national family planning policy in post-*reformasi* Indonesia, not least because the top-down approach of centralized government was exchanged for a system in which local authorities had more say in managing local budgets, which had damaging effects on the availability of contraceptives and other health-related issues in some provinces. The central government's response to these deleterious effects of decentralization was to make special budget allocations to encourage the various regions to uphold their family planning policy.

According to the 2012 Indonesian Demographic and Health Survey, 62 percent of all married women in Indonesia use contraception, as opposed to less than 10 percent in the 1970s (Hull 2012). Hormonal injections are now by far the most popular contraceptive method (used by 32 percent), followed by the birth control pill (used by 14 percent) (Misnaniarti and Ayuningtyas 2016, p. 1681). Despite the widespread availability of modern contraceptive methods, some women cannot afford to use them, some still lack sufficient knowledge on the risks of pregnancy, and some are prohibited from using them by their husbands or family for religious reasons.

Although there are no reliable data on pregnancy terminations, it is estimated that more than 2 million abortions take place each year in Indonesia (Hull and Widyantoro 2010, p. 175). Abortions are only permitted in exceptional circumstances, such as when pregnancy is the result of rape or when a mother's life is in danger. The law states that these abortions can only take place in the first six weeks of a pregnancy. For more than four decades, activists and health professionals have lobbied the government to reform laws regulating pregnancy termination and to improve clinical procedures, but little has been achieved so far. Neither the revised Health Law (2009) nor the Regulation on Reproductive Health (No. 61/2014) contains any new policy. In 2018, this law became the focus of national attention and further calls for reform when a fifteen-year-old girl from Jambi, Sumatra, was sentenced to six months in prison for undergoing an abortion performed by her mother after being raped by her brother (Treat Rape Victim 2018).

Terence Hull and N. Widyantoro (2010, p. 177) note that relatively few criminal actions are taken against abortion practitioners and their clients and argue that the legislation is, therefore, more of a "moral statement than a practical tool of social control," yet the secrecy and poor hygiene under which many abortions are carried out put the health of many women at risk. Between 11 and 14 percent of the maternal mortality rate in Indonesia (392 in 100,000 live births) is the result of unsafe abortions, which translates to the death of between forty-three and fifty-five women from unsafe abortions for every 100,000 live births (Sundawa 2014; Sedgh and Ball 2008). Of the approximately 4.5 million births per year in Indonesia, only 67 percent are registered. Child and infant mortality rates have consistently declined in Indonesia in the last few decades as health services for mothers and children have improved and become more widely available (Trisnantoro et al. 2010). Yet chronic malnutrition continues to affect more than one-third of all Indonesian children, leaving them stunted and inhibiting their cognitive development (World Bank 2015).

Even though the broad trends in fertility and contraceptive use in Indonesia since 2000 might suggest that fertility will continue to decline and that population growth will slow, there are some indications that such predictions should be approached with skepticism. For example, although the size of Indonesian families has generally shrunk, recent data show that the average age for first marriage of both men and women has gone lower again (Hull 2016, p. 145). Urban women tend to marry at age twenty-four (men at twenty-seven), but their rural counterparts are only twenty-one on average (men around twenty-five). Age differences between spouses are also said to be widening. According to the Marriage Law (1974), the legal age for marriage in Indonesia is twenty-one, but with written parental consent, girls can marry at sixteen (boys at nineteen). Allowing marriage at such an early age impedes the protection of girls as children, prevents them from fulfilling their potential, and compromises their rights to education and reproductive health. It is estimated that one in four girls is married before turning eighteen, as there is substantial social and religious pressure, particularly in rural areas, for young girls to be married to prevent premarital liaisons (UNICEF 2015). Attempts to change Indonesia's Marriage Law and increase the minimum age for girls to marry to eighteen have been unsuccessful because of the increasing influence of religious conservatism, which has also stifled calls for an end to polygamy.

Health

Although life expectancy is lengthening in Indonesia, many people still die before they reach the age of seventy of degenerative and preventable diseases. Twenty-one percent of all deaths in Indonesia in 2012 were caused by strokes, with ischemic heart disease (8.9 percent), diabetes (6.5 percent), respiratory infections (5.2 percent), and tuberculosis (4.3 percent) being other main causes of death (World Atlas 2017). Increasing environmental pollution, lack of clean water, malnutrition, and unbalanced nutrition cause serious damage to the health of Indonesians and increase the risk of premature death. Compared with food in other Asian countries, Indonesian food tends to be high in cholesterol. The growing prevalence of a more Western diet also has the potential to increase the number of deaths from obesity, diabetes, and coronary artery disease.

For Indonesian men, smoking tobacco is the number one killer, causing strokes, heart attacks, lung cancer, and other cardiovascular and respiratory diseases. About 400,000 die each year from smoking-related illnesses (Britnell 2015, p. 46). Although alcohol abuse is lower in

Indonesia than in non-Muslim societies, not least because of religious sanctions on drinking alcoholic beverages, there has been a signficant increase in drug abuse in the last two decades. According to reports by the National Narcotics Agency (Badan Narkotika Nasional [BNN]) from 2008, there were between 3.1 to 3.6 million drug users in Indonesia, amounting to roughly 2 percent of the total population. In recent political debates in regard to the death penalty, these numbers were inflated to 4.5 million drug users, of whom an estimated forty to fifty people died every day as a result of drug abuse; these numbers were, however, projections based on the 2008 study and not on real counts. The BNN statistics have been criticized widely as imprecise and as promoting political outcomes such as the Indonesian government's strong support for the death penalty. Indonesia is one of three Asian countries—the others being Pakistan and the Philippines—with growing HIV/AIDS infection rates; in 2013, an estimated 640,000 Indonesians were living with HIV/AIDS. Religious sensitivities regarding homosexuality and premarital and extramarital liaisons impede the delivery of public-health education.

According to the World Health Organization (2017b), Indonesia's total expenditure for 2014 on health care services amounted to 2.9 percent of its gross domestic product (GDP), or US$299 per capita. Despite substantial improvements since *reformasi*, access to health care is limited for many Indonesians. In 2013, there were 2,454 public and private hospitals around the country (Badan Pusat Statistik 2017), of which only twenty-five had been accredited by Joint Commission International by 2017 (Joint Commission International 2017). With a total capacity of 305,242 beds, Indonesian hospitals in 2012 could not quite offer one bed for every 1,000 of its population (World Health Organization 2017a). The Indonesian capacity is one of the lowest in the Asia and Pacific region, below that of countries with a much lower GDP, such as Vietnam, which had two beds for 1,000 people in 2010. Many hospitals still lack sufficient, adequately trained medical practitioners, and their equipment is often out of date. There is 0.2 of a physician and 1.2 nurses and midwives available for every 1,000 inhabitants (World Atlas 2017). The lowest level of health care is offered by integrated health service posts (*posyandu, pos pelayanan terpadu*), run by communities and focused on providing basic maternal care. As these statistics reveal, the Indonesian government needs to invest more in its public-health system, as well as in preventative health-care education.

Some crucial developments have taken place in recent years, but not all are as beneficial as they might appear at first glance. In 2014,

Indonesia introduced a system of universal health-insurance coverage, partly in response to a 2000 addition to the constitution (Article 28H[3]), which stipulates every person's "right to social security to enable their full development as dignified human beings." Previously, under the New Order, only a small number of Indonesians, such as civil servants and members of the military, had access to health insurance and pension plans. Some employees were covered by health care funded jointly by employers and employees under the Jamsostek plan (Jaminan Sosial Tenaga Kerja [labor social insurance]), which was undermined by underreporting of staffing levels to the agency and corruption in the administration of fees. The majority of working people had to pay out of their own pockets for any health-care services they required.

Initiatives to implement laws for a national social-security system to cover health services, pensions, and compensation for workplace death and injury began as early as 2004 but were delayed during the presidency of Susilo Bambang Yudhoyono, who took relatively little interest in the issue, until 2011. The Yudhoyono government launched a social-insurance plan for poor households (*asuransi kesehatan masyarakat miskin*), which gave health-card holders free treatment in public-health centers. By 2009, about 76.4 million people, almost one-third of the population, were covered by this plan (Tadjoeddin 2014, p. 25). Serious efforts to craft a national social-security system resumed only when a broad coalition of trade union and nongovernmental organization (NGO) activists, lawyers, students, journalists, and other professionals sued the government for negligence and lack of commitment to implementing the 2004 legal provisions within the stipulated five-year time frame (Jung 2016, p. 488). Under the new Law No. 24 of 2011 on Social Security Administering Bodies, health-care, workplace accident, old age, and death benefits are guaranteed for all Indonesian citizens through a compulsory insurance, with the government obliged to pay premiums for those who cannot afford it.

With decentralization, social-welfare programs, including free health-care programs, proliferated in parts of Indonesia. Local reformist politicians competing for votes in Indonesia's more than 500 subnational entities started to introduce local health-care plans financed by local budgets (Tadjoeddin 2014; Aspinall 2014). One of the first such plans was introduced in Bali in 2003. These local initiatives were known as Jamkesda (Jaminan Kesehatan Daerah [regional health insurance]) and were replicated in many other districts in the following years. Some were open to all residents, but most were free only for the poor. For example, in late 2012, the Jakarta Health Card (Kartu Jakarta

Sehat) was launched by Joko Widodo, then governor of the Special
Capital Region of Jakarta, to provide health insurance for Jakarta residents, especially the underprivileged. By 2012, 245 districts across
Indonesia had some sort of local health-care financing plan for the poor
at the *puskesmas* (*pusat kesehatan masyarakat,* or local health center)
level and sometimes even third-class hospital treatment (Sparrow et al.
2017; Pisani, Kok, and Nugroho 2017). Yet the identification of who
fell under the definition of being poor and was, therefore, deserving of
free services was complicated, as the poorest people often found it hard
to prove the precariousness of their livelihoods.

Despite considerable misdirection of health-care services to people
who clearly were ineligible to access them and the collection of illegal
fees by some health-service providers, the overall outcome of the local
initiatives was a substantial increase in health-care coverage. Eighty-six
million people out of a total population of 245 million had coverage in
2013, at a total cost of Rp8.29 trillion (US$861 million) (Rosser 2012;
Aspinall 2014, p. 808). In addition, NGOs and religious associations,
such as Nahdlatul Ulama (NU) and Muhammadiyah, have been involved
in providing health-care services to people in need. Islamic parties, such
as Partai Keadilan Sejahtera (Prosperous Justice Party [PKS]), started to
offer welfare services in areas where local administrations failed to do
so, not least to garner political support in local and national elections
(Jung 2016). Yet these free or low-cost services are not equivalent to
good-quality services, which, after all, the political, vote-buying motives
of those proposing the services could not guarantee (Aspinall and Warburton 2013). In 2014, a universal social health-insurance plan (Jaminan
Kesehatan Nasional [JKN]) was finally established, but the challenge
for the government remains to achieve actual health coverage throughout Indonesia. Until this has happened, those with serious health conditions who can afford to will continue to seek treatment in Malaysia, Singapore, Australia, and Europe.

Education

When Indonesia declared independence in 1945, there were just ninety-
two high schools and five universities for 72 million people, 95 percent
of whom could not read or write. Seventy years later, the UN Educational, Scientific and Cultural Organization (UNESCO) reported literacy rates in 2015 of 96.3 percent for men and 91.5 percent for women,
which represents a considerable achievement, as few nations have been
able to combat illiteracy in such a short period of time. Although there

have been major changes in education in Indonesia since the end of the New Order, its education system, like its health-care system, suffers from a strong rural-urban divide that continues to contribute to inequality. Education plays a key role in shaping future national development, and any investment in education made now will have long-term consequences for the Indonesian workforce in the twenty-first century.

Basic Education

Indonesia's formal education system has three levels of schooling: primary school (six years), junior secondary school (three years), and senior secondary school (three years). Senior secondary schooling may be at a general senior high school or a vocational training school. Each level of schooling is separated by a national examination. In 2017, there were approximately 170,000 primary schools, 40,000 junior secondary schools, and 26,000 high schools in Indonesia. Eighty-four percent of these schools operate under the Ministry of National Education and the remaining 16 percent under the Ministry of Religious Affairs.

Between the 1970s and the 1990s, educational provision and attainment improved greatly, not least because of Indonesia's heavy investment in education using economic gains from the oil boom (Suryadarma 2015). In 1973, for example, a program to build a primary school in every village began, and 138,940 schools were constructed across the country over the following ten years. Private schools do not play a huge role in primary schooling, as demand is fully met by public schools; they do, however, meet some niche demands for faith-based education. At the junior and senior secondary level, the state is still unable to provide capacity for increasing enrollments, which gives space at secondary levels for private schools to enter, although most parents prefer public schools over the private system (Suharti 2013). Altogether, private schools make up about 7 percent of the total number of schools. There is a significant lack of specialized schools providing education for students with special needs and with special talents. In 2013, 70 percent of students with disabilities did not have proper access to education (Majority of Disabled 2013). Many observers agree that improving the quality of secondary education is one of Indonesia's top priorities, not least because most students do not proceed beyond secondary school (di Gropello 2013, p. 262; Suharti 2013, p. 34).

Since 1984, school attendance has been compulsory for the first nine years, and, since decentralization, has become compulsory in some provinces for twelve years, but there is little enforcement of this requirement, and those who do not or cannot comply are not sanctioned. Boys and girls enroll in primary schools at the same rate. Although universal enrollment in primary school education became a reality in Indonesia in the early 1980s, it still falls short in terms of universal completion of primary schooling (Suryadarma and Jones 2013, p. 2; Suharti 2013). In order to improve school attendance, assistance programs for the poor (*bantuan siswa miskin* [BSM]) were launched under President Yudhoyono (Yusuf and Sumner 2015). They provide cash transfers of up to Rp450,000 to the families of vulnerable and poor students to ensure their retention at primary school. In 2004, nearly 20 percent of primary students and 26 percent of junior high school students relied on these payments (Manning and Sumarto 2011, p. 9). In 2005, the Bantuan Operasional Sekolah (BOS) school operational assistance grant was introduced to increase the funding for expenses other than salaries in primary and junior secondary schools. Upgraded in 2009, the BOS program sought to focus more on the provision of quality in education through spending on such things as better teaching and better learning materials, but schools still lack many requirements for the delivery of quality education.

In an evolving economy such as Indonesia's, primary education is no longer deemed sufficient, as it cannot produce a workforce with adequate skills and competencies for the modern labor market. Secondary and tertiary education were once perceived as a privilege reserved for a talented or affluent few, but it has now become essential for anyone seeking an adequately paid job in contemporary Indonesia. Although secondary school enrollment had increased to 86 percent in 2016, higher education remains expensive, and many of those who have enrolled have had to abandon their studies halfway through because they cannot afford to continue (Suharti 2013). Only 55 percent of children from poor families are enrolled in secondary school (Oxfam International 2017). The difference in school enrollment between urban and rural areas remains extreme at higher school levels, with rural areas in eastern Indonesia lagging furthest behind (Slater 2013). In many remote parts of Indonesia, students' access to education remains blocked and talent is wasted because of the state's failure to provide adequate facilities.

The school dropout rate is about 3 percent per year, and as it applies for each of the six years of primary schooling, the cumulative figure is therefore 18 percent (Suharti 2013, p. 27). Many of the children who drop out of primary school are functionally illiterate. Although it is commonly assumed that early school-leavers will become child workers, many in fact do not work immediately and remain economically inactive (Utomo et al. 2014). However, some do join the workforce as, for example, domestic helpers or petty traders. The informal economy can absorb many poorly educated workers, but these people will be poorly paid for many years, thus continuing the vicious circle of poverty for their families. Girls who leave school early are likely to be economically and educationally inactive for a longer time during their formative years, tend to marry earlier, and are less likely to reengage in education later on in life, compared to their male peers (Utomo et al. 2014).

The government of Joko Widodo initiated a range of programs for social assistance for those in or close to poverty, including the issuing of the smart card (*kartu Indonesia pintar*). This program is expected to substantially extend the BSM plan, as smart-card holders are guaranteed twelve years of free education and free higher education for poor students who pass the university entrance exams (Jokowi Launches 2014). The Indonesia smart card is targeted at 24 million poor students, including students eligible for scholarships and others who cannot afford to attend school. Primary school students can receive Rp225,000 (US$18.50) per semester, junior secondary school students Rp375,000 per semester, and senior secondary or vocational school students Rp500,000 per semester. To upgrade the skills of the Indonesian workforce and restructure employment so that it no longer focuses on agriculture but instead on trade, administration, and services, the Indonesian government needs to dedicate more effort and more public spending to improving secondary and tertiary education.[1] However, additional spending on education does not automatically improve the quality of teaching and learning. In terms of spending available resources more efficiently and more transparently, Indonesian schools have a long way to go.

When Indonesia faced a serious shortage of teachers in the early 2000s, particularly in remote rural areas, the central government allowed the hiring of teachers on short-term contracts. Increasing the number of teaching staff did not result in increasing teaching quality. Lack of transparency in the recruitment process, overhiring, and general corruption in the administration of BOS funding have meant that many teachers and school principals, who are appointed directly by the district head (*bupati*), ended up in prison (Junaedi 2016). Compared with neighboring countries, too many of Indonesia's teachers are poorly paid, and to make things worse, there are no sanctions for their frequent absence from class (Suharti 2013; World Bank 2010). In 2010, competency tests were introduced to motivate teachers to upgrade their skills through incentive programs. Those who passed were given double salary payments, whether or not they fulfilled their duties in the classroom. To pass the test all they needed to do was to take a short intensive course, and many certified teachers performed no better than their uncertified colleagues (Suharti 2013, p. 47). Teacher absenteeism continues to be a significant problem, particularly in remote areas; for example, in some highland areas in Papua, one out of every two teachers is absent on any given day (OECD/ADB 2015, p. 110; Munro 2013). However, this figure does not even include those teachers who are at school but do not enter the classroom to teach. Moreover, locally appointed contract teachers (*guru honorer*) are exempt from the many new standards for teachers with full civil-servant status. Although they are mostly underpaid, there are at least 1 million contract teachers all over the country, many of them hired by local politicians to reward them for their support in local elections (Pisani 2013). Rather than being driven by any motivation to educate Indonesia's youth, many of these teachers are more interested in the prospect of getting secure jobs as civil servants. Promotion depends on loyalty and time served, and not necessarily on motivation and competency (Rosser 2018).

A number of initiatives in Indonesia are aimed at improving primary education in remote areas (Slater 2013). Following models from the 1950s, such as Pengerahan Tenaga Mahasiswa (Higher Education Student Deployment Program), the NGO Indonesia Mengajar (Teaching Indonesia Movement) set up by Anies Baswedan, who later became minister for education and culture and then governor of Jakarta, has sent dozens of university graduates to some of the country's most isolated and underresourced communities since 2010. Yet, despite exceptional achievements, such programs are insufficient to properly address the deep structural inequalities in contemporary Indonesia (Gellert 2015).

Although Indonesia spends more on education than many other countries, including the United Kingdom and the United States when expressed as a percentage of government spending, the quality of education is very low according to international standardized tests. Of the sixty-five countries participating in the Programme for International Student Assessment (PISA) test in 2015, Indonesia ranked sixtieth in reading skills and sixty-fourth in math and science, well below Thailand and Malaysia. Needless to say, students from poor families performed worse than children from families of higher socioeconomic status. Generally, the blame for Indonesian students' poor PISA and other test scores is directed at poor training of teachers, many of whom do not have university degrees, at teacher absenteeism, and at insufficient and poor-quality textbooks and classroom equipment.

But the material side of learning is only one factor in poor education outcomes. The common mode of instruction in Indonesia favors rote learning and memorizing from textbooks, with little nurturing of critical and creative skills by teachers. Curriculums are developed centrally. In recent years, science subjects were removed from the primary school curriculum, and history and geography from the junior high school curriculum, and the extra space was allocated to more teaching of religion, citizenship, and Bahasa Indonesia (the official Indonesian language) (Palatino 2013). In fact, the overall shift within the national education system from secular to more religiously inspired instruction is very obvious, particularly after the passing of Law 20/2003 on the National Education System, which is regarded as accommodating rather more the interests of conservative Muslims, such as state funding for accredited religious schools.[2]

Despite the poor results in international tests, a majority of students tend to pass the national exams, which raises serious doubts about actual student achievement in the Indonesian education system. How fit are young Indonesians to navigate effectively in the modern world? How equipped are they for the requirements of the modern workplace?

Religious Schools

The regulation of education in Indonesia is exceptional in that there is not one ministry but two with responsibility for administering education across the archipelago. The Ministry of Religious Affairs oversees most public and private religious schools (*madrasah*), of which there are more than 45,000, mostly at the primary and junior high school level (Kingham and Parsons 2013, p. 68). Religious schools are set up either by local communities or Islamic organizations in lieu of state-funded schools, and they are attended by about 6 million students, often from poor families in disadvantaged areas. The quality of these schools and the education they provide is significantly lower than in public schools, as they are disadvantaged in terms of financial support, both at the national and the district level (Manning and Sumarto 2011; OECD/ADB 2015, p. 121).

In theory, religious schools teach the same core curriculum of general subjects as state schools, in addition to religious instruction, which makes up roughly one-third of all lessons. In reality, most of the schools lack the capacity to meet minimum requirements, such as providing classrooms, qualified teachers and principals, compliant lesson plans and assessments, and sufficient books and other equipment. To receive state funding, a religious school must be accredited, but the accreditation process is often very complicated in decentralized and hyperbureaucratic Indonesia, and many *madrasah* have failed to get financial support (Kingham and Parsons 2013, p. 74). Private *madrasah* cater to the children of the poorest families, but without accreditation, they receive less support than public *madrasah* and public schools. Students at unaccredited *madrasah* that get no public funding not only get a poor education but also graduate with diplomas that are not recognized elsewhere and, therefore, these students do not have access to further education.

Not all Islamic education institutions are under the Ministry of Religious Affairs, as some schools and universities are funded entirely from private sources, which raises ongoing concern about the ideological orientation of many of these institutions (Tan 2012). In fact, experts, such as Sidney Jones, estimated that about 40 *madrasah* and *pesantren* (Islamic boarding schools) can be considered hotbeds of fundamentalism and violent extremism (Aiyar 2015). The Al-Mukmin *pesantren*, located in a suburb of Surakarta in Central Java, has gained particular notoriety. The International Crisis Group (2003, p. 26) has called it the "Ivy League" for Jemaah Islamiyah recruits, not least because its founders, such as Abu Bakar Bashir and Abdullah Sungkar, and several alumni, including Amrozi bin Nurhasyim, Ali Ghufron, and Ali Imron, were implicated in a series of terrorist attacks in the early 2000s. Around 200 or so religious schools emphasize an orthodox Wahhabi philosophy but tend to not preach violence.

Tertiary Education

Indonesia's tertiary education sector, which includes universities, institutes, colleges, polytechnics, and community academies, has grown tremendously since the 1980s, in part because of privatization in the sector. In 2001, only 15 percent of youth eighteen to twenty-two years old were enrolled at a university. By 2010, that figure had risen to 23 percent (Suryadarma and Jones 2013, p. 9). Since 2000, more women have begun to participate in tertiary education, thus reducing their gender inequality. In fact, in 2008, at the undergraduate level, the number of enrolled female students surpassed the number of male students. At the masters and PhD levels, numbers of male and female students are almost equal, although in Islamic institutions the number of female postgraduate students remains substantially lower (Suharti 2013).

Most universities—about 3,400—are private institutions, about 100 are state-operated, and about fifty are Islamic institutions. The large number of unaccredited tertiary-education institutions and study programs poses the greatest challenge. Accreditation is valid for five years, but because of the inefficiency of the accreditation system, a large backlog of institutions awaiting accreditation has built up. There continue to be striking differences in quality between public and private institutions. Geographic inequity persists, as most tertiary education institutions are located in Java, although ambitious plans are in place to expand tertiary education to the main outer islands, so that, for example, every province will have at least two polytechnics and every district at least one community academy. As of 2015, all Indonesian teachers are required to have a four-year university bachelor degree, and many new universities have cashed in on this requirement, among them Indonesia's Open University, which had more than 400,000 students in 2016 (Padmo et al. 2017).

Attending a university is extremely expensive, costing an average Indonesian household one-third of its annual expenditure to fund one family member's higher education. Admission fees at Indonesia's elite universities can reach Rp250 million (US$25,000). Although some universities have scholarship programs generated by their own revenue, there are no student loan programs of any kind in Indonesia, which prevents many from pursuing the tertiary education that could lift disadvantaged students and their families out of intergenerational poverty. State funding for universities remains sparse, despite the fact that Indonesia's economy needs more workers with tertiary education (OECD/ADB 2015). Total tertiary education expenditure was about 1.2 percent of GDP in 2011, which is lower than in Malaysia (1.69 percent), but higher than in Thailand (0.71 percent), where enrollment numbers are much higher than in Indonesia (OECD/ADB 2015, p. 205).

On the whole, higher education in Indonesia is underfunded by international standards, in both teaching and research. In fact, most Indonesian universities do not yet have the capacity to achieve innovation through applied research and technology transfer (di Gropello 2013, p. 256). Generally, research money is channeled to selected universities in the form of competitive grants and also to some universities as small block funding based on their track record in research. Currently the Ministry of Education and Culture directs its support first and foremost to the research-focused elite institutions, ignoring the important role of regional universities in training the future workforce. Outcomes in patents, technology licensing, and journal articles show that Indonesia is starting slowly from a very low base (OECD/ADB 2015).

The quality of university education is still considered problematic, with standards even at the most prestigious universities often being suboptimal, resulting in Indonesia's poor showing in university global leagues tables (Rosser 2018). In 2018, no Indonesian universities were in the *Times Higher Education* World University Rankings of the world's top 500 universities. In the QS World University Rankings, three Indonesian universities were among the top 500, with the University of Indonesia the highest ranked at number 277.

The internationalization of higher education is seen as an important tool for raising quality. In 2016, 40,000 Indonesians were studying overseas, which amounted to less than 1 percent of the total number of students, a figure substantially lower than its neighbors. Around the same time, 6.1 percent of all Malaysian tertiary students and 1.9 percent of Vietnamese were studying overseas (OECD/ADB 2015, p. 197). In 2016, the top five overseas destinations for tertiary students were Australia, the United States, Malaysia, Japan, and Egypt. In 2012, the Indonesian Ministry of Finance established the Endowment Fund for Education (Lembaga Pengelola Dana Pendidikan [LDPD]) and since then has given over 16,000 scholarships to masters and PhD students to pursue their studies overseas; outcomes have, however, been disappointing, as many students have not graduated on time. For those not lucky enough to win a scholarship and unable to afford to study at home or abroad, false certificates and diplomas are widely available on the internet. It comes as no surprise that the Ministry of Research and Higher Education receives hundreds of reports of local politicians using fraudulent university diplomas when they run for office (Kemenristekdikti 2017; Rosser 2018).

Troubled Education-to-Work Transitions

Entry into the labor market and achieving financial independence marks the transition into adulthood. It is a prerequisite for marriage and parenthood for young men and, increasingly, for women in Indonesia. Longer periods of learning do not necessarily result in the graduation of better-qualified entrants to the workforce. Many graduates, whether from secondary or tertiary institutions, face significant challenges when they try to enter an increasingly competitive job market. In other words, the expansion of the education system has not yet resulted in better opportunities and widespread upward social mobility. Despite the fact that more middle-class families are investing in longer education for their children, the chances that their children will benefit from their schooling seem to be declining. Moreover, although formal education is important in applying for jobs, it is often not enough to actually get hired. Personal networks and the ability to pay bribes (often as much as several months' wages) are prerequisites for getting into the job market (Naafs 2013, p. 240).

With the national overall unemployment rate running at about 7 percent in 2010 and continuing at that rate, youth unemployment, which is at almost 40 percent, is rampant, particularly among high school graduates (di Gropello 2013, p. 249). Although Indonesian universities are generally considered to provide graduates of better quality than secondary schools and vocational-training institutions, many university graduates still do not possess the marketable academic, behavioral, and technical skills required by potential employers, and the unemployment rate among young people with tertiary education remains around 12 percent (Tadjoeddin 2014, p. 19).

Despite high youth unemployment, many employers complain that they cannot find adequate professional staff to fill vacant positions. There are several reasons for this contradiction. On the one hand, a growing number of graduates with university diplomas are competing for a small pool of jobs deemed appropriate for their level of education, such as entry-level jobs in public administration (Schut 2015). Even though decentralization has seen the creation of new provinces and districts and the proliferation of publicly funded jobs in their bureaucracies, many university graduates have difficulty finding jobs in these new bureaucracies unless they are well-entrenched in the respective networks and can afford to pay the informal, often exorbitant, hiring fees; they seem to have little interest or are ill-equipped for work in other employment sectors. Consequently, many young graduates move to Jakarta and other metropolises to find work, competing with their unskilled peers and contributing to Indonesia's high rates of urbanization and urban youth unemployment (Tadjoeddin 2014, p. 16). Because of their financial insecurity and difficulty in planning their future, many young people have to delay marriage and family formation.

On the other hand, Indonesian educational institutions keep producing graduates without the basic skills that make them employable. The skills that students acquire at school and those that employers look for, such as independent thinking, negotiating skills, creative thinking, problem solving, computing skills, English language skills, and general practical knowledge, often do not match. Even in the manufacturing and services sector, employers have difficulty finding adequate staff. To make matters worse, vocational education (*sekolah menengah kejuruan* [SMK]) continues to have a bad reputation, as it is typically perceived as being for those who have failed academically and as a second chance for the poorest groups in the population. Dropout rates from SMKs tend to be high, in part because many SMK students are from families of low economic status and face financial difficulty. Although SMKs are supposed to provide their students with practical and technical skills, they have been criticized for the poor quality and irrelevance of the training they provide, which does not match what the labor market demands (OECD/ADB 2015, p. 165). To combat the lack of skills and to reduce youth unemployment and underemployment, more on-the-job training is needed. In 2015, there were about 55 million skilled workers, but by 2030, Indonesia will need at least 113 million skilled workers in order to progress (OECD/ADB 2015, p. 156). With about 2 million people entering the job market each year, there is an urgent need to prepare these workers with better skills so that they have a chance of succeeding in life and of competing in an increasingly skills- and knowledge-based economy (World Bank 2016).

Employment

At independence, the majority of Indonesians worked in agriculture. Employment in the state administration was often reserved for the educated elites. While more than half of Indonesia's working population was still in agriculture in the 1980s, jobs began to shift into other sectors, thus driving urbanization. In the second half of the 1980s, labor-intensive exports triggered economic growth (Aswicahyono, Hill, and Narjoko 2010). Although Indonesia's economy has made a remarkable recovery from the financial crisis of 1997, the recovery has not generated many new and urgently needed jobs in the formal economy. Indonesia can no longer rely on creating jobs for workers in low-productivity agriculture and services, as it could before the crisis, but needs to create jobs in other sectors (Manning and Sumarto 2011). As in some other middle-income developing countries in the region, a slow and poorly performing bureaucracy and economic nationalism have, however, stalled the creation of new jobs underwritten by the help of foreign direct investment.

In 2015, almost 33 percent of the Indonesian labor force (122 million people) was active in agriculture, while 22 percent worked in industry and manufacturing and the remaining 45 percent were employed in the services sector (Statista 2017). The poorest of the poor usually work in fishing and farming, earning wages that are often stagnant or even declining, particularly in the mid-2000s (Yusuf and Sumner 2015, p. 340). Employees in low-skilled jobs in manufacturing also often receive low wages and have little job security and little hope of ever progressing into better-paid jobs. The official unemployment rate in 2015 was 6.2 percent, with a higher rate among urban populations (7.3 percent) and 4.9 percent among rural populations (Indonesia Investments 2017). Underemployment, which includes the underutilization of skills and people working part-time jobs when full-time work is preferred, is also a huge problem for Indonesia's workers (Tadjoeddin 2014, p. 20).

These labor statistics do not, however, indicate how many people were engaged in formal employment and how many worked in the informal economy without access to basic social benefits, such as pensions or paid sick leave. Economists assume that between 60 to 70 percent of all Indonesian workers are self-employed or work under informal conditions and thus have no job security (Naafs 2013; Rothenberg et al. 2016). Moreover, tax payments from the informal economy are often not made, which gives informal enterprises unfair business advantages and limits the government's ability to provide more public goods and services to larger segments of society (Rothenberg et al. 2016). Yet the informal economy is also an important safety net for workers who lose their employment in the formal economy. Trade unions represent less than 4 percent of workers (Tadjoeddin 2014, p. 28).

When it comes to salaries and wages, Indonesia's labor market is characterized by high levels of inequality. With a gross national income at a purchasing power parity of US$11,220 per capita in 2016, Indonesia is no longer considered a lower middle-income economy, yet poor-quality employment and low wages remain the norm. The minimum wage is set at the district level, and in some parts of Indonesia wages have risen in the last decade, but payment of a minimum wage is not systematically enforced. Being employed does not guarantee economic security, and some reports have shown that the minimum wage fails to cover household expenditure of workers living in some urban areas where the cost of living tends to be higher (Oxfam International 2017). Although the situation for formally employed workers is not good, self-employed workers and those in the informal sector are even more likely to have a low income that does not cover their basic living costs. A number of labor-rights organizations have campaigned for the revision of the minimum wage, which supposedly covers the living costs of 1.5 persons, to turn it into a living wage that covers the living costs of 2–3 persons. Any adjustment of minimum wage standards, however, needs to be consistent across Southeast Asia so that adjustment in one country does not undercut wage levels in other parts of the region.

The Indonesian labor market is heavily gendered. In general, the state encourages women to take up employment in government, manufacturing, and services (Caraway 2007), so far, though, the participation rate of women (older than fifteen years) in the formal employment sector in Indonesia is only about 51 percent. Most manufacturing jobs are located in the greater Jakarta area and other urban agglomerations, which requires thousands of workers to move to already congested areas to find work. A growing number of young, unmarried, and low-skilled women are among this urban workforce. Some observers claim that because of women's increasing attainment in both education and work, male workers now risk being pushed out of certain sectors, which, in turn, could feed a crisis of masculinity that cuts across the stereotypical understanding of men as the main breadwinners of the family. Unemployment statistics for men and women do not, however, support this claim, although male unemployment tends to be more publicly visible, as unemployed women are more likely to engage in unpaid domestic tasks. Women are also more likely to be underpaid and employed in the informal economy, as confirmed by Indonesia's ranking in the Global Gender Gap index at 88 out of 144, and, more specifically, at 107 for the gap between men and women in terms of economic participation and opportunity, in 2016 (World Economic Forum 2016). Because they are more likely to be employed in the informal economy, women are exposed to more precarious work conditions. According to Mohammad Tadjoeddin (2014, p. 26), more than 10 million Indonesians, mostly women, are domestic workers who work many unpaid hours of overtime, do not get the minimum wage, and often do not get a day off each week.

Next to women, children are the most vulnerable to exploitation in the workforce. Although Indonesia has signed the Convention on the Rights of the Child (1990), it was not until 2001 that the Indonesian government set up its National Action Committee on the Elimination of the Worst Forms of Child Labor. Its first survey on child labor in 2009 found that of the 58.8 million Indonesians between the age of five and seventeen, about 4.05 million, or 6.9 percent, were considered as working children (Tadjoeddin 2014, p. 27).

Because of its large surplus of workers and a scarcity of jobs, Indonesia is a significant labor exporter to the Middle East, East Asia, and other Southeast Asian countries. Official figures of documented overseas labor migrants give the number as approximately 4.5 million; the number of undocumented migrants is estimated to be two to four times greater (Tadjoeddin 2014, p. 27). According to the World Bank, migrant workers compose 7 percent of Indonesia's workforce (only China and the Philippines have larger proportions of migrant workers) and in 2016, remittances from these workers accounted for 1 percent of Indonesia's gross domestic product. The sector is controlled by a few powerful groups in business and politics, and the rights of workers have often been neglected. Overseas employment in manufacturing, agriculture, and low-skilled services, such as domestic work, has been particularly attractive to poor women from rural areas in eastern Indonesia (International Organisation for Migration 2010). Not only are women overrepresented in the overseas migrant-worker population, they also earn the largest share of the remittances. Recruitment for overseas work differs widely across Indonesian provinces, but many female migrant workers lack proper legal protection both in Indonesia and abroad (Palmer 2012) and are exposed to trafficking and forced labor practices throughout the migration cycle. The exploitation, mistreatment, and abuse of men, women, and children working abroad have been widely documented, and the Indonesian government has responded by implementing in 2015 a moratorium on labor migration from Indonesia to twenty-one Middle Eastern countries. This decision, however, was criticized by many labor rights groups, arguing that this attempt to protect the Indonesian workforce is inadequate and may even lead to a growth in undocumented overseas labor migration. In October 2017, following a lengthy process, the Indonesian legislature passed a new law (Law 18/2017) that seeks to strengthen protection for the millions of Indonesians working overseas.

Poverty and Inequality

During the New Order, poverty in Indonesia declined significantly and living standards improved substantially, thanks to steady economic growth and to efficient programs to help lift people out of poverty (Manning and Sumarto 2011; De Silva and Sumarto 2014). According to Haryo Aswicahyono, Hal Hill, and Dionisius Narjoko (2010), industrial growth was at least 9 percent in every year but two between 1970 and 1996. During that period, absolute poverty fell by around 50 percentage points, accompanied by substantial gains in education and health standards (Sumarto, Suryahadi, and Bazzi 2008). The 1997 financial crisis—the worst economic crisis in Indonesia's postindependence era—caused the economy to contract by 14 percent, which resulted in an escalation of poverty (di Gropello 2013, p. 236). Many people lost their jobs, incomes, and savings. The International Monetary Fund (IMF) and the World Bank imposed a number of measures, including the abolition of subsidies for many essential commodities and enforced greater labor market flexibility, which further increased poverty levels. Real wages declined, while prices for stable food and commodities skyrocketed.

By the end of 1998, almost one-fourth of the population was deemed to be living below the official poverty line (Perdana and Maxwell 2011, p. 276), and many migrated from the cities back to rural areas.

In order to ease some of the worst impacts of the 1997 crisis, the Habibie government set up a number of social security programs, referred to as Jaring Pengaman Sosial (Social Safety Net [JPS]), focusing on health-care assistance (*kartu sehat* [health cards for the poor]), food (*beras miskin*, or *raskin* [subsidized rice]), and education (scholarships). The scope of these programs, which were entirely funded by external donors, was unprecedented in Indonesian history (Perdana and Maxwell 2011, p. 276). The JPS brought about visible improvement in household welfare. In 2002, the poverty rate fell to 12.2 percent—lower than it had been before the 1997 crisis (Sumarto, Suryahadi, and Bazzi 2008). However, the benefits of economic growth after the 1997 crisis have not been shared equally, and millions have been left behind.

Most administrations after the Habibie interregnum of 1998–1999 continued efforts to reduce poverty, enabled by gradually cutting fuel subsidies and using the savings to target social security and poverty alleviation. The rising price of oil in the early 2000s put extreme pressure on the Indonesian budget, as payment of fuel subsidies increased to more than 20 percent of total government spending. Although there was widespread protest against these cuts, which led to increases in fuel and transport prices, the government's decision was wise, as rich people, who owned cars, tended to benefit more from the subsidies than the poor.

Having made substantial savings, Yudhoyono initiated infrastructure development programs to stimulate economic development, particularly in rural areas (Sumarto, Suryahadi, and Bazzi 2008). Moreover, in order to help the poor to adjust to the fuel-subsidy cuts, the Yudhoyono government introduced a substantial compensation package in 2005 that included unconditional cash transfers, health support, and educational assistance to prevent poor people from slipping deeper into poverty. At that time, direct cash transfers (Bantuan Langsung Tunai [BLT]) worth Rp100,000 (US$10) were made to more than 15 million poor households, as emergency payments that were only available for a few months (Perdana and Maxwell 2011). The distribution of BLT was impaired, however, as the funds were absorbed more often than not by those who did not really deserve them.

Having learned from the shortcomings of the distribution of unconditional cash transfers, in 2007 the Yudhoyono government set up conditional grants under the Hopeful Family Program (Program Keluarga Harapan [PKH]), which required recipients to send their children to school and to attend regular health checks (particularly for pregnant women). In 2010, PKH covered 798,000 households across twenty provinces (Manning and Sumarto 2011, p. 14). It was targeted to reach 4.5 million households by 2014 and had a budget allocation of Rp9 trillion (US$1 billion) (Tadjoeddin 2014, p. 26), but difficulties in accessing and identifying the real poor, fundamental to the PKH's effectiveness, persisted, largely because of variation in poverty across the archipelago. In Badan Pusat Statistik's 2018 data, poverty rates were highest in the provinces of Papua and Maluku (both at 21.2 percent). Regions with very high poverty rates tend to have lower educational attainment, more restricted access to clean water and sanitation, and poorer access to public health care. Despite the regional disparity in poverty rates, the greatest number of Indonesia's poor people live on densely populated Java (Aji 2015). In 2009, more than 30 percent of rural households still did not have access to clean sanitation (Manning and Sumarto 2011, p. 11). Although rural populations tend to be poorer, since 2000 inequality has been consistently higher in the cities than in rural areas. For millions of people who have moved to the city to escape poverty, their standard of living has not necessarily improved.

During Yudhoyono's second term in government (2010–2014), the government's poverty-reduction strategy had three foci: direct assistance to poor households for basic necessities; community empowerment by funding poor communities to improve basic social and economic services; and microenterprise empowerment through credit that is not collateralized. To demonstrate the government's commitment to this strategy, Vice President Boediono, an economist, was appointed as head of the National Team for the Acceleration of Poverty Reduction. Evaluation of poverty-reduction programs has indicated that outcomes were mixed, mostly because of difficulties in getting the assistance to targeted populations and because of the effects of food price shocks (Aji 2015). Consequently, Yudhoyono's ambitious aim when he became president to halve the poverty rate (and the unemployment rate) remained unfulfilled at the end of his two presidential terms (Tadjoeddin 2014, p. 14).

In 2000, along with 188 other nation-states, Indonesia signed up to eight Millennium Development Goals to be achieved by 2015 in the eradication of poverty, which ranged from halving extreme poverty and providing universal primary education to halting the spread of HIV and promoting gender equality (Index Mundi 2000). Eighteen years later, results in meeting these goals remained mixed at best, owing to the many political, economic, structural, and cultural challenges that Indonesia faces. When Joko Widodo became president in 2014, his previous successes as mayor of Solo and governor of Jakarta raised hopes that he would make an effort to improve the welfare of the poor. One of his first official acts as president was to cut fuel subsidies further and reallocate the savings to infrastructure projects and social welfare. Jokowi has since delivered on many of these projects, including development of airports, railways, and roads, using state-owned enterprises to push them along. However, the anticipated boost to the economy from an expectation of added employment from these projects has not eventuated, and his critics point to the rather stagnant annual GDP of around 5 percent per annum, which falls well below the 7 percent he promised during his presidential campaign in 2014.

In 2018, Indonesia's Badan Pusat Statistik published data indicating that fewer Indonesians—just under 26 million, or slightly less than 10 percent of the population—were living in poverty than ever before in the history of Indonesia. These people were still living below a poverty line set by the government at consumption outlays of Rp387,000 per month, or US$0.89 a day, per person—a line that differs from an international poverty line of US$1.90 a day used by the World Bank and others. If the international line is applied in Indonesia, the number living in poverty rises to about 70 million (36 percent of the population) (Standar Garis 2018). Although poverty rates have been decreasing in the 2010s, thanks to macroeconomic stability, there are still enormous challenges to sustainably reduce the number of chronic poor and near poor. Significant inequity across regions and the rural-urban divide persists; for example, urban poverty rates are well below the national average at 7.02 percent, whereas rural rates are at 13.2 percent, and in the eastern provinces of Papua and Maluku poverty rates are 21.2 percent, compared to Java's 8.94 percent and Kalimantan's 6.09 percent (Kusuma 2018). Moreover, Indonesia needs to make a greater effort to reduce the gap between the rich and the poor, as inequality is a threat not only to poverty reduction but also, in the long term, to economic growth.

Across various measures of inequality, Indonesia's story is one of increasing disparity between rich and poor. Oxfam International (2017) lists Indonesia as the sixth-most-unequal country in the world in terms of wealth. The Gini coefficient, a different measure of inequality based on the distribution of income or consumption in a nation's population, shows increasing if less pronounced inequality. Indonesia's Gini coefficient rose from 0.33 in 1998 to 0.41 in 2015, before decreasing slightly to 0.384 in 2018 (Yusuf and Sumner 2015; Aisyah 2019).

Between 2002 and 2016, the number of billionaires increased from one to twenty, all of whom were men, with the wealthiest 1 percent of the population controlling nearly half of the nation's wealth. The 1997 crisis reduced the overall inequality gap slightly, as inflation meant that the rich lost more than the poor, but in the post-*reformasi* period, wealth became more clearly concentrated among the wealthiest Indonesians. The superrich achieved and consolidated their position, either by selling the country's economic resources and commodities (palm oil, coal, minerals, oil, and gas) and concentrating land ownership in their hands, or through multimedia, communications technology, and finance businesses. Their economic power has been cemented in the many roles they now play in politics or the media, or in both.

The drivers of inequality are complex, as they stem from a variety of interconnected structural factors, such as low wages and insecure work, limited access to education and health services, and infrastructure generally. A poor system for collecting taxes has failed to redistribute wealth from the rich to the poor, in large part because tax compliance remains low and tax evasion among high earners is common. A tax amnesty was launched in mid-2016 to achieve greater compliance with taxation law and the repatriation of undisclosed offshore assets to provide funds for the government's national budget. Without doubt, this approach has the potential to increase revenue so that more can be invested in social programs and thereby redistribute wealth. With the amnesty that ran from July 2016 until March 31, 2017, the additional revenue paid to the Ministry of Finance was significant. More than 800,000 tax evaders declared Rp4,700 trillion (US$350 billion) in assets previously hidden from the authorities. That is equivalent to 40 percent of Indonesia's GDP and 90 percent of the money supply. The windfall helped fund the government's key infrastructure spending, but it remains to be seen if necessary legal reforms can be implemented and taxpayers' behavior changed in the long term.

Conclusion

According to the fifth national principle of Pancasila, there should be "social justice for all Indonesian people." This chapter has shown that inequality in Indonesia is not only pervasive but is on the rise. It stems from a basic inequality in opportunity for Indonesians from early in their lives. Poor children suffer more from poor nutrition and inadequate sanitation. They get sick more often but do not have access to quality health care, and their physical growth and cognitive development are impeded by malnutrition. Poor children attend poor schools and are more likely to drop out with fewer formal qualifications and are poorly prepared for the job market and their future more generally. Although Indonesian children in the twenty-first century spend more time in school than children of previous generations did, there has been no observable increase in their knowledge and skills. Despite curriculum change, teacher training, and scholarship programs, there continues to be an extreme mismatch between the skills produced by the education systems and the skills needed in the labor market. Bad outcomes in education influence Indonesia's international competitiveness negatively. There is high demand for skilled workers in high-salary formal jobs, but most available workers are low-skilled and receive low wages. Most of the employed are still far from having decent work, let alone a decent standard of living. Workers in the informal economy lack the social security of those in formal employment and tend to be more deeply affected by misfortunes, such as sickness, accidents, and other sudden misadventures in life.

Given the demographic change taking place in Indonesia, it is becoming more necessary than ever to attend to the needs of young people—the largest cohort of the population, after all—and their well-being and edification, as their prospects will determine the nation's future. Young people are considered the "hope of the nation," but if the state fails to support them, they will become agents of social protest and political transformation (Parker and Nilan 2013, p. 5). All post-*reformasi* governments have attempted to implement social welfare programs to alleviate poverty. In decentralized Indonesia, poverty reduction is no longer a matter for the central government alone, but increasingly also for provincial and local government administrations. This potentially will have benefits for some, but the nature of local politics and existing infrastructure and services provisions is such that there is the risk that populist politicians will use anti-poverty rhetoric to get into power and then fail to deliver any sound policies, thus exacerbating existing inequality.

Notes

1. The constitution had been amended in 2002 to require, under Article 31, all central and regional governments to allocate 20 percent of their annual expenditure to education. The subsequent Law 20/2003 on the National Education System further strengthened this requirement, but it was not actually met for the first time until 2009.

2. The infiltration of religious values can be traced back to the constitution as amended in 2002, which stipulated that the national system of education should include religious values (Yusuf and Sterkens 2015, p. 125).

7

Civil Society
and Human Rights

UNDER THE NEW ORDER THERE WERE FREQUENT VIOLATIONS OF human rights in Indonesia. In 2019, two decades after the fall of the New Order regime, activists and civil society groups continue to struggle for a better human rights framework for Indonesia, encompassing justice and truth-seeking for historic human rights violations and stronger legal and institutional instruments to protect these rights. The efforts of these civil rights activists have met with varying degrees of success. In this chapter, we examine the most significant cases of human rights abuse in the New Order and post–New Order eras and the ongoing challenges in the pursuit of truth, justice, and a stronger civil society in Indonesia.

In short, the persistence of human rights abuses associated with the security forces since Suharto's fall continues to be a major challenge to Indonesian democracy. Why has it been so difficult for elected governments to hold the military and police accountable? Why has it been so difficult to change the institutionalized culture of violence in the security forces? The answers lie within an analysis of Indonesia's failure to deal with past abuses and the structures and individuals responsible for them. Ongoing impunity for crimes against humanity committed by the security forces and sanctioned by government ensures that a culture of violence within those institutions remains in place.

The list of human rights violations under the New Order begins with the mass killings of Communists, both known and alleged, in 1965–1966, and includes repression of political opponents, military violence against and torture of civilians, repression of basic rights to freedom of speech and assembly, and discrimination against minority ethnic and religious groups. Discrimination of Indonesia's small ethnic Chinese minority of 1.2 percent of the population (Coppel 2017) was institution-alized and systemic under this regime. Laws restricted use of Chinese language, names, script, and customs and excluded those Indonesians with Chinese ancestry from entering public office, including the presi-dency, all while the government kept some of this minority close in busi-ness dealings (Purdey 2006). As Ariel Heryanto (2006) describes it, the ethnic Chinese minority were "under constant erasure," and anti-Chinese sentiment was ever-present.

The military oppression of movements and groups seeking inde-pendence from Indonesia was a notable characteristic of the New Order. Among those targeted were the guerrilla fighters of Organisasi Papua Merdeka (Free Papua Movement [OPM]) and Gerakan Aceh Merdeka (Free Aceh Movement [GAM]), also known as Acheh-Sumatra National Liberation Front (ASNLF), and members of Frente Revolucionária de Timor-Leste Independente (Revolutionary Front for an Independent East Timor [Fretilin]) in East Timor. The Indonesian military fought these separatist movements with brutal determination. As a conse-quence, civilian populations in the provinces where guerrillas pursued separatist agendas suffered great losses, not only because of military repression in the designated militarized zones (*daerah operasi militer* [DOM]), but also through poverty and a lack of medical services, basic infrastructure, and food supplies.

After the fall of Suharto in May 1998, activist and victim organiza-tions seized the moment to renew their calls to revisit human rights vio-lations committed under the New Order. Despite some initially promis-ing steps, hopes for measures to redress this violent past were soon dashed. In his short term as president, B. J. Habibie facilitated the release of political prisoners, lifted political controls, and more impor-tant, built a new system of human rights instruments by amending the 1945 constitution and adopting the Human Rights Law.[1]

The Human Rights Law (No. 39/1999) adopted the principles of equality and nondiscrimination and of protecting the right to life, jus-tice, freedom of the individual with regard to slavery, and freedom of religion, political beliefs, and speech. Although initiated by Habibie, it was his successor, President Abdurrahman Wahid, who adopted the Human Rights Court Law (No. 26/2000), but the courts set up under this new law cannot deal with cases of human rights abuse that predate the law's enactment, unless the president establishes a special proce-dure for an exception to be made (Herbert 2008). During his first term as president, Susilo Bambang Yudhoyono signed the International Covenant on Civil and Political Rights and the International Covenant on Economic, Social and Cultural Rights in October 2005, but there was little expectation that the former general would make any serious attempt to address atrocities committed by the military.

When Joko Widodo was nominated as a presidential candidate in 2014, hopes grew in civil society that past human rights abuse would be addressed. During his election campaign, Widodo reached out to human rights activists for support, and the protection of human rights featured prominently in his nine-point agenda (Nawa Cita). He identified a number of cases for further investigation, such as the 1965–1966 massacres and the disappearance of students in 1997–1998, promising that the "just finalisation of past human rights violations would be of utmost importance to his government" (Setiawan 2016). As this chapter will show, following his election to the presidency in 2014, Widodo failed to deliver on his promises.

Although there were some significant reforms in the years immediately after Suharto's fall, such as constitutional amendments, legislative hearings, and some concessions on human rights courts, it has become more difficult to make similar reforms in contemporary Indonesia. Successive governments have refused to come to terms with the nation's violent past, allowing poorly healed wounds to fester in the collective memory and failing to prevent further violations of human rights.

The failure of transitional justice and reconciliation measures in postauthoritarian Indonesia can be blamed on domestic political elites who are unwilling to put time and resources into bringing justice to victims and who have stymied efforts by civil society to implement global norms of transitional justice. Immediately after the fall of the New Order regime, millions of dollars, expertise, and knowledge flowed from foreign donors to foster a democratic transition in Indonesia but did not necessarily help Indonesia to come to terms with its past. This is not surprising, given the continued influence of elites and dynasties, including the Suharto family, in Indonesia's politics and economy. Furthermore, opponents of transitional justice made effective use of many legislative, religious, and cultural strategies to undermine justice initiatives (Ehito 2015).

In this chapter, we seek to direct attention to continuing violation of human rights, such as in Papua and among other minorities, and to the ongoing impunity of perpetrators of past violations, primarily members of the security forces, though this also includes members of vigilante groups and militias close to the security forces and other political elites. Human rights issues have too often been disguised in the general euphoria of human rights meetings, committees, declarations, and the like (Hadiprayitno 2010), and Indonesia now faces the dilemma of a gap between policy and practice in the protection of human rights (Azhar 2014). We pay special attention to Komisi Nasional Hak Asasi Manusia (National Commission on Human Rights [Komnas HAM]), established under Suharto in 1993, but for many years it was a toothless institution with limited powers of investigation and recommendation.

In addition, we investigate the state of civil society in contemporary Indonesia. In response to the repression of the New Order in the 1980s and 1990s, civil society organizations (commonly known as LSM [*lembaga swadaya masyarakat*]) and activism grew. Two of these groups were formed in 1980 as Lembaga Bantuan Hukum (Legal Aid Institute [LBH]) and Yayasan Lembaga Bantuan Hukum (Indonesian Legal Aid Foundation [YLBHI]); the third one, Lembaga Studi dan Advokasi Masyarakat (Institute for Policy Research and Advocacy [ELSAM]), was formed in 1993. They are still leading national organizations in defending human rights.

Under the various governments since Suharto's regime, civil society has undergone wide-reaching transformation, not all of which has favored people living in Indonesia. Some former well-known activists have joined political parties and entered elite politics. Others who were less accommodating of government policy were silenced, including the former head of the Commission for the Disappeared and Victims of Violence) (Komisi untuk Orang Hilang dan Korban Tindak Kekerasan [KontraS]), Munir Said Thalib, who was poisoned on a Garuda flight from Singapore to Amsterdam on September 7, 2004, and whose murder has never been fully explained. In post-Suharto Indonesia, despite a number of formal government commitments to human rights, many minorities, whether religious, ethnic, or of sexual orientation, continue to be marginalized, repressed, discriminated against, and stigmatized today. In recent years a shift to conservatism in Indonesia has resulted in increasing discrimination against religious and sexual minorities.

Dealing with the Past: Seeking Justice for New Order Human Rights Violations

1965–1966

The New Order was born out of a mass killing of unknown proportions that some historians and legal experts claim amounted to genocide (Melvin 2017; International Peoples Tribunal 2017). General Suharto seized power during an alleged coup by the Partai Komunis Indonesia

(Indonesian Communist Party [PKI]) on September 30, 1965. Subsequently, large-scale massacres and the systematic killing of PKI members and attacks on affiliated organizations and their suspected sympathizers were carried out by the military and police, as well as by Muslim youth and student groups supplied with weapons by the military. Estimates of the number of people killed range from 500,000 to 1 million (Cribb 2001a). Mutilated bodies were thrown into mass graves or deliberately left where the public could see them as a warning. Intellectuals and artists aligned with the left, or suspected of being so, were imprisoned along with more than 1 million suspected Communist sympathizers for long periods in camps on remote islands, such as Buru, often without ever being brought to trial. In the four decades that followed the massacres, those who survived imprisonment and torture and their families were explicitly excluded from public life. As a number of scholars have argued, on the one hand, the Suharto regime prided itself for having quashed all Communist activity, while on the other hand, it needed to perpetuate the potential for Communist resurgence to justify its deeds.

In post–New Order Indonesia, with the Cold War a distant memory, propagation of Communist ideology remains outlawed under the 1966 regulation prohibiting its spread (TAP MPRS XXV/1966). Anti-communist propaganda continues to be used by various groups, not only against left-leaning groups and activists but also in denouncing a range of activities, including those that promote the protection of human rights. In September 2017, the Jakarta offices of YLBHI, the legal aid foundation, were attacked by fundamentalist Islamist groups attempting to stop a meeting of academics discussing the 1965–1966 killings. Protesters claimed that the meeting had been called to reestablish the outlawed PKI. Police initially failed to stop the demonstrators and the meeting was not able to proceed, after which human rights activists claimed they had become the new enemies of the state (Wieringa 2017).

Since the fall of the New Order, many victims' groups, NGOs, and Komnas HAM have attempted to document the mass graves of those killed in 1965–1966. Among the most vocal advocates for justice for the dead and the recovery of the remains of those killed are the founders and members of Yayasan Penelitian Korban Pembunuhan 1965–1966 (Foundation for Research into Victims of the 1965–1966 Killings [YPKP]). Despite evidence gathered from a number of excavations of mass graves, fact-finding missions, and testimonies of witnesses and victims, not a single perpetrator has yet faced justice (Wahyuningroem 2016).

Since 1998, there have been several failed attempts to achieve truth-seeking and justice. In 2000, during Megawati's presidency, the MPR called for the creation of a national truth and reconciliation commission (TRC), and Law 27 on a Truth and Reconciliation Commission was passed by the DPR in 2004, requiring the government to establish formally such a body. Not only did it take several years for the law to be passed, but the final version was significantly different from early drafts, much to the disappointment of NGOs and victims' families. Under the law, the TRC was empowered to recommend an amnesty for perpetrators of serious crimes, and victims could only receive compensation in exchange for their concurrence in the amnesty (International Centre for Transitional Justice and KontraS 2011, pp. 29–30). Several NGOs filed a lawsuit against these provisions of Law 27/2004 at the constitutional court. Rather than eliminate the particular provisions mentioned in the suit, the constitutional court struck down the law in 2006, thereby annulling the entire basis of a TRC.

In post–New Order Indonesia, one of the main obstacles to justice for these historic crimes against humanity is the fact that the courts established in 2000 following the passing of the Human Rights Law (No. 39/1999) cannot deal with crimes committed before 2000, which fall under the jurisdiction of ad hoc human rights courts. To set up an ad hoc court to prosecute a particular case, Komnas HAM must first conduct an investigation, the recommendations of which are then sent to the attorney general. If approval to proceed is granted by the attorney general, an ad hoc human rights court is established, through a recommendation to the DPR committee and to the president. There are many shortcomings inherent in these provisions for establishing ad hoc courts, such as the lack of any guarantee of the impartiality of the appointed judges and of any mechanism for appeal. It is, therefore, not surprising that only two ad hoc human rights tribunals have been established so far—one for East Timor and one for the Tanjung Priok Massacre (see below). The recommendation of Komnas HAM's wide-ranging and later embargoed report into the 1965–1966 killings (Komnas Perempuan 2012) that the attorney general use this legal mechanism has been ignored.

In 2014, in response to the lack of political will within Indonesia to take any action to redress perpetrators of the 1965–1966 killings, human rights activists, academics, and Indonesian exiles established the International People's Tribunal (IPT) on Crimes Against Humanity in Indonesia 1965, timed to coincide with the fiftieth anniversary of the beginning of the killings. The IPT, held in The Hague in November 2015, was presided over by seven international judges, led by South African Zak Yacoob. It reported in July 2016, finding that gross crimes against humanity had occurred, that the violence was state sanctioned, and that a case for genocide against the ethnic Chinese minority could be made (McGregor and Purdey 2016). The IPT's process and findings were immediately rejected by the Indonesian government, which claimed it had its own procedures for dealing with past crimes. In an effort to demonstrate its desire to handle this issue "at home," Joko Widodo's government announced in May 2016 the establishment of a Reconciliation Committee (Setiawan 2016). Key members of the committee were the coordinating Ministry of Politics, Law and Security; the National Police; the military; and the State Intelligence Agency; among other members were people who were themselves suspected of involvement in serious human rights abuse, such as retired general Luhut Panjaitan. The committee initiated a government-sponsored seminar in Jakarta at which victims had the opportunity to put their case for the first time to academics and members of the military. Televised and broadcast live across the nation, the gathering was considered an important example of open public hearing of this issue after decades of silence and denial, but it achieved nothing in terms of support for truth-seeking or justice for victims. Since that seminar, there has been an escalation in anti-communist propaganda and attacks on events related to 1965–1966, including the banning of films by Joshua Oppenheimer and the disruption of book discussions and gatherings of victims and their supporters (McGregor, Melvin, and Pohlman 2018). When the New Order ended in May 1998, the specter of anti-communism remained as a powerful, although increasingly ludicrous, tool to discredit political opponents and evoke fear (Pohlman 2017).

Papua

The conflict in Papua remains the longest-running violent dispute between the central government and local resistance. As described in Chapter 3, Indonesian control of Papua rests on the New York Agreement signed in August 1962 by the Netherlands and Indonesia, under UN auspices and pressure from the Kennedy administration for a resolution in favor of Indonesia. The agreement made provision for an "Act of Free Choice"—a vote on becoming part of the Indonesian nation. In 1969, the western part of New Guinea was annexed as Indonesian state territory with the Act of Free Choice (Penentuan Pendapat Rakyat [PEPERA]). One thousand and twenty-two Papuan representatives were delegated authority on behalf of all Papuans to choose whether they agreed to integration with Indonesia, and they opted unanimously in favor of integration (Saltford 2003). The delegates were allegedly selected by the Indonesian central government in Jakarta, and closely monitored, and intimidated, by the military. In the twenty-first century, not only does the Papuan independence movement continue to dispute Indonesia's sovereignty over Papua, but it also draws attention to political and economic inequality, ongoing human rights violations, and the perpetrators' impunity (Munro 2013). In late 1999, a report prepared by ELSAM documented 921 deaths resulting from military operations between 1965 and 1999 in various parts of the provinces of Papua and West Papua (Human Rights Watch 2007b). Others believe that the number is several times that figure because of indirect consequences of the military counterinsurgency, such as disease, malnutrition, and starvation. None of these violations have been addressed so far by the human rights instruments now available in Indonesia, including the ad hoc human rights courts. Amnesty International (2018) continues to document casualties from security forces operations since 1998, as well as the continuing impunity enjoyed by the security forces responsible.

Since 1969, armed resistance to the Indonesian government has been limited to small units of guerrillas loosely organized under the OPM and the Tentara Pembebasan Nasional (National Liberation Army [TPN]). Poorly equipped armed insurgents launch sporadic hit-and-run ambushes at Indonesian security force posts and have on a few occasions taken hostages to draw attention to their cause. Most notoriously, in 1996 a guerrilla group kidnapped twelve members of an international scientific expedition to the area and held them hostage for four months. Indonesian military retaliation was and continues to be severe. As in other "rebellious provinces" in Indonesia, security forces have free rein to combat resistance to Indonesian rule. Papua offered a quick career enhancement to soldiers and military experts, with little accountability for their actions. In their sweeping searches for OPM guerrillas, the security forces have used excessive violence and have not spared women and children (Human Rights Watch 2007a).

The remoteness of the area and the lack of reliable reporting under the New Order made it very difficult to find out what was going on inside the restive province. Despite a relatively strong network of Catholic and Protestant churches and their infrastructure, it often took weeks if not months for news of forced displacement, retaliative killing of civilians, and other cruelties to come out, thus offering fertile ground for rumor and unfounded speculation. Some of the most eminent Papuan leaders moved overseas—to Australia and Europe—and their day-to-day connections with the insurgents remained sporadic, but as symbolic leaders they have sought for many years to direct the world's attention to the Papuan cause (Chauvel 2009, 2017).

A broad independence movement across Papua, encompassing various religious denominations, students, and other civil-society groups emerged at the end of the New Order. Their activities have mainly involved nonviolent resistance to authorities in Papua through flag raisings, mass mobilization for demonstrations, and the publication of political manifestos for an independent Papua. As in the other restive provinces, East Timor and Aceh, the withdrawal of Suharto and the political reorientation in Jakarta opened up expectations that secession from Indonesia could be achieved. However, these movements were often suppressed by the Indonesian military, which feared losing its grip over some of the most resource-rich provinces. Because Papua is rich in gold, copper, and many other natural resources, the Indonesian military and police have benefited by forming protection rackets to offer "security" to mine operators (Misol 2006).

The Biak Massacre of July 1998 was an indication that despite the *reformasi* era, the Indonesian military would not allow the breakup of the unitary state. Members of the OPM and civilians raised the Morning Star flag (Bintang Kejora), the symbol of the independence movement, near the water tower in the city of Biak and camped there for several days. Early in the morning of July 6, the Indonesian military began shooting at participants in this protest. Although a few managed to escape, the military rounded up about 200 protesters, many of them wounded, and forced them onto two Indonesian boats. They were taken to two different locations and thrown into the ocean. Days later, their bodies washed up on the shore or were caught up in fishing nets (Rutherford 1999). The Indonesian military claimed that the dead bodies on the beaches were not Papuan demonstrators but victims of the Aitape tsunami from more than 600 miles (1,000 kilometers) away.

In February 1999, early in the *reformasi* era and buoyed by developments toward an independence vote in East Timor, an attempt was made to promote a more peaceful dialogue between the Indonesian government and representatives from Papua. The Forum Rekonsiliasi Masyarakat Irian Jaya (Forum for Reconciliation for the People from Irian Jaya [FORERI]) was established and met President Habibie and senior military officers in Jakarta to convey their plea for independence, but their pleas were rejected outright and any form of national debate was shut down (Rutherford 1999). In 2000, Papuan nationalists formed the Dewan Papua (Papuan Council), a key political platform in support of independence, and held a National Congress from May 29 to June 4, attended by more than 3,000 people.

In October 2001, President Abdurrahman Wahid sought to quell demands for independence by offering a high level of autonomy through the Papua Special Autonomy Law, which explicitly allowed symbols of Papuan identity such as flags and songs (International Crisis Group 2003). Wahid had agreed that the Morning Star flag could be flown in Papua as a "cultural" symbol, as long as it was flown below the Indonesian national flag. Indonesian courts have, however, continued to treat raising the Bintang Kejora as a pro-independence statement. Since 2001, dozens of activists have been charged with *makar* (treason, or rebellion) and convicted under antisubversion legislation that allows a very wide interpretation of what it means to spread hatred or instigate rebellion (Human Rights Watch 2007b).

The long history of repression continued through the 2000s, with dozens of protesters against Indonesian rule arrested, often ill-treated, and convicted for peacefully expressing their discontent through flag raising and other activities of political resistance. During that time, people in Papua were subjected to ongoing violence and injustice, including extrajudicial executions, sexual assaults, and forced displacement from villages. In December 2000, the police raided student dormitories in Abepura and tortured some of the students.[2] Most significant, in November 2001, Theys Eluay, the chairman of Dewan Papua, was killed under circumstances that have still not been properly investigated.[3] In 2002 alone, forty-one people were arrested in Papua for peaceful independence activities (Human Rights Watch 2007a, 2007b). In May 2005, Filep Karma and Yusak Pakage, two independence supporters, were charged and convicted of spreading hatred and rebellion and sentenced to fifteen-year and ten-year prison sentences, respectively (Human Rights Watch 2007b).

In the 2010s, these abuses and cases of arbitrary detention and intimidation of pro-independence groups have continued. In January 2018, twenty-seven-year-old West Papuan Yanto Awerkion, a member of the civil-society organization West Papua National Committee, was convicted of treason for his part in organizing a pro-independence petition that gathered more than 1.8 million West Papuan signatures and was presented to the United Nations in September 2017 (Cochrane 2018). In July 2018, Amnesty International Indonesia reported that since 2010, security forces have unlawfully killed at least ninety-five people in Papua and West Papua, with the overwhelming majority of perpetrators never being held to account for these crimes (Amnesty International Indonesia 2018). Inhuman and degrading treatment and torture continue to be widespread in Papua and West Papua, in addition to the lack of freedom of expression, severe restrictions on freedom of assembly, and arbitrary detention (Hernawan 2018).

In terms of economic, social, and cultural rights, Papua remains stagnant. In 2003, Papua was split into two provinces (Papua and West Papua) so that better services could be offered to those living in this large area and to guarantee more participation by Papuans in the local government structure. The split was also a response to high levels of transmigration from other parts of Indonesia, which meant non-Papuans started to outnumber Papuans, especially in urban areas. Economic and social dominance of transmigrants persists, however, even though decentralization policies that are supposed to empower indigenous Papuans have been adopted (Munro 2013).

As explained in Chapter 6, the quality of education in Papua remains low compared to the rest of Indonesia, owing to poor management of the education system, incompetence, high levels of absenteeism among teachers, and inadequate funding. Access to health care and government services is also very poor in Papua, which has the highest HIV/AIDS infection rates in Indonesia (Anderson 2013). In spite of several development efforts and reconciliation attempts, such as the Papua Road Map, with its focus on dialogue, which was given tacit support by President Yudhoyono in 2011–2012, and Widodo's 2014 campaign promise to invest in Papua, there has been little improvement in the everyday lives of Papuans (Institute for Policy Analysis of Conflict 2017a). Papua remains the poorest province in Indonesia, according to the 2016 Human Development Index. A combination of limited economic improvement, political failure in peaceful lobbying for independence, and the persistence of state-sanctioned violence and impunity has ensured that violent resistance continues to spiral.

In November 2006, armed groups in Papua convened under a united framework to hold the first congress of the Tentara Pembebasan Nasional–Papua Barat (TPN–PB, West Papuan National Liberation Army), at which they declared their commitment to fight colonialism, imperialism, and global exploitation until they have reclaimed sovereignty over Papua and its people (Human Rights Watch 2007b). However, Papuan guerrillas are not a united force and Papuan nationalism is complicated by significant ethnic diversity and geographic division between the lowlands and highlands. Furthermore, it continues to be difficult to get detailed and trustworthy information about the situation in Papua because foreign journalists and diplomats cannot travel freely there, and local reporters and defenders of human rights continue to face intimidation and obstruction from security forces.

President Widodo initially made many welcome gestures after his election in 2014. Among them was an offer of clemency to political prisoners, which backfired, as only five prisoners accepted the offer, with others rejecting it on the grounds that accepting it would be an acceptance of guilt. Pledges to investigate and complete some of the most serious cases of human rights violation—including those in Wamena (violent security force operations in twenty-five villages after two Indonesian soldiers had been killed by OPM in 2003), in Wasior (violent retaliations by paramilitary police after five police were killed by OPM in 2001, resulting in four dead, five disappeared, and thirty-nine tortured Papuans), and in Paniai (shootings in which five teenagers were killed and seventeen other protesters wounded in December 2014)—have been criticized for misinterpreting and underestimating the complexity of these cases and, more significantly, for showing "little interest in dealing with the much larger issue of holding security forces accountable at the command level for human rights violations in Papua" (Institute for Policy Analysis of Conflict 2017a, p. 1). During its Universal Periodic Review (UPR) at the UN Human Rights Council in May 2017, Indonesia pledged to finalize a criminal investigation into alleged gross human rights violations in Wasior in 2001 and Wamena in 2003, and forward the case to the human rights court established under Law No. 26/2000 (Amnesty 2018). However, by mid-2018, nothing had been done.

In 2015, Widodo promised to open West Papua and Papua to foreign journalists and international observers; although the number of journalists granted permits to visit the province rose from twenty-two in 2014 to thirty-nine in 2015, this remains a very low and restricted number (United Nations Human Rights Council, National Report 2017, p. 19). International human rights organizations continue to report on the frequent use of torture and inhumane treatment by security forces in response to political protest and alleged disturbances of public order. Extrajudicial killings often occur as acts of revenge or retaliation for violent acts and nonviolent interactions with members of the security forces; an example of such a killing was the murder of well-known human rights defender Joberth Jitmau in May 2016 (International Coalition for Papua 2017, p. 3).

International attention focused on this part of Indonesia is growing. Since 2014, the establishment of a broad coalition of pro-independence groups working overseas—the United Liberation Movement for West Papua (ULMWP); its main partner inside Papua, the Komite Nasional Papua Barat (West Papua National Committee [KNPB]); and the regional support group Pacific Decolonization Solidarity Movement (PDSM)—have brought a new dynamic to the independence movement. The movement's short-term objective is to move from observer status to full membership of the Melanesian Spearhead Group (MSG), a subgroup of the Pacific Islands Forum consisting of Vanuatu, the Solomon

Islands, Papua New Guinea, and Fiji, with one nongovernment member, the Kanak Socialist National Liberation Front of New Caledonia. In 2016, much to the disdain of the Indonesian government, members of the MSG raised their concern about human rights violations against the Papuan population at the UN General Assembly, supported by other bodies, such as the Committee on the Elimination of Racial Discrimination (CERD). Since then, Indonesia has invested significant diplomatic and aid efforts to suppress momentum on this issue and has so far succeeded in blunting the independence groups' push. In October 2017, the Institute for Policy Analysis of Conflict (2017) concluded: "In trying to resolve past human rights cases . . . the Jokowi government's commitment to addressing grievances became mixed up with trying to stop a pro-independence Papuan bid for membership in a Pacific subregional organisation." Shortly after, ULMWP activists presented the UN Special Committee on Decolonization with a petition signed by 1.8 million people from Papua, pressing for the issue of Papua's self-determination to be addressed internationally (Chauvel 2017).

Aceh

The conflict between the Indonesian government and separatists in Aceh began in 1976 after GAM declared Acehnese independence. Over almost three decades of conflict, an estimated 15,000 to 30,000 people died and another 100,000 were displaced (McCulloch 2005). Out of hundreds of documented incidents of human rights abuse in Aceh, very few of the perpetrators have been brought to trial, and only in military or *koneksitas* courts (civil-military courts), away from public scrutiny and with very disappointing outcomes. Senior military officers were usually spared from standing trial, and only lower and mid-ranking officers were punished, although, because of a lack of transparency, it remains unclear whether those who were found guilty actually served their sentences (International Centre for Transitional Justice and KontraS 2011).

The Boxing Day tsunami of December 26, 2004, had a devastating impact on Aceh and altered the course of its history. With an epicentre off the west coast of northern Sumatra, the tsunami claimed 230,000 lives in 14 countries around the Indian Ocean with the highest number of losses suffered in Aceh. Following the tsunami, international negotiators brokered a memorandum of understanding (the Helsinki MoU) between GAM and government forces in 2005 to end the decades of conflict (Aspinall 2005b). The peace agreement contained four mechanisms to implement peace between GAM and the Indonesian military. First, it called for an amnesty for the rebel fighters of GAM. Second, it outlined a timetable and benchmarks for demobilization, disarmament, and decommissioning of GAM and Indonesian forces. Third, it established an agenda for the reintegration of combatants, political prisoners, and civilians involved in the conflict and a foundation for compensation payments to victims of the conflict. Fourth, it recommended the establishment of a human rights court and a truth and reconciliation committee for Aceh, though it provided no details or a time line on how to establish it (Ehito 2015; Aspinall 2008b).

In 2005, President Yudhoyono signed a presidential decree (No. 22 of 2005) granting general amnesty to persons involved in GAM activities, and more than 1,400 prisoners were granted amnesty and released (Aspinall 2008b). Armed conflict in Aceh has ended, human rights abuses linked to the security forces have been reduced, and the province is now mostly peaceful, but the justice and reconciliation agenda has failed completely. Despite a law calling for it to be established, the proposed human rights court for Aceh has not been established, and if it had been, it would have no retrospective authority, so it could not deal with cases on events that occurred before 2006.

As outlined in the Helsinki MoU, it was agreed that there would be a truth and reconciliation commission in Aceh as part of a national Indonesian TRC. This was also provided for in the 2006 law for the governing of Aceh, but the TRC for Aceh has not been established because, as mentioned earlier, the national TRC was ruled unconstitutional in 2006 (Aspinall 2008b). In 2013, in the absence of a national TRC, Aceh's provincial parliament mandated the establishment of a local Komisi Kebenaran dan Rekonsiliasi (Commission for Truth and Reconciliation [KKR]), even though not all local political leaders supported it. Among those who opposed it were a number of former GAM leaders, no doubt concerned about the possibility that former GAM members could be held accountable for human rights abuses during the conflict. Despite severe shortfalls in funding for the KKR, the commissioners were elected in late 2016. The KKR is mandated to design a reconciliation mechanism incorporating dispute-resolution practices based on local Acehnese *adat* (custom). These mechanisms are expected to be established at the local level and will only be used to adjudicate cases that do not involve gross human rights violations (Kent and Affiat 2017). Because it has no power to extract detailed information from the Indonesian military about its role in the conflict, the KKR may have only a very limited chance of proving human rights abuse and initiating prosecution of the perpetrators.

In the absence of juridical redress, a range of alternative forms of justice and economic compensation have so far dominated post-conflict transformation in Aceh. The Helsinki MoU provided for economic assistance for those most affected by the conflict, identified as former combatants, political prisoners, and civilians who suffered demonstrable loss. However, embedding reparation for victims within a reintegration program for former combatants proved problematic. Compensation was to include suitable farmland, employment, or social security for victims unable to work. In February 2006, the Badan Reintegrasi-Damai Aceh (Aceh Peaceful Reintegration Agency [BRA]) was set up to implement an extensive reintegration program and offer funds to local victims and their families. After calling for livelihood proposals from former combatants and victims, BRA received approximately 48,500 applications. By mid-2007, 20,000 payments to victims' families, averaging about U$200–300 per family had been made (Clarke et al. 2008, p. 27). Widespread corruption was reported, however, so it is likely that some of these payments never reached those entitled to them. Instead of truth-seeking and institutional justice, what could be observed in Aceh was "a sort of 'monetisation of justice'" (Aspinall 2008b, p. 22).

Besides compensation, great hope was placed in local traditional practices of reconciliation, such as *diyat* (compensation for the family of people killed) and *peusijuek* (ritual to symbolize reconciliation), to overcome grievances (Avonius 2009). These do not satisfy many victims, however, leaving a sense of injustice that might have long-term implications for the sustainability of peace in Aceh. Any failure to provide justice to victims while perpetrators evade punishment has the potential to remain a potent source of grievance that might reignite the struggle for secession in the future.

Since Aceh began to enforce its sharia criminal code in late 2015, human rights groups have raised concerns about the use of the code and its associated bylaws to carry out public canings and to criminalize consensual same-sex sexual acts and all *zina* (sexual relations outside of marriage). This has resulted in particular concern about the loss of basic rights for members of the LGBTQI (lesbian, gay, bisexual, transgender, queer, and intersex) community in Aceh, to the extent that Human Rights Watch (HRW) has described that loss as a violation of basic human rights as agreed in the Helsinki MoU (Harsono 2017a).

East Timor

The Comissão de Acolhimento, Verdade e Reconciliação de Timor Leste (Commission for Reception, Truth and Reconciliation in East Timor [CAVR]) has documented an estimated minimum of 102,800 conflict-related deaths in East Timor between 1974 and 1999, comprising 18,600 violent killings and 84,200 deaths from disease and starvation. Indonesian forces and their auxiliaries were held responsible for 70 percent of the killings. Because of East Timor's remoteness and the difficulties news media had in gaining access to the island, most of this violence initially went unnoticed by the outside world. This changed on November 11, 1991, when Indonesian military opened fire on a crowd of peaceful mourners in a procession to Dili's Santa Cruz cemetery. In what became known as the Dili, or Santa Cruz, Massacre, at least 250 East Timorese pro-independence demonstrators were shot. Coverage of the killings by foreign journalists and the death of a foreigner in the shooting meant the event reached a worldwide audience, resulting in significant international pressure on the Indonesian government.

There was another spike in deaths in East Timor at the time of the independence referendum in late August 1999, when a resounding majority of Timorese voted in favor of secession from Indonesia. Despite the presence of international observers and the UN Transitional Administration in East Timor (UNTAET) following the referendum, violence erupted, perpetrated by local militia sponsored and equipped by the Indonesian military. Fourteen hundred people died and between 60 and 80 percent of East Timor's infrastructure was destroyed in a scorched-earth program of systematic destruction. An estimated 400,000 people were displaced from their homes, many of them forced into West Timor by the militia.

In May 2002, Timor-Leste, as the new nation was now called, achieved full independence. It faced three significant legal challenges. First, it had to rebuild an administrative and juridical apparatus from scratch to establish the rule of law and enable democratization and internal sovereignty. Second, the new state had to create institutions and mechanisms to support internal reconciliation, which was deemed necessary for the successful integration of those who had previously opposed Timor's independence. Third, it had to fulfill its international human rights obligations in order to be accepted as a legitimate member of the international community (Strating 2014). Despite several promising attempts at the local, national, and bilateral level, most achievements in bringing justice to the Timorese have not been entirely satisfactory.

UNTAET operated as the interim governing authority in East Timor from October 25, 1999, until independence on May 20, 2002. The CAVR was established in 2001 and began operating the following year, its main focus being to record minor human rights abuses, such as looting, burning, and minor assault, and to promote nonjudicial ways of dealing with low-level offenses in order to pave the way to community reconciliation, rather than restorative justice. Reconciliation had different meanings for different people. For some, it implied forgiveness, forgetting, and closure on the violent past to enable everyone to move forward; for others, it meant acknowledging the past without any proper compensation to the victims of past abuse (Kent 2009). CAVR presented its full report, called *Chega!* (Portuguese for "no more, stop, enough!"), to the Timor-Leste parliament in 2005 and to the United Nations in 2006, and it was subsequently published in the Tetum, Portuguese, and Indonesian languages. The government of Timor-Leste has implemented some of its recommendations, including establishing an institute for memory, the Centro Nacional Chega! in Dili.

Within a month of the 1999 referendum, Komnas HAM established the Komisi Penyelidik Pelanggaran Hak Asasi Manusia di Timor Timur (Commission for Human Rights Violations in East Timor [KPP-HAM]) in Jakarta (Linton 2004). Its report, published early in 2000, found "widespread collaboration between Indonesian military and police and pro-autonomy militia" and identified high-ranking officials, including General Wiranto, the commander in chief, as responsible for crimes against humanity (Strating 2014, p. 237). It also named twenty-nine military, police, militia, and civilians suspected of responsibility for the violence. As had the international commission of inquiry set up by the United Nations, KPP-HAM's report also recommended that an international tribunal should try crimes committed in 1999.

On September 15, 1999, the UN Security Council issued a binding resolution that called upon the Indonesian government to bring the perpetrators to justice, giving them two options—to accept an international tribunal, or to establish a national human rights court. Timor-Leste lacked the resources for such an extensive tribunal, but in any case, Indonesia was very much opposed to an international tribunal, preferring to establish its own human rights tribunal to investigate and prosecute crimes committed in Timor-Leste. Indonesia's foreign minister, Alwi Shihab, worked to convince the UN Security Council and Secretary-General to agree to an ad hoc human rights court model (Hadiprayitno 2010). The Human Rights Court Law (No. 26/2000), adopted in November 2000, was the result of strong international pressure, but also behind its adoption was the sincerity of President Abdurrahman Wahid, who had apologized to Timor-Leste when he visited in March 2000. The ad hoc human rights court was established in August 2001, but it could not adequately address human rights violations committed in 1999. Prosecutors charged eighteen mid-level and senior-level officials, most of them members of the security forces. Six senior police, military, civilian, and militia leaders were convicted, but all were acquitted on appeal (International Centre for Transitional Justice and KontraS 2011; Linton 2004; Azhar 2014). A report presented by three experts appointed by the UN Secretary-General to monitor the implementation of the Security Council's recommendation led commentators to describe the court proceedings as "sham" trials (Jolliffe 2005).

Not only was Indonesia reluctant to pursue perpetrators with the greatest responsibility for crimes committed during and after the referendum within its own justice processes, it was also reluctant to extradite suspects to Timor-Leste. The Serious Crimes Unit established by the United Nations indicted 380 people; of those, about fifty have been convicted, mostly East Timorese militiamen unable to flee to Indonesia. Like other Indonesian senior military figures, General Wiranto enjoyed sanctuary in Indonesia, despite an international warrant for his arrest. Wiranto pursued a political career unhindered and has never faced any legal repercussions, being appointed coordinating minister for political, legal, and security affairs in Joko Widodo's cabinet in July 2016. Timor-Leste's reliance on imports of rice, ammunition, and other goods from Indonesia and its need to foster a friendly relationship with Indonesia have mitigated against putting pressure on the Indonesian government for extraditions. It was, therefore, not unexpected that, in late 2004, Indonesia and Timor-Leste jointly established a Commission for Truth and Friendship (CTF) to investigate the 1999 violence, independently of UN recommendations and intervention. The CTF was made up of an equal number of Indonesian and Timor-Leste representatives. Four years later, after interviewing only eighty-five people and collecting statements from only sixty-two witnesses, the CTF produced its final report, which recommended four major actions relating to institutional reform, development of joint policies, establishment of new human rights institutions, and reparation. The CTF recommendations contained no detailed estimates for reparations amounts and nothing about how to distribute the cost of establishing the proposed institutions between the two countries. Both Indonesia and Timor-Leste have demonstrated a lack of political will in implementing many of the CTF's recommendations (Strating 2014).

Having observed little serious effort to bring those responsible for crimes against humanity to justice, the UN Security Council set up the Serious Crimes Investigation Team in 2006 to resume the investigative functions of the former Serious Crimes Unit, established under UNTAET.

Its task was to help Timor-Leste's prosecutor-general complete outstanding investigations into cases of serious crimes committed in 1999. The UN Integrated Mission in Timor-Leste (UNMIT) was established in August 2006 to support the new government in enforcing security and democratic governance in the country. It completed its mandate at the end of 2012, citing good progress on key developmental indicators in the country and peaceful elections earlier that year. Timor-Leste again held peaceful national elections in 2017.

Tanjung Priok

In September 1984, Indonesian security forces opened fire on civilian protesters at Jakarta's port, Tanjung Priok, killing at least twenty-four people, although local observers estimated the number of deaths as being up to ten times higher. The protest broke out after a military officer had tried to remove from the local mosque written material that was critical of the Suharto regime and of the imposition of Pancasila as the sole state ideology. Angry members of the mosque burned his motorbike. The military arrested four people, which led to a protest march to the office of the military district command, joined by more than 1,500 protesters. In the aftermath of the shooting, dozens of protesters were disappeared, others were arbitrarily arrested and detained, and some tortured and subjected to unfair trials. In 1999, a Komnas HAM investigation into the incident led to the establishment of the Commission for the Investigation and Examination of Human Rights Violations in Tanjung Priok, the membership of which included several New Order military figures. Its final report found that there had been no systematic massacre at Tanjung Priok (Junge 2008). The report enraged members of the Front Pembela Islam (Islamic Defenders Front [FPI]), who attacked the office of Komnas HAM. In a follow-up report, published in October 2000, Komnas HAM called for the establishment of an ad hoc trial, singling out twenty-three members of the military, including some high-ranking officers, to be investigated for their involvement in the Tanjung Priok Massacre. The most prominent of these was retired general Try Sutrisno, former commander in chief of the military and vice president under Suharto.

In April 2001, President Abdurrahman Wahid issued a presidential decree (No. 53 of 2001) to establish the Ad Hoc Human Rights Court for Tanjung Priok. The decree was revised by Presidential Decree No. 96 of 2001, issued by Megawati Sukarnoputri, which emphasizes the location and the time of the atrocities (Hadiprayitno 2010). The trial commenced in September 2003 and all defendants were indicted for crimes against humanity under the Human Rights Court Law (26/2000). However, all defendants were low- and middle-ranking officers, while the actual decisionmakers and more senior military figures, such as Try Sutrisno and the former armed forces commander, retired general L. B. Murdani, escaped trial. The outcome of the trial was further weakened a year later when the twelve (of fourteen retired and active military personnel tried), who were initially found guilty, were acquitted on appeal (International Centre for Transitional Justice and KontraS 2011).

The trial itself came under heavy criticism for other reasons. Members of the military had threatened victims and witnesses, both inside and outside the courtroom, and the judges had not dared interfere. Such blatant intimidation caused several defendants to alter their testimonies from the statements they had initially made to investigators and lawyers (Hamid 2009). According to the International Centre for Transitional Justice and KontraS (2011), prosecutors failed to consider those responsible for planning the action, drafted weak indictments, and failed to ensure protection of witnesses or victims. The military made known its disdain for the legal process and the ad hoc court, expressing preference for the issue to be settled in accordance with *islah* (traditional Islamic practice to achieve reconciliation in a dispute). Before the trial had started, the military distributed cash grants of between Rp1.5 and 2 million and motorcycles to Tanjung Priok victims (Waterson 2009). Moreover, to make the process more credible, the military invited well-known and respected Islamic scholar Nurcholish Madjid to oversee the signing of the Islah Charter, a document drawn up to confirm reconciliation between the people in Tanjung Priok and the military (Ehito 2015).

Victims and their representatives asked President Susilo Bambang Yudhoyono to further investigate the issue, without success. During his election campaign in 2014, Joko Widodo promised to look into the Tanjung Priok Massacre, along with other gross human rights violations, but four years into his presidency, this and other commitments to human rights had fallen from his list of priorities. Despite his implication in the Tanjung Priok case, Try Sutrisno was appointed in June 2017 by Widodo to be his adviser for a presidential working group tasked with the enforcement of Pancasila (Batu 2017).

Post–New Order Human Rights Violations and Ongoing Impunity

Every Thursday afternoon from four o'clock to five o'clock, a group of people wearing black shirts and carrying black umbrellas stand silently facing the presidential palace in a demonstration known as Kamisan

(*Kamis* means Thursday). They assemble to protest against a range of human rights abuses, such as the mass killings in 1965–1966 and the disappearance and murder of activists in 1998, in an effort to prevent the nation from forgetting past abuses. Why have calls for transitional justice for historical crimes against humanity committed under the New Order been more or less dismissed by successive governments in democratic Indonesia? Human rights advocates point to the ongoing impunity of perpetrators of these crimes, many of whom have resumed positions of power and influence in contemporary Indonesia (Hadiz 2017b; Purdey 2016b). As the East Timor and Papua cases demonstrate, human rights violations did not cease with the fall of the New Order government and the *reformasi*, and intimidation of and violence against defenders of human rights has persisted.

Violence Against Human Rights Defenders: The Case of Munir

On September 7, 2004, Munir Said Thalib, a leading human rights lawyer, died on a Garuda flight from Singapore to Amsterdam, where he planned to undertake postgraduate studies. He had been poisoned with arsenic while in transit in Singapore, so he did not survive the flight. More than a decade later, there has been no progress in identifying those behind his murder. As one of Indonesia's most prominent human rights campaigners, Munir Said Thalib (known simply as Munir) had taken up the cause of dozens of activists who were disappeared. He cofounded two human rights organizations; helped uncover evidence of military responsibility for human rights violations in Aceh, Papua, and Timor-Leste; and made recommendations to the government for bringing high-ranking officials to justice. In September 1999, he was appointed to KPP-HAM in East Timor.

In December 2004, Presidential Decree No. 111 responded to public outrage by establishing a fourteen-member team, headed by a high-ranking police official and including senior human rights activists, to conduct a six-month investigation of Munir's murder. Two agencies whose members were implicated through phone records and internal memos—Badan Intelijen Negara (State Intelligence Agency [BIN]) and Garuda, the national airline—would not cooperate with the team's investigation, but the team completed its task and submitted a report to the president, which implicated senior Garuda and BIN officials and recommended establishing a new team with a more robust mandate. The government did not release the report, contravening an explicit provision in the decree for its public release; nor did it establish a new team, despite domestic and international pressure to do so (International Centre for Transitional Justice and KontraS 2011).

Three employees of Garuda were convicted of Munir's murder, but it is unlikely that they acted alone, and those responsible at the highest levels for his death have allegedly not been brought to justice. In 2008, former BIN official Muchdi Purwopranjono faced trial but was acquitted. The findings of an independent investigation in 2005 were ignored by the government and never published. Successive governments have shown little political will to reopen the case.

In 2014, Joko Widodo, then president-elect, appointed Abdullah Mahmud Hendropriyono to his inner-circle transition team. Hendropriyono headed BIN at the time of Munir's murder, and many human rights groups believe he was involved in planning the assassination, although Hendropriyono has always denied the allegations. Outrage from Munir's widow at the appointment forced Jokowi's camp to reaffirm their commitment to resolving Munir's case, but there has been no progress in doing so during the first term of Jokowi's presidency. The 2013 opening of a museum commemorating Munir's life and work in his hometown, Batu, has ensured that his murder will not be erased from the collective memory.

Gender Discrimination and Violence Against Women

Some aspects of gender inequality and their consequences for women's health, education, and work have been identified in Chapter 6; this section elaborates further on discrimination and violence against women. During the New Order, most women in Indonesia played a subordinate role in public life; their roles were limited to being mothers, housewives, and supporters of their husbands. Under the notion of *azas kekeluargaan* (literally, family principle), an approach used by the state to convey a vision of the nation as one big happy family (Aisyah and Parker 2014), Indonesian women were largely "normatively gendered and essentially depoliticized" (Pohlman 2017). Any contribution to family income was usually expected only from lower-middle-class women and the working poor. In reality, of course, millions of households were headed by women in the absence of or through the incapacity of a male family member.

Employment in public office and membership in political organizations were largely reserved for men, although most public institutions had a subsidiary branch reserved for the wives of key stakeholders, such as Dharma Wanita (for civil servants' wives) and Dharma Pertiwi (for wives of the armed forces), which were largely quiescent and conformed to the government agenda (Blackburn 1999). Independent political activism by women was largely discouraged, as evidenced by the demonization and destruction of the Communist women's movement, Gerakan Wanita Indonesia (Gerwani) (Pohlman 2017). An example of such discouragement is the case of Marsinah, a factory worker and union activist, who was abducted, tortured, raped, and murdered following a protest in May 1993. Although Marsinah became a symbol in the struggle against violence against women, her killers never faced justice. The cases of many women who were suspected Communists or simply relatives of supporters of the left, and who were therefore subjected to sexual assault, arbitrary arrest, torture, stigmatization, and marginalization under the New Order stand as further examples. Under the New Order regime, women not only lacked state protection from violence of many kinds but were even subjected to certain kinds of gender violence encouraged by the regime itself, particularly against those it depicted as leftists or rebels. Under the New Order, the Indonesian army used rape as an instrument of torture and intimidation in Aceh, Papua, and East Timor.

It was not until near the end of the New Order that young urban women, influenced by international debate on gender equality and supported by funding from international sources, began to set up organizations. One of the main focuses of their activities was state-driven and domestic violence against women, and their activism was driven mainly by the government's inertia. Violence against women in public and private spheres simply had no place in the government's perception of a harmonious society based on contented families and a just state (Blackburn 1999). Sexual violence and rape outside of the domestic sphere were often blamed on the victims and their assumed looseness, both by the police and the courts, thereby exposing victims to shame and humiliation and explaining why so few cases were reported.

Although a number of serious cases of sexual violence were reported, there has been a striking lack of indictments for sexual crimes. Under the Indonesian criminal procedural code, two witnesses must corroborate any allegation of rape, and a medical examination must be ordered by police within twenty-four hours of the crime for the perpetrator to be convicted. In the aftermath of mass violence and gang rapes in May 1998, all kinds of violence against women and the relationship between the state and women were debated more openly in Indonesia, but the debate revealed a need for more public education to change public attitudes toward victims.

The union between husband and wife under Indonesian law is unequal, not least because the 1974 Marriage Law states that a husband is the head and main breadwinner in a family. Most domestic violence occurs within marriage (Aisyah and Parker 2014), but reporting it has long been problematic, partly because domestic issues are not considered public matters requiring the intervention of outsiders. Groundbreaking change came with Law 23/2004 on the Abolition of Domestic Violence, which introduced the terminology of domestic violence (*kekerasan dalam rumah tangga*) for the first time and outlawed marital rape (Aisyah and Parker 2014). Although much needs to be done by government agencies and NGOs, the Indonesian people are now more aware of widespread domestic violence. According to data collected by Komnas Perempuan (2012), 113,878 cases of domestic violence were reported in 2011, 97 percent of which were of violence toward wives. In the 2010s, there have been increases in divorce rates and more cases initiated by women citing their husband's infidelity, financial problems, and polygamy as grounds for divorce (Sumner and Lindsey 2010), but women who leave their husbands are still stigmatized in Indonesia. The stigmatization of *janda* (widow or divorcée) arises because of their autonomy as women not under a man's control, and because the sexual desire (*nafsu*) of widows and divorcées is viewed as a threat by the wider public (Aisyah and Parker 2014).

After the collapse of the Suharto regime, conservative Islam gained in influence, enabling conservative Muslims to gain control over important institutions and to strengthen reactionary interpretations of women's position in society. This was particularly apparent when Megawati Sukarnoputri ran for the presidency. As a daughter of Sukarno, the nation's founder, she was very popular, but there was widespread consensus among Muslim leaders that a woman could not lead a Muslim nation (Blackburn 1999). Against the common expectation that *reformasi* would increase gender equality and improve the situation of women in Indonesia, many of the new political parties were very reluctant to nominate female candidates. Consequently, even fewer women entered parliament than there had been in the final New Order assembly.

However, during the early *reformasi* years, more young women became active in civil-society organizations and religious institutions, which gave them a platform on which to be heard in the public sphere. Many religious women used revisionist interpretations of Islam to encourage gender equality and challenge the legal grounds of polygamy. At the same time, other pious Muslim women drove agendas seeking to strengthen heteronormative discourses and conservative agendas (Rinaldo 2008), such as the prohibition of pornography (see Chapter 8) and in sexual health and abortion (see Chapter 6). Another indication of regressive trends in contemporary Indonesia has been the debate on female circumcision, a practice that is still pervasive among Indonesian Muslims (Baumgardner 2014). Although female circumcision in Indonesia is less destructive than the female genital mutilation common in some African countries, the Indonesian Ministry of Health banned the practice in 2006 in the face of significant opposition. The powerful Majelis Ulama Indonesia (Council of Indonesian Ulama [MUI]) released an edict in 2008 declaring that female circumcision was part of religious practice, leading the Indonesian Health Ministry to repeal the ban in 2010 and to issue instead regulations for medical practitioners, rather than traditional practitioners, to perform circumcisions under more sanitary conditions. The medicalized approach backfired, as medical practitioners tend to use scissors and make real cuts, rather than scratching and rubbing the skin with a penknife as traditional circumcisers do. In regulating female circumcision, the Indonesian government is caught between international pressure to ban the practice and pressure from Muslim authorities within Indonesia seeking to continue it. Despite public education and campaigning to discourage female circumcision, many Indonesians are still in favor of the practice.

The Islamist revival and growing Islamization of Indonesian politics and society have brought new obstacles and challenges for women. Although several attempts to introduce sharia law on a national level failed in 2002, under the Law on Regional Autonomy (22/1999) and later under the Law on Local Government (32/2004), local governments began to implement sharia law (*perda sharia*) in their districts, municipalities, and provinces. Between 1999 and 2008, of 470 districts and municipalities, fifty-two enacted seventy-eight *perda sharia* (Bush 2008, p. 176). In fact, only nine of Indonesia's thirty-four provinces have not passed any *perda sharia* (Afrianti 2016, p. 350). Muslim women activists and local female parliamentarians have complained that they have not been consulted or involved sufficiently in drafting the *perda sharia*, but complaints of any sort are generally dismissed by accusing the complainant of being un-Islamic.

Generally, *perda sharia* seek to regulate public order and social problems by, for example, prohibiting prostitution, gambling, and alcohol consumption. Others prescribe religious duties, including regularly reading the Quran and paying religious tax (*zakat*); a number of *perda sharia* relate to religious symbols, such as requiring Muslim civil servants or all Muslim women to wear Muslim clothing. The content of *perda sharia*, however, varies widely from place to place. Women are affected more negatively than men by the *perda*, not only because they regulate their dress and morality more vigorously, but also because they restrict their mobility. Many cases have caught the media's attention, such as that of a waitress in West Java who was arrested by local police on her way home from work one evening and detained for three days on suspicion of being a prostitute, as she had lipstick in her purse (Bush 2008). Women's groups have repeatedly complained about gender discrimination inherent in many *perda sharia*. Komnas Perempuan data from 2009 to August 2016 show that 421 discriminatory by-laws were issued by local governments, including some that regulate morality and restrict women's control over their own bodies. Although many of these regional laws are in blatant violation of national regulations that prescribe equality between men and women and prohibit gender-based discrimination, the supreme court has been hesitant to review and revoke problematic *perda sharia* (Parsons and Mietzner 2009; Lindsey and Butt 2016). Furthermore, following a ruling of the constitutional court in early 2017, the central government now has reduced powers to revoke regional by-laws.

LGBTQI Community

LGBTQI (lesbian, gay, bisexual, transgender, queer, and intersex) movements in Indonesia were started by the transgender male-to-female (*waria*) groups in Jakarta and Surabaya in the 1970s, with Himpunan Waria Djakarta (Waria Association for Jakarta) actually established with the support of Jakarta governor Ali Sadikin (Boellstorff 2004a, pp. 176–177). At that time, Indonesian society seemed more open to gender identities and sexual orientations that were not heteronormative, partly because many ethnic groups had additional social gender constructions beyond the male-female dichotomy. The term *homosexual* was an import that entered Indonesia in the 1970s and was initially strongly associated with diseases such as HIV/AIDS (Khanis 2013).

Despite experiencing many setbacks, these early *waria* groups inspired LGBTQI people to establish organizations and media outlets in the 1980s and late 1990s, of which GAYa Nusantara is one of the oldest and best known. Until the 2000s, there was no unified or coordinated approach among the LGBTQI groups, which fought for their rights separately. Because they all faced strong, often religiously inspired, resistance to their struggle and their specific concerns, many of these small groups came together in larger networks. In 2004, the Directorate-General of Human Rights under the Ministry of Law and Human Rights formally included LGBTQI people as a group in need of protection, a stipulation that was set out in the Rancangan Hak Asasi Manusia (National Human Rights Plan of Action [Ran HAM]), although little action followed to put any protection in place. LGBTQI people increasingly face violence, harassment, discrimination, and stigmatization in Indonesia (Boellstorff 2004b). Islamic fundamentalist groups have attacked LGBTQI events and activists on many occasions, often under the eye of Indonesian police. Some observers have noted that Indonesia is still relatively tolerant of homosexuality, bisexuality, and transgenderism in comparison with many other Muslim countries. Although this may be the case, tolerance of ideas and practices that are not heteronormative is not only defined by the absence of prohibition or by the shadowy underground existence of those ideas and practices. For example, Indonesian television and films in 2019 include gay characters in minor roles, although they are usually depicted with ridicule in a way that reinforces heteronormative and patriarchal social dominance.

The Indonesian criminal code does not prohibit homosexual acts between consenting adults, as long as they are private and do not involved commercial gain. A national bill that sought to criminalize homosexuality failed twice to be enacted, first in 2003 and again in 2017. Nevertheless, some local governments have passed by-laws based on traditional Islamic morality that criminalize homosexuality. The *perda sharia,* described above, introduced by the Acehnese provincial government in 2002, criminalizes *liwath* (sodomy) with a maximum punishment of 100 lashes, 100 months in jail, or a fine of 1,000 grams of gold. The first conviction was in 2017, when two young men were sentenced to public caning with eighty-three lashes each (Rompies and Topsfield 2017). Anti-LGBTQI sentiments are widespread, not only in regions that have adopted conservative *perda*, but also in cities that have generally been more open and safe for LGBTQI. Homophobic violence that is both politically and religiously driven is on the rise. For example, in 2017 the police in Jakarta launched multiple raids on gay saunas under the pretext of pornography law; those arrested were paraded before the media and morally condemned.

Religious Minorities

Religion plays an important role in the private and public lives of Indonesians. For many decades, Indonesia has been praised for its tolerance of religious diversity and for its active promotion of pluralism. Although the constitution acknowledges and protects freedom of religion, only six religions are officially recognized in Indonesia and protected by the state—Islam, Protestantism, Catholicism, Buddhism, Hinduism, and Confucianism. In November 2017, a constitutional court decision ruled that articles in the 2013 Civil Administration Law requiring Indonesians to adhere to one of the six religions or face restrictions in education, employment, and marriage were discriminatory (Topsfield and Rompies 2017). Thus it should now be legal and permissible for adherents of indigenous religions to include their religion on their identity cards. In the 2000 census, 400,000 Indonesians identified as following faiths other than the six official religions, among them a number of traditional beliefs and indigenous religions. The constitutional court ruling effectively gave official recognition to these faiths and was heralded as a significant win for religious freedom (Harsono 2017b). Atheism is prohibited and punishable under the 1965 Presidential Instruction on Blasphemy (commonly known as the Blasphemy Law). In theory, the state in Indonesia should be neutral toward all religions, but in reality it often is not. Muslims, as adherents of the state's majority religion, demand privileges, and when the state consents to those privileges, it discriminates against adherents of other beliefs.

Nearly all Muslims in Indonesia are Sunni, the largest branch of Islam globally. Sunni Muslims are represented by several organizations that cut across the political spectrum, and some have strong international ties. Salafism and Wahabbism, both of which originated in the Middle East, have influenced both the ultraconservative and violent strains of Sunni Islam in Indonesia since the 1980s. Under the New Order, any political opinion that diverged from the official national narrative on religion and ethnicity was prohibited in order to prevent religious conflict and strengthen national cohesion. Nevertheless, a number of violent attacks on Christian churches took place on Java, particularly in the mid-1990s (Purdey 2006; Intan 2012), and similar attacks have persisted in the democratic era.

After the fall of Suharto, however, many long-repressed views, some of them radical and even militant, began to emerge and flourished, undisturbed by the state (Colbran 2010). During the sectarian conflict on the Maluku Islands between 1999 and 2004, hundreds of Christian and Muslim victims lost their lives (Bräuchler 2003). Violence between Christians and Muslims also erupted in Poso on Sulawesi (McRae 2013a). Annual reports by the Setara Institute on religious freedom and the repression of minorities show that there were 216 violent attacks on religious minorities in 2010, 244 in 2011, 264 in 2012, 177 in 2014, and 236 in 2015. Among the victims were Christians, Shias, Ahmadis, members of Gafatar, and many unrecognized animist groups, such as Sunda Wiwitan. Extremists also targeted foreign "infidels," as in the Bali bombings of 2002 and 2005 and the attacks on Jakarta's Marriott Hotel in 2003, on the Australian Embassy in 2004, and in the city center on Jalan Thamrin in 2016. In May 2018, a family of suicide bombers carried out coordinated attacks on three churches in Surabaya, killing forty-one Indonesians.

In addition to physical assaults and the forced displacement of minority religious groups, hundreds of churches and other places of worship have been closed and the construction of new facilities denied (Crouch 2012). Post-Suharto governments have, overall, failed to respond decisively to religious intolerance, acts of harassment, intimidation, and open violence, particularly against the Ahmadis (Colbran 2010). Not only has the state limited freedom of religion by determining how religions must be interpreted and practiced, but its legal structure has supported harassment and violence directed at minority religious groups in the interests of maintaining orthodox interpretation of rituals, religious harmony, and public order (Human Rights Watch 2013).

Religious extremists and militias, such as FPI, have committed many violent acts in the name of Islam, and the FPI is known to have close connections with some police and army generals. Its leaders, such as Rizieq Shihab and Munarman, received relatively lenient sentences for violence they had instigated, such as an attack on an interfaith gathering in Jakarta in 2008. Besides the new radical groups, the performance of the established Muslim mainstream organizations, NU and Muhammadiyah, the most dominant promoters of moderate Islam in Indonesia, has left a lot to be desired. Although both have occasionally condemned violence against minorities in the name of Islam, they have done little to prevent legal discrimination against religious minorities, such as the Shia and the Ahmadis. In fact, MUI has issued a fatwa urging a ban of Ahmadiyah, Shia, and Gafatar. It has also condemned secularism, pluralism, and liberalism in one of its fatwas, combining them in the acronym SIPILIS to invoke their association with disease. By April 2011, nearly half of Indonesia's then thirty-three provinces had banned Ahmadiyah, thus diminishing the rights of its adherents, including the right to register their marriages.

One of the most effective instruments used in preventing members of religious minorities from exercising their religious beliefs and in punishing deviant believers is the 1965 Blasphemy Law, enacted under President Sukarno in response to requests from Muslim conservatives. Before 1998, there were only a few notable convictions for religious defamation, but since then, more than fifty cases have been tried, mostly for insulting Islam (Crouch 2012). Among more recent cases was that of Sebastian Joe, a Muslim sentenced to four years' imprisonment for blasphemy in November 2012, increased to five years in 2013 under the Information and Electronic Transactions Law, by the Ciamis court, West Java, for comments about Islam on his Facebook page (Human Rights Watch 2013). A very prominent case was that of former Jakarta governor Basuki Purnama (Ahok), a Chinese Indonesian Christian, sentenced to two years in prison in May 2017 for allegedly insulting Muslim believers by including a Quranic verse in an election campaign speech.

In October 2009, NGO activists challenged the Blasphemy Law in the constitutional court. Led by former president Abdurrahman Wahid, the petitioners argued that the law violates the constitutional right to freedom of expression and Indonesia's obligations under international human rights treaties (Crouch 2012). Members of Islamist militias attended the hearings in the constitutional court, and some of them harassed the petitioners' lawyers and witnesses at the court building, without facing any consequences. In 2010, the constitutional court, whose decisions cannot be appealed, confirmed the validity of the Blasphemy Law and placed restrictions on minority religious beliefs in the interest of maintaining public order (Crouch 2012; Human Rights Watch 2013). The UN Human Rights Council criticized the ambiguity of the Blasphemy Law several times in its Universal Periodic Review of Indonesia in 2017, but the Indonesian government has repeatedly rejected its recommendations. In July 2018, Indonesia's constitutional court dismissed for a third time since 2010 a petition to revoke the Blasphemy Law. This particular petition was filed by members of the Ahmadiyah community who sought the law's abolition on grounds that it fuels discrimination and abuse of religious minorities. However, the court ruled that such abuses had nothing to do with the Blasphemy Law but were linked to subsequent regulations derived from the law and from "local regulations" (Human Rights Watch 2018).

In 2017, the radical Islamic organization Hizbut Tahrir Indonesia (HTI) was banned in the interest of protecting Indonesian unity, soon after Joko Widodo signed a presidential decree giving the government powers to ban groups incompatible with national unity. In a move criticized by human rights groups, for the first time in the post-Suharto era the government disbanded an organization without due process of law, thus setting a disturbing precedent.

People with Disabilities

According to a national survey conducted by the Indonesian Ministry of Health in 2013, 17 percent of Indonesians have a disability, and an estimated 6 percent live with a "mental emotional disorder" or a mental health condition (Human Rights Watch 2016). Most of these people are unable to access adequate health services, and they are very vulnerable to human rights violations. The law that currently governs the Indonesian government's approach to disability is Law No. 4/1997, which situates people with disabilities as helpless and in need of charitable assistance. For years disability activists have demanded new regulations that better reflect contemporary understandings of how people with disabilities can contribute to and participate in society (Dibley 2016). In 2011, Indonesia ratified the UN Convention on the Rights of Persons with Disabilities. During the run-up to the 2014 presidential elections, Joko Widodo promised that his government would implement a new national law on the rights of people with disabilities to help overcome negative perceptions of disability in Indonesia; the Persons with Disabilities Law was introduced in 2016 (Fuad 2018). Basic improvements, such as barrier-free access to public buildings, the use of braille, and even the use of simultaneous sign language interpretation on television during presidential debates, have been introduced very gradually (Dibley 2014), though significant challenges remain.

The situation of the mentally ill in Indonesia is particularly dire, as the provision of mental health care and special services for them lags behind in the absence of adequate services, competent health-care specialists, and adequately funded institutions. In 2013, there were only forty-eight mental hospitals and between 600 and 800 trained psychiatrists across Indonesia (Human Rights Watch 2016). A number of studies have found that people living with a mental illness are far more likely to experience human rights violations, including physical restraint or shackling (*pasung*), and to have limited access to basic rights, such as shelter, food, proper hygiene, and medicine; they are also more likely to experience physical and sexual abuse (Nurjannah et al. 2015; Human Rights Watch 2016).

Shackling is often the last resort for families that have limited resources and fear violence. According to estimates by the Indonesian Ministry of Health, more than 20,000 people were shackled in 2011 (Safitri 2011), and some were locked in rooms, sheds, cages, or even animal shelters for periods of time ranging from a couple of hours or days to years. Although shackling was officially banned in 1977, the practice continues. Recently, the Indonesian Ministry of Health has condemned shackling as an inhuman and discriminatory treatment of the mentally ill, but it has not succeeded in eradicating the practice. A government campaign, Indonesia Bebas Pasung 2014 (Indonesia to be free of shackling by 2014), was launched in 2010 but has faced set-backs because local authorities have not allocated adequate funding to existing facilities. The practice has also been underreported, which has prevented authorities from intervening and providing alternative treatment.[4] The number of mentally ill people who are not shackled but are neglected or disowned by their families or communities and left to wander, sometimes naked and dirty, on the outskirts of major cities or in rural areas is also underreported. Living on the streets exposes mentally ill people to bullying, mocking, physical abuse, and sexual exploitation by strangers.

Although the provisions of Law 36/2009 on Health clearly spell out that human rights of the mentally ill are to be respected, health-care workers and academics have observed a disconnect between Indonesia's mental health legislation and local policy and procedures (Nurjannah et al. 2015). According to Human Rights Watch (2016), unmodified electroconvulsive therapy, without anaesthesia or muscle relaxants, continues to be practiced in Indonesia, often causing dental damage, spinal and pelvic fractures, and muscle injuries in patients. Restraint, forced seclusion, involuntary treatment, and medication also remain in widespread use. Furthermore, it has been reported that patients in mental institutions are beaten by guards and staff, sexually harassed by staff and other patients, and administered contraception without prior consent (Human Rights Watch 2016). Although Indonesia is a party to most major international human rights conventions and, therefore, obliged to respect the human rights of persons with disabilities, successive governments have done little to ensure meaningful compliance with those conventions.

Conclusion

Some say the past should be forgotten and, rather than dedicating time and resources to dealing with past human rights abuse, Indonesia should focus on preventing future abuse. Such thinking becomes problematic when one considers the many different types of human rights abuse and discrimination that still prevail in contemporary Indonesia. The experience of transitional justice in Indonesia illustrates some of the larger continuing problems of governance in post-Suharto Indonesia, where the rules of the game may have changed but many of the players have not. Many from the New Order era have little interest in looking either backward or deeper into the larger social forces at play (Ehito 2015).

The failures of transitional justice since the end of the New Order reflect the incomplete reform of the military and a lack of will among political elites who fear incrimination for historical human rights abuses. Moreover, the weakness of the judiciary is perhaps a key reason that there has been so little justice in the post-Suharto era. Pressure from civil society has also been inconsistent, with calls for justice at times uneven and even muted, notably in the case of Munir's murder in 2004 and, more recently, in attacks on the offices of the YLBHI in 2017.

In the early *reformasi* period, Indonesian civil society flourished and new laws intended to protect the rights of all, including minorities, were adopted. However, in the late 2010s, legal and political commitments made at home and internationally to addressing past and present human rights abuse have so far been no guarantee of effective action. The enforcement of human rights legislation remains problematic. For those within civil society for whom human rights, gender equality, and minority and disability rights are of central concern, the struggle has in recent years become more difficult as conservative forces within and outside government bring pressure to bear on advocates for universal rights for all Indonesians.

Notes

1. In the fourth amendment to the 1945 constitution, the range of human rights protection was expanded. Article 28 of the amended constitution guarantees the universally accepted human rights—the right to freedom of assembly, to life, to establish a family, to personal development, to be treated equally before the law, to work and employment, to religion and freedom of expression, to information, to freedom from torture and inhuman and degrading treatment, to a healthy environment, and to freedom from discrimination (Hadiprayitno 2010).

2. According to Komnas HAM investigations, early on December 7, 2000, unknown people attacked a police post in Abepura, killing two officers and a security guard and setting fire to some shops. The police responded by conducting a sweeping operation through student dormitories, taking more than 100 students into custody, many of whom were injured and three of whom died. Komnas HAM found that there had been torture, summary executions, and assault, and it recommended prosecution of twenty-five police officers, twenty-one for their direct role in the violence and four for operational responsibility. Komnas HAM forwarded the file to the Office of the Attorney General, which charged two senior officers two years later. Almost 100 witnesses provided evidence of systematic arrests and beatings, but both officers were acquitted in 2005 and the victims' claims for compensation were dismissed (International Centre for Transitional Justice and KontraS 2011).

3. In 2003, seven low-level Army Special Forces (Kopassus) soldiers were found guilty, not of murder, but of mistreatment and battery leading to Eluay's death.

4. In 2014, 1,274 cases of *pasung* were reported across twenty-one provinces and in 93 percent of cases, people were rescued, but there are no data on how many were successfully rehabilitated and how many returned to being shackled once they went home to their families (Human Rights Watch 2016, p. 38).

8

Media and
Popular Culture

UNDER SUHARTO'S NEW ORDER REGIME, THE DENIAL OF HUMAN rights and freedoms placed restrictions on the distribution of information. The media was rigidly controlled and manipulated, and viewpoints and voices opposing the regime were suppressed. In the two decades since the end of the New Order, there has been widespread change in freedom of expression, which has benefited both the media and popular culture. Indonesia has a more vivid and diverse media landscape than ever before and a booming media industry with dozens of national and regional television stations (both public and commercial), hundreds of radio stations and press outlets, and countless online media sites. The enhanced freedom of expression and consequent media freedom are achievements of *reformasi*, yet they have, to a certain extent, also fostered fierce contestation and social instability. Whether the proliferation of media outlets has democratized media content and public debate, as is often widely assumed, remains open to question. Serious doubts persist in the evaluation of the depth of the transition from Suharto's authoritarian regime toward a more open pluralistic and deregulated political system in which the media fully acts as the fourth estate.

Despite democratic reforms and political deregulation, some skeptics argue that social and political transition has not been as deep as was hoped for, because media outlets "have become a crucial site for the proliferation of money politics" (Tapsell 2012a, p. 228). As described in Chapter 4, kinship politics has continued over the last two decades in Indonesia, supported by the "cartelisation of media ownership" in the hands of the rich and their political and economic allies. Old Indonesian oligarchies have built powerful multiplatform media oligopolies (Tapsell 2015, p. 32), which, because they lack diversity in their content, are

167

seriously impeding access to impartial news coverage and, therefore, to freedom of expression. Currently, Indonesian print, broadcast, and online media are dominated by twelve media conglomerates: MNC Group; Kompas Gramedia Group; Elang Mahkota Teknologi; Visi Media Asia; Jawa Pos Group; Mahaka Media; CT Group; BeritaSatu Media Holdings; Media Group; MRA Media; Femina Group; and Tempo Inti Media (Jurriëns 2016, p. 39). The recipe for their success lies in their multiplatform portfolio, or "digital ecosystem" as Ross Tapsell (2017, p. 39) calls it, which goes beyond the production of news and increasingly connects news outlets to e-commerce, gaming, travel, and event management, as well as to housing, job, and communication portals. Not only have these media oligarchs become even richer during the digital era, but most of them have now placed their sons in vital positions in their oligopolies, often in their media headquarters rather than in other business portfolios, which will guarantee their future meddling in politics to spur their own ambitions for political positions or, at least, as kingmakers.

Indonesians no longer have to rely on news that has been sanitized by the state, as under the New Order, but they may not be getting the media coverage they hope for yet. Given the influential media conglomerates and their respective political agendas, it is hardly surprising that Indonesians have embraced social media so enthusiastically in order to access alternative news reports and to produce their own news content. According to the Asosiasi Penyelenggara Jasa Internet Indonesia (Indonesia Internet Service Provider Association [APJII]), in 2017 the number of internet users was estimated at 143.2 million, with a 54.68 percent penetration rate (the percent of users in the whole population).

Although the state no longer regulates media outlets through a strict licensing process as it did under the New Order, and the much-feared Ministry of Information was abolished during Abdurrahman Wahid's presidency, other state institutions and nonstate actors have taken control of media content. For example, the Lembaga Sensor Film (Film Censorship Institute [LSF]), formerly the Badan Sensor Film, has continued to ban local and foreign films and TV productions (van Heeren 2007, p. 218). Moreover, as an outcome of the 2002 Broadcasting Law (Undang-Undang Penyiaran), an independent Indonesian Broadcasting Commission has been set up to monitor the broadcast media in the public interest.

The culture of censorship that evolved under the New Order has not suddenly disappeared, and its legacy is still rather pervasive (Barkin 2014). As of 2019, it is not only the state and its institutions that censor the media and the actions of citizens; many other agents within society censor by acting as moral police, harassing individual activists; intimidating artists; disturbing performances, exhibitions, and shows; and issuing violent threats to media outlets. One of the most prominent examples of such censorship was the cancellation of a Lady Gaga show in Jakarta in 2012. In response to protests and threats of violence from Muslim hard-line groups, such as Front Pembela Islam (Islamic Defenders Front [FPI]), the Indonesian police, citing security risks, refused to issue a permit for the American pop star to perform in Jakarta (Wilson and Nugroho 2012). According to those hardliners, Indonesian youth must be protected from the degenerate West, which symbolizes sexual liberty, obscenity, hedonism, feminism, anarchy, and identity politics more broadly (Allen 2007).

The growth of Islamic pop culture (*pop Islam*) is seen as a result of the success of Islamic politics in post–New Order Indonesia (Heryanto 2011). In line with the wider Islamization of Indonesian society, but primarily driven by conservative and fundamentalist Muslims, a grim anti-pornography debate reemerged in the post–New Order era, which had negative impacts on the media and the publishing industry, as well as on popular culture and the arts more broadly (Allen 2007; Lindsay 2011; Weintraub 2008). In 2006, the Indonesian legislative assembly proposed a bill on Pornography and Pornographic Acts (Rancangan Undang-Undang Anti Pornografi dan Pornoaksi), which, even though it was fiercely criticized by women's groups, moderate Muslims, representatives of ethnic minorities, and artists, was eventually passed in October 2008 as the Pornography Act (Undang-Undang tentang Pornografi 44/2008). One of the first artists to be hit by the full force of this law was the very successful singer Nazriel Irham (alias Ariel Peterpan), whose private sex tapes were uploaded to the internet without his knowledge or consent (Pausacker 2014). The law has, however, had very little impact on the output of Indonesia's burgeoning underground porn DVD/VCD industry, whose products are widely available (Barker 2015).

Indonesia's deepening Islamization has not only shaped the media through its most extreme acts, such as censorship. Its influence on media and popular culture, including music, fashion, film, and other art forms, has in many respects been much subtler. In fact, Muslim-themed popular culture has become an important arena in which Muslims in contemporary Indonesia constitute and contest ideas about Islam (Hoesterey and Clark 2012; Barkin 2014). Muslim-themed TV programs and movies have gained in popularity in the second decade after *reformasi*. The development of distinct genres, such as *film Islami, sastra Islam,* and *sinetron Islam* (soap operas), has exposed a range of Muslim intellectuals, novelists, televangelists, musicians, and filmmakers who claim to speak on behalf of Islam and create new publics and new articulations of Islam (Hoesterey and Clark 2012; Rakhmani 2014a, 2014b). Inspired by an urge for proselytization (*dakwah*), these people aim to promote aspirational norms of (normative) piety and present a Muslim modernity that can function as an alternative to Western ideas and societal models. The so-called *dakwah*-tainment has, however, caused many skeptics to lament the outright commodification and commercialization of Islam by the media and popular culture entrepreneurs. In their view, such "feel-good commercial Islam" embraces Islamic aesthetics but lags behind in providing clear theological guidance.

In this chapter, we argue that the post–New Order era exhibits remnants of the previous authoritarian media culture, not only because of its continued ownership by and the influence of some of the old elites groomed under Suharto, but also because of the authoritarian legacy of the New Order that persists in adherence to New Order values, such as censorship, patriarchy, and social conservatism. We aim to provide an overview of the main changes in and challenges to Indonesia's media landscape, in regard to both form and content, and we discuss a number of indicative media events that have had a lasting impact on Indonesia's wider media politics and on popular culture.

Print Media

Journalism was among the first major sectors to be corporatized under Suharto's New Order. Throughout his presidency, the print media in Indonesia were closely watched and regulated by the Departemen Penerangan (Ministry of Information); the Indonesian military also kept a tight grip on the media (Tapsell 2012a; Sen and Hill 2000). Although there were periods of relative openness during Suharto's rule, the Ministry of Information often arbitrarily banned newspapers, books, and magazines if they were considered to be out of line with official state propaganda. For example, in 1994 the Ministry of Information revoked the license of *Tempo*, the most significant weekly magazine in Indonesia (next to *Detik* and *Editor*), alleging it threatened national security. *Tempo* had been founded by Goenawan Mohamad and Yusril Djalinus in the 1970s, and for a long time it managed to balance reliable reporting with the constraints of very limited press freedom under the New Order. Its reporting of the purchase of old, overpriced East German warships revealed the massive waste of state funds as well as conflict between two ministries. This was considered to have triggered the unexpected clampdown on *Tempo*'s activities (Team of *Tempo* journalists 2009).

After the bans, Aliansi Jurnalis Independen (Alliance for Independent Journalists) was founded and became the prime defender of press freedom in Indonesia, while *Tempo* went underground until it resumed its print version after Suharto's resignation.

Indonesia's "Islamic turn," which started toward the end of Suharto's reign, is also apparent in the newspaper landscape. One of the best-known newspapers to target a more conservative Muslim readership is *Republika*, founded in 1992 and closely affiliated with the modernist think tank Ikatan Cendekiawan Muslim Indonesia (Association of Indonesian Muslim Intellectuals [ICMI]). The establishment of this newspaper, along with greater tolerance of religion in politics and society, was deemed a concession to the growing Muslim elites and the extent to which they were embedded in Suharto's circle of power. Suharto had, after all, hitherto vehemently sidelined political aspects of religion. Throughout his New Order, certain topics that touched on ethnicity (*suku*), religion (*agama*), race (*ras*), and intergroup relations (*antargolongan*), commonly referred to as SARA, were taboo in the media and invited censorship for the sake of superficial social harmony. So too did critical reporting on corruption, collusion, and nepotism that involved members of the presidential family or high-ranking members of the military.

The Indonesian military and police frequently threatened, intimidated, and harassed members of the Indonesian and foreign press. Australian journalist Hamish McDonald, for example, was banned from reentering Indonesia after publishing a critical account of how Suharto's family managed its power and wealth in 1980. The former foreign editor of the *Sydney Morning Herald*, David Jenkins, was similarly banned from entering Indonesia for eight years from 1986 to 1994 after publishing a book about Indonesian military politics and an article about the wealth of the Suharto clan. With their liberty very much decreased, some Indonesian journalists leaned toward self-censorship to avoid disciplinary measures by their superiors and outright injunctions; others were open to receiving bribes for favorable coverage of certain issues, establishing a culture that persists in Indonesia today. The pervasive control over journalists and media gave rise to a media landscape that distracted readers from significant political developments by reporting on relatively unimportant matters, such as the private lives of celebrities and other gossip.

After the end of the New Order, state interference and censorship in Indonesia eased. The new developments were brought in by the 1999 Press Law (Undang-Undang Tentang Pers, 40/1999), which offered greater press freedom through various measures, for example, ending the restrictive limitations on the number of pages that newspapers and magazines could publish and removing limits to the number of press corporations that could coexist in any given region (Armando 2014, p. 393). Moreover, the new law supported reductions in production costs and made it easier to establish new press corporations, resulting in growth in print media and mass media outlets across the archipelago. Increased news coverage and freer reporting helped, in turn, to empower civil society to a certain extent. Although Indonesian journalists engage increasingly in investigative journalism and manage to bring to light well-hidden secrets, such coverage tends to be one-off case stories that are insufficiently connected to Indonesia's wider political context, and the underlying causes and processes (Steele 2011).

Although the Ministry of Information was disbanded by President Abdurrahman Wahid in 1999, the Indonesian press and its news contributors are still not entirely free of state intervention. In 2015, Freedom House judged Indonesia's press as only "partly free," and Reporters Without Borders World Press Freedom ranked Indonesia at 130 out of 180 countries surveyed in 2017 (Reporters Without Borders 2018). Although the government now rarely interferes with press freedom, journalists and editors are more frequently faced with defamation lawsuits, protests, and even violent attacks, especially from vigilantes and extremist groups (Steele 2011). According to the Committee to Protect Journalists (2018), at least seven Indonesian journalists were killed in Indonesia between 2003 and 2018. Despite wider press freedom post-*reformasi*, Indonesian journalists continue to be intimidated, beaten, and murdered, not only in provinces known for their separatist violent conflicts, such as Aceh, Maluku, and Papua, but increasingly for their reporting of environmental topics, especially the destruction of forest for palm oil plantations, and corruption cases. Examples of violent retaliation against journalists and media outlets include the murder of Alfrets Mirulewan, who investigated allegations of unlawful fuel sales in Maluku in 2010. In another incident, the *Tempo* office was fire-bombed by two men on a motorcycle in June 2010, after the magazine had published a story about police corruption, secret bank accounts, and excessive salaries for senior police officials. *Tempo* had already been sued for libel and defamation in 2003, after alleging that Tomy Winarta, an Indonesian businessman with strong links to the military, had benefited from an accidental fire in the Tanah Abang textile market, where he planned to build a shopping center. *Tempo*'s office was also attacked by Winarta's followers, causing *Tempo* to take out a lawsuit against them. Although little came out of those trials in the end, they had a discouraging impact on investigative journalists, who were reminded once again of the need to be extremely cautious when reporting on business-military links in Indonesia (Steele 2011).

The ongoing threats to press freedom, paired with the elitist media ownership that serves the political ambitions of the owners rather than diversity in media content, are responsible for an enduring lack of investigative journalism and news reporting. Freedom of the press has also been limited for several decades by visa restrictions on foreign journalists that have prevented them from visiting Papua officially and reporting on increasing violence in that province. In 2014, two French journalists, who had entered on tourist visas, were detained and sentenced to prison. Although President Widodo announced in May 2015 that accredited journalists were no longer restricted from entering Papua, the Indonesian military and intelligence have resisted his announcement by surveillance of journalists and by interfering with their work, particularly if they are reporting on sensitive issues, such as the violation of human rights, land grabbing, and corruption.

The legacy of New Order secrecy persists, even after the enactment of the 2008 Freedom of Information Law and the establishment of the Komisi Informasi Pusat (Central Information Commission [KIP]) in 2009, which adjudicates in information disputes between the public and government bodies. The KIP, however, remains a toothless institution; many government bodies ignore its decisions, as it has no legal authority to enforce its rulings. For example, in October 2016, KIP ruled that the report of an investigation into the 2004 murder of human rights activist Munir Said Thalib was public information that needed to be disclosed and more light finally shone on this crime, but relevant government agencies claimed to have no knowledge of where the report, produced in 2005 under the Yudhoyono government, was stored and could not, therefore, hand it over to the public.

Additional impediments to freedom of expression in Indonesia include pro-decency sentiment and the anti-pornography legislation "spearheaded by rightwing political Islam and facilitated by post–New Order political structures of regional autonomy," which allows for local *sharia* by-laws and similar prohibitions (Lindsay 2011, p. 178). One of the standout test cases for this conservative social trend was the publication of the Indonesian version of *Playboy*, launched in 2006. Although it never published photos of nude women, the magazine became the frequent target of hostile demonstrations by Islamist groups, and *Playboy*'s office was repeatedly subject to violent attacks (Heryanto 2011).

Former *Playboy* editor Erwin Arnada faced accusations of violating the indecency provisions of the criminal code. In 2011, the supreme court accepted Arnada's appeal against a two-year jail sentence on indecency charges, overturning its own decision. Arnada was freed after eight months in prison. Despite the success of Arnada's appeal, Indonesia has been more widely affected by the conservative attitudes underlying his trial and conviction.

As of 2019, the top-selling newspapers in Indonesia are *Kompas* and *Jawa Pos*. The former dominates the Jakarta readership, and the latter is most dominant in densely populated East Java. Among other influential publications are *Tempo, Pos Kota,* and the English-language *Jakarta Post*. Like the owners of the TV conglomerates, newspaper owners in Indonesia are also important political and economic players who "brazenly push their respective owners' interests" (Tapsell 2012a, p. 234). From the mid-2000s on, several daily broadsheet newspapers have been established in Indonesia, and some existing newspapers have been saved from extinction after being bought and restructured by people eager to invest significant sums of money in print media. For example, the *Surabaya Post* was bought by politician and businessman Aburizal Bakrie in 2008 to ensure more favorable reporting on the Lapindo mud flow in Siduarjo, which had resulted in the eviction of thousands of inhabitants and for which his company was held responsible (Tapsell 2012b, pp. 110ff). A newcomer was the English-language *Jakarta Globe*, launched in 2008 and owned by James Riady's BeritaSatu Media Holdings (Tapsell 2012a, p. 227). The Riady family is not only listed as one of the twenty richest families in Indonesia but also has distinct interests in other media outlets, including broadcasting, print, digital, online, social and mobile media, an online news portal with live streaming, and mobile phone applications (Tapsell 2017). Bakrie and Riady are also owners of broadcast companies and, therefore, deeply involved in shaping Indonesia's media landscape.

Post–New Order Indonesia has seen a proliferation of Islamic media, both in number and diversity of content (Irawanto 2011). As new Islamic publications emerged and existing ones were revitalized and redesigned, the Islamic press in Indonesia became more pluralistic and polyphonic and not just a medium for Islamic proselytizing. Since *reformasi*, Jakarta is no longer the main center for Islamic publishers, as other cities, such as Bandung, Yogyakarta, Semarang, Sukoharjo, Surabaya, Gresik, and Bangil have become hubs of the Muslim press. Among the subgenres of the Islamic press are Sufism and mysticism publications (*Hidayah* and *Kisah Hikmah*, as well as *Cahaya Sufi*),

Islamic women's magazines (*Noor* and *Paras*), and the voice of Islamic youth culture (*Annida*); there are also publications dedicated to political activism (*Sabili, Suara Hidayatullah,* and *Media Dakwah*), some of which offer outspoken Salafi points of view. The close linkages between Islamic print media and their online platforms and other fundamentalist online websites are unmistakable.

Islamic media outlets often tend to be short-lived, as many newly established newspapers and magazines, including *Kiblat, Suara Azan,* and *Ummat,* have gone bankrupt because of poor management, a failure to capture the aspirations of their readers, and their use of old-fashioned adversarial journalism (Irawanto 2011, p. 74). Islamic media have had no success in developing advertising models that are both commercially viable and religiously justifiable (Tapsell 2017). They often fail to attract sufficient revenue from advertising, as they cannot promote certain products, such as alcohol, cigarettes, and anything not deemed *halal* (permissible according to Islamic teaching). Thus, many Islamic press products have to rely on donations. Some *pesantren* (Islamic boarding schools) publish their own magazines, for example, *Al-Furqon, Al-Hawari,* and *Almuslimun,* which resemble in-house bulletins rather than commercial publications, as they are managed unprofessionally and appear irregularly. The economic sustainability and political viability of the Islamic press depends on its ability to appropriate popular culture and Islamize it, and to articulate the politics of Islam within the overall context of contemporary Indonesia (Irawanto 2011, p. 78).

Television

The reach of television in Indonesia cannot be underestimated. Televisions are ever-present and switched on in private and in public spaces. Indonesians are voracious consumers of TV, watching an estimated 251 minutes of TV every day per person (Austin, Barnard, and Hutcheon 2015, p. 91), leading some observers to conceptualize Indonesia as a "televised world" (Jurriëns 2016). By 2010, television penetration in Indonesia had reached 93 percent of the total population, whereas radio penetration was at only 40 percent, and newspaper penetration at approximately 25 percent (Indonesia Media Guide 2010, cited in Armando 2014). Consequently, the content of TV programs and the politics behind the TV screen have considerable influence on Indonesian viewers.

Indonesian public TV began in 1962 when Televisi Republik Indonesia (TVRI) formed to broadcast the Asian Games (Kitley 2000), and it continued to be the only state-owned TV broadcaster for some time under the New Order. Between 1989 and 1995, a commercial private TV station system was established, with broadcasters such as Rajawali Citra Televisi Indonesia (RCTI), Indosiar, Surya Citra Televisi (SCTV), Televisi Pendidikan Indonesia (TPI), and ANTV emerging (Sen and Hill, 2000). Even though these were privately owned, Suharto kept a tight grip on these broadcasters. Jakarta's RCTI was owned by Suharto's son, Bambang Triatmodjo, and TPI, an educational channel, by his daughter, Siti Hediati Hariyadi (Titiek). Moreover, SCTV in Surabaya was owned by Henry Pribadi and Suharto's cousin Sudwikatmono; ANTV was owned by Aburizal Bakrie, a successful businessman and newspaper owner close to Suharto, who later extended his involvement in cross-media ownership (Armando 2014, p. 399).

During *reformasi*, President Habibie issued five more permits for new commercial television stations. Hary Tanoesoedibjo, a businessman of Chinese descent, bought RCTI and TPI from Suharto's son and daughter, and Eddy and Fofo Sariaatmadja, also of Chinese descent, bought SCTV. The media industry expanded—one of few industries to do so during the economic downturn triggered by the 1997 financial crisis (Heryanto 2011). In 2019, there are ten main national stations: RCTI, SCTV, Media Nusantara Citra Televisi (MNCTV), Indosiar, ANTV, TransTV, Trans7, Global TV, Metro TV, and TVOne. The owners are prominent in Indonesian politics and business affairs. Hary Tanoesoedibjo, one of the ten richest Indonesians, owns three stations (Global TV, MNCTV, and RCTI); Chairul Tanjung owns two; Fofo and Eddy Sariaatmadja own two; Aburizal Bakrie owns two (ANTV and TVOne); and Surya Paloh owns Metro TV. Bakrie and Paloh are both politicians, Bakrie having served as coordinating minister for economics and then coordinating minister for people's welfare during the Yudhoyono presidency, before standing as Golkar's presidential candidate in the 2014 elections. Surya Paloh is founder and chairman of Partai Nasional Demokrat (Nasdem) and has nurtured an ambition to become president. Although Chairul Tanjung claimed for a long time to have no interest in politics, he eventually became spokesman for Yudhoyono's Partai Demokrat and served as coordinating minister for economics under Yudhoyono (Tapsell 2015, 2017).

Unlike the regional newspapers and radio stations that flourished under decentralization, the main national television stations remain centrally based in Jakarta. Regional TV has so far not succeeded in attracting funding, which means that there is little coverage of regional news throughout Indonesia. Instead of watching regional political debates and shows, viewers from Sabang to Merauke consume more or less the same broadcasts, which originate in Jakarta. Although there are local and regional TV stations, they cannot compete with the big giants, as they lack the funding to improve their offerings to viewers. A draft of the Broadcasting Bill was proposed in 1997, which sought to diffuse the power of the Jakarta-based privately owned TV channels, but they firmly resisted it. It was, in fact, the first bill that President Suharto refused to sign during the New Order (Armando 2014, p. 400). A Broadcasting Act (32/2002) was eventually passed in 2002, however, little effort was made to enforce the law and increase regional coverage because of continued resistance from the close-knit TV ownership system in Jakarta and its political leverage. Ten years later, after a judicial review of the Act in the constitutional court, the Indonesian parliament announced its intention to revise it, but no action has been taken. In this respect, democratization of the media in Indonesia continues to lag behind.

Leaving aside the ownership and structure of Indonesian TV, it is worth noting some of the main features of its programming content, summarized by Heryanto (2011, p. 71) as "consisting primarily of gross violence, vulgar sexual allusions, hyper-sentimental dramas, horror-cum-superstition suspense, and talk shows with bad jokes." When scrutinizing commercial TV in post–New Order Indonesia, the success of *sinetron* (soap operas), which are shown on most channels, stands out. Mocked for their "dumbing down effect" and for "selling dreams," *sinetron*, with their melodramatic portrayal of the wealthy upper class and their love affairs, seem to satisfy a widespread desire for TV watchers to escape from their everyday struggles. Because of the legal requirement that 80 percent of content broadcast on Indonesian TV channels must be domestic, locally produced *sinetron* have flourished (Jurriëns 2016, p. 43). At the height of the financial crisis, it became too expensive to import Western media products, and consqeuently, growth in the domestic TV industry, first and foremost *sinetron* series, was boosted. Even though most *sinetron* are low-budget productions, relying on rather simplistic formulas in terms of plot, casting, and equipment, they can be very lucrative enterprises for the producers. It is estimated that between US$351 million to US$1 billion were spent on the production of *sinetron* in Indonesia between 2009 and 2014 (Rakhmani 2014a, p. 441). The commercial significance of *sinetron* has attracted and produced many Indonesian stars. The most popular and highest-earning TV stars and Indonesian film actors and actresses tend to be young people of mixed ethnicity, with noticeably Caucasian facial features, such as Cinta Laura (Indonesian German), Pevita Pearce (Indonesian British), Chelsea Islan (Indonesian American), Hamish Daud (Indonesian Australian), Keenan Pearce (Indonesian British), Aliando Syarief

(Indonesian Arab), and Stefan William (Indonesian American), partly because their looks continue to be associated with wealth and modernity (Heryanto 2011, p. 64).

Compared to the 1980s and 1990s, when mainly token coverage of Islam was shown, in the post–New Order period the commodification and commercialization of Islamic images and themes in TV content steadily increased (Rakhmani 2014b). Whereas TV had previously only featured evening prayers and sermons, societal changes have led to an increase in the screening of Muslim TV content, which goes beyond the call for prayers. There is debate among long-term observers about whether the increase in Muslim-themed content was a reaction to popular demand from the Muslim majority audience or whether it was the preemptive action of risk-averse producers, intent on showing some public goodwill, which generated much greater commercial success than they ever anticipated. Although Indonesian commercial TV stations offered little Muslim-oriented programming during the 1990s apart from the occasional holiday-themed quiz and variety programs during major Muslim festivals, such as the fasting month of Ramadan, toward the end of the decade the media elites in Jakarta discovered its commercial potential "despite (or perhaps because of) the rise in religiosity among wealthy and educated Muslims" (Barkin 2014, p. 7). During the early 2000s, Indonesian TV shifted visibly toward screening more Islamic content.

Although Korean and Taiwanese soap operas have been extremely popular in Indonesia (Heryanto 2014b), during the 2010s another kind of *sinetron*—Muslim *sinetron*—has made its way onto the Indonesian screen. These productions of melodramatic romance stories have played a significant role in increasing the emphasis on Islam in television programming (Rakhmani 2014a, p. 436). Generally speaking, the plots of Muslim *sinetron* are similar to those of conventional secular family-centered dramas about the trials and tribulations of young people's romance, but they tend to place greater emphasis on fulfilling parental expectations and filial duties. When it comes to disentangling love triangles among the main male and female characters, the solution in these Islamic melodramas is usually polygamy.

One of the first successful Muslim *sinetron* was the supernatural drama *Rahasia Ilahi* (God's Secret) in 2003. After the successes of *Pintu Hidayah* (The Door of Guidance, 2005) and *Buku Harian Nayla* (Nayla's Diary, 2007), both aired by RCTI, Muslim *sinetron* productions appeared on other commercial TV channels. During Ramadan, extended versions of many popular *sinetron* are provided for viewers. The popularity of Muslim *sinetron* was further enhanced by the commercial success of the

Islamic-themed, melodramatic cinema hit *Ayat-Ayat Cinta* (Verses of Love) in 2008, based on a 2004 novel by devout Muslim writer and proselytizer Habiburrahman El Shirazy (Heryanto 2014b).

Typical of Muslim *sinetron*, regardless of whether they fall into the supernatural, melodramatic, or more humorous subgenres, is a specific set of obvious Islamic aesthetics, composed of Islamic symbols (calligraphy) and speech (Muslim greetings), costumes (*jilbab* and *peci*), and settings (mosques or *pesantren*). Some Muslim *sinetron* also feature religious figures, such as an *ustad* (teacher), partly guaranteeing that the show represents mainstream rather than unconventional Indonesian Islamic ideas and practices, or they integrate recitation of short passages from the Quran in an effort to educate their audiences. Yet overall, these shows serve more as entertainment for their audience than as a means of proselytization—a fact that is criticized by some of the more conservative Muslim activists, who are particularly critical of the more humorous *sinetron* productions tailored to the tastes and preferences of the Muslim proletariat, such as *Pesantren Rock 'n' Roll* (The Rock and Roll Islamic Boarding School) and *Islam KTP* (ID Muslim [more broadly translated as Superficial Believer]). Although other religiously inspired TV formats, such as Islamic talk shows, Islamic music shows, or *dakwah* talent shows, might tend more toward proselytization, critics are tireless in bemoaning the commercialization of Islam by Muslim-themed shows and programs.

Other popular TV programs in Indonesia include reality, talent, and horror shows. Currently, almost every TV channel broadcasts reality TV programs, which are locally produced but often inspired by foreign formats, such as the extremely successful *Indonesian Idol* (on RCTI), *Akademi Fantasi Indosiar* (Fantasy Academy, on Indosiar), and *Kontes Dangdut Indonesia* (Dangdut Contest Indonesia, on MNCTV) (Coutas 2006, p. 371). In Indonesian media culture, the horror genre has a history that is much longer than that of reality and talent shows. Even before *reformasi,* private TV stations broadcast a variety of horror films (usually on Thursday nights) and mystery shows. Relatively new subgenres are the horror reality show and horror infotainment programs, which present the supernatural as part of the everyday life and reality of Indonesians (van Heeren 2007). Gossip, infotainment, and comedy shows, such as *Newsdotcom*, have enjoyed wide popularity in recent years.

Cinema

Indonesian cinema has endured many ups and down since the early 1950s. In the postindependence period, particularly during the Guided

Democracy era, cinematic production peaked. In the early years of Sukarno's presidency, heroic films about the revolutionary years and struggle for independence, such as Usmar Ismail's *Darah dan Doa* (The Long March, 1950), *Enam Djam di Djogdja* (Six Hours in Jogja, 1951), and *Lewat Djam Malam* (After the Curfew, 1954), were popular, as were the films of leftist filmmakers such as Bachtiar Siagian and Basoeki Effendi. Their popularity was a result, in large part, of a partial ban on the import of Western movies. During the political conflict of the early 1960s, film production in Indonesia declined (Hanan 2010).

The Indonesian film industry did not recover until Suharto's presidency. Once it had lifted bans on Western film imports, the government was able to collect import taxes on foreign films that, in turn, helped local filmmakers and the emergence of highly commercial and apolitical cinema. The production of horror movies dominated the 1970s (van Heeren 2007). Nevertheless, a range of institutional and quasi-institutional repressive measures continued to control what could or could not be shown on the silver screen. Under the Suharto regime, anti-communist propaganda films, such as the four-hour *Pengkhianatan G30S/PKI* (The Treachery of the Indonesian Communist Party in the Thirtieth of September Movement, 1984), were produced, which provided the official view of the role of the PKI in the abortive coup of 1965 but was a complete distortion of reality. Until 1997, *Pengkhianatan G30S/PKI* was shown on TV every year and all Indonesian students had to watch it (Heryanto 2014b). Interestingly, other propaganda films were made, such as *Djakarta 1966,* which depicted the collaboration between the Indonesian military and student groups against the Communists and their sympathizers, but were never released to the public, as it was feared that they might give the students the wrong idea about how to handle their president.

Noteworthy films of this era included Sjuman Djaya's *Si Doel Anak Betawi* (Betawi Lad, 1973) and Eros Djarot's *Tjoet Nja' Dhien* (1988), a film about an Acehnese female freedom fighter, which was the first Indonesian film to be screened at the Cannes Film Festival. However, from the mid-1980s on, the Indonesian film industry, except for the production of horror films, went in decline again, not only because of the wider penetration of TV but particularly because of the monopoly that Suharto and his family held over the TV industry. Later, the spread of pirated videotapes, VCDs, and DVDs damaged the Indonesian film and cinema industry (Heryanto 2011).

Following Suharto's resignation in 1998, the Indonesian film industry slowly revived, turning into an industry that was smaller in scale but notable for its more innovative projects and the production of more independent short films and documentaries, which were used to advocate for human rights issues. In post–New Order Indonesia, new film genres, such as Islamic cinema, emerged, but there were also changes in existing genres and formats, such as the ever-popular horror movies. One of the icons of Indonesian arthouse cinema, both before and during *reformasi*, is Garin Nugroho, who directed numerous internationally acclaimed features and documentaries, many of which were set in Indonesia's peripheries, such as Papua. In choosing such settings, Nugroho sought to shift attention to political realities on the periphery, using allegory and metaphor rather than open criticism to achieve this. Among his most famous works are *Surat Untuk Bidadari* (Letter for an Angel, 1993), *Daun Di Atas Bantal* (Leaf on a Pillow, 1998), and *Aku Ingin Menciummu Sekali Saja* (Bird-Man Tale, 2003). The 2003 film tells the story of a young Papuan and his obsession with a weeping, lighter-skinned Indonesian woman against a background of increasing political repression in West Papua after the Second Papua People's Congress of June 2000.

Given its greater political openness and new media developments, the post–New Order era meant that the 1965–1966 anti-communist violence could be revisited both in fiction and in documentaries, including *Terlena: Breaking of a Nation,* by Andre Vltchek (2004), and Robert Lemelson's documentary *Forty Years of Silence: An Indonesian Tragedy* (2009), as well as Ifa Isfansyah's *Sang Penari* (The Dancer, 2011), a film based on the trilogy *Ronggeng Dukuh Paruk* (Ronggeng Dancer from Village Paruh), by novelist Ahmad Tohari. The films that attracted the most critical attention were, however, Joshua Oppenheimer's fascinating but disturbing *Act of Killing* (2012) and *The Look of Silence* (2014), which documented the 1965–1966 killings through the eyes of both the victims and the perpetrators (Heryanto 2014b).

Since *reformasi,* there has also been an increase in the creative participation of women in the Indonesian film industry—as directors, producers, trainers, publicists, and distributors (Hughes-Freeland 2011). Many have been educated overseas and now teach in a growing number of film and media courses of study offered at Indonesian universities. Well-known female producers and directors in contemporary Indonesian cinema include Christine Hakim and Nan Achnas, whose film *Pasir Berbisik* (Whispering Sands, 2001) was the first art film made in Indonesia by women. Following more popular film formulas, the commercially highly successful melodramatic love story *Ada Apa*

Dengan Cinta? (What's Up with Love? 2002) was directed by Rudi Soedjarwo, but workshopped, produced, and cowritten by Mira Lesmana and her colleagues. Lesmana's subsequent and equally successful production was *Laskar Pelangi* (The Rainbow Troops, 2008, directed by Riri Riza), about the destinies of a group of children from a poor Islamic regional school on Belitung, a small island, and their relationships with the teachers. Although Indonesia now has a new generation of very prolific female writers, who write what is commonly referred to as *sastra wangi* (fragrant literature), very few of their successful and highly acclaimed novels have been turned into movies, exceptions being *Mereka Bilang, Saya Monyet!* (They Say I'm a Monkey, 2008) and *Supernova* (2014). In 2017, indicating an important moment for international recognition of Indonesian film, the Mouly Surya–directed and Nugroho-written drama, *Marlina, Murderer in Four Acts,* became the fourth Indonesian film to be featured at the Cannes Film Festival, and the first since Nugroho's *Serambi* in 2006. Described as a "feminist satay western" (that is, an Indonesian take on the classic spaghetti western film with a feminist twist), it is one of several depictions of strong women on film in this period.

Consistent with the general increase in religiously oriented cultural productions in Indonesian society, cinema also took a Muslim turn. Although there had previously been a few Islamic-themed films, such as *Sunan Kalijaga* (1983), about a promoter of Islam in fifteenth-century Java, and *Sembilan Wali* (Nine Saints, 1985), popular cinema now has a more comprehensive depiction of Muslim characters on celluloid. Nia Dinata's *Berbagi Suami* (Love for Share, 2006) is a film that tells three stories from different social milieus in Jakarta and explores, with a hint of irony, the limitations of polygamous marriage. The aforementioned *Ayat-Ayat Cinta* (Verses of Love, 2008), the story of a smart and pious young Indonesian Muslim from a modest family who goes to study in Egypt, where he meets his two wives (a German Turkish Muslim woman and an Egyptian convert), was viewed by 3.5 million people and achieved the second-highest revenue from ticket sales in Indonesia as of July 2019. It is interesting to note that the producers and directors of these Muslim-themed films were non-Muslims who had made a career in Indonesian secular films before they decided to try something new (Hoesterey and Clark 2012). Their commercial success was often held against them, as critics accused them of commercializing Islam. The unexpected success of *Ayat-Ayat Cinta* was emulated in cinema and TV productions alike; one of the copycat cinema productions was *Perempuan Berkalung Sorban* (Woman with a Turban, 2009), which did not draw such large audiences. More recent productions included Chaerul Umam's *Ketika Cinta Bertasbih* (When Love Glorifies God, 2009), which, with a budget of US$4 million, has been one of the most expensive Indonesian film productions (Heryanto 2014a).

The prolific production of horror films in Indonesia, both for the cinema and for TV, has already been mentioned. According to Katinka van Heeren (2007, p. 213), Indonesian horror movies have their own distinctive format; not only do their plots not have to make much sense, but they also have as common ingredients religious and erotic elements, with the religious supposedly balancing the erotic. The sleazy reputation this genre has earned is further supported by the sexually explicit posters used to advertise the films, which have almost nothing to do with the films' stories. Traditionally, horror films appealed to lower-class tastes rather than to the middle classes, which means that they have been screened in rural and lower-class cinemas more often than in high-end theaters and malls. This has now changed, not least because post–New Order horror film productions no longer rely entirely on the old formulas. Modern Indonesian horror films have left their conventional rural settings and replaced them with urban settings with young middle-class urbanites as the protagonists (Heryanto 2011). One of the modern horror films to become a box office hit was *Jelangkung* (The Uninvited, 2001), which reached an audience of 1.3 million. After *Jelangkung*, more horror films, mainly produced by young filmmakers, were released and screened, including *Titik Hitam* (Black Spot, 2002) and *Peti Mati* (The Coffin, 2003).

As well as the many horror movies and romantic comedies (known for their inclusion of erotic elements [*tante girang*], rape, and promiscuity) produced every year, a small number of less conventional films are made and released, such as *Arisan!* (The Gathering, 2004), which raised the topic of the homosexual relationships of men maintaining a heterosexual facade. The topic of homosexuality was briefly alluded to in *Ayat-Ayat Cinta* but was dealt with in a very conservative understanding of sexuality. Most recent Indonesian films continue to endorse traditional gender bias, as their characters seldom have nuanced roles and usually represent stereotypical sexuality. If homosexual characters appear on the screen, they are usually subjected to ridicule, which is one way of overcoming censorship. Other film directors have had less luck in challenging moral norms and avoiding censorship. Findo Purwono, for example, and his *Buruan Cium Gue* (Kiss Me Quick, 2004), a rather dull teenage comedy, triggered a scandal on the strength of its title alone. Members of Majelis Ulama Indonesia (MUI) and influential individuals, such as TV preacher Aa Gym, thought it encouraged pre-marital sex and adultery among teenagers and called for its ban. After fierce debate, the film was recalled from national distribution, even though it had already been passed by the Censor Board; it was then reworked and rereleased as *Satu Kecupan* (One Smooch) (van Heeren 2012). Censorship issues were also played out when community groups protested the screening of films on grounds of their lack of morality. In 2007, for example, a group calling itself Warga Peduli Moral Sulsel (Citizens Concerned for South Sulawesi Morality) achieved a local ban on the film *Maaf, Saya Menghamili Istri Anda* (Sorry, I Got Your Wife Pregnant) (Lindsay 2011, p. 182).

The political documentary genre has also seen a number of changes, as the New Order censorship and widespread depoliticization of public life had prevented anything resembling independent or critical political filmmaking. One of Indonesia's leading documentary filmmakers is Aryo Danusiri, whose first documentary, *Kambing Kampung Yang Kena Pukul* (Village Goat Takes the Beating, 1999), was about human rights violations in Aceh. His documentary *Di Antara Gajah-Gajah* (Playing Between Elephants, 2007), on the humanitarian intervention in post-tsunami and post-conflict Aceh, won the Human Rights Award at the Jakarta International Film Festival. Another well-known documentary filmmaker is Lexy Junior Rambadeta, who founded Offstream Films and Images, as well as Recording the Future Projects. His documentaries include *Mass Grave* (2001), on the exhumation of a mass grave of executed Indonesian Communist Party members in Yogyakarta, and *The Indonesian Student Revolt* (2001), about the Trisakti killings. One of the best-known female documentary filmmakers is Ariani Djalal, who has produced, written, and directed documentaries and news features for TV. She produced *Bade Tan Reuda* (Aceh's Never-Ending Tragedy, 2003), which was directed by Lexy Junior Rambadeta and won Best Documentary at the Jakarta International Film Festival in 2003. Ariani Djalal and Aryo Danusiri are part of a group called Ragam in Banda Aceh, which trains young women to be filmmakers. A documentary that has won several prestigious awards and, more important, the hearts of its audiences is Daniel Ziv's *Jalanan* (Streetside, 2013), which features the lives of three Jakarta buskers.

Whereas Indonesian documentary filmmakers have met with success and recognition, some of their foreign colleagues have faced censorship for their films about conflict, poverty, health, and social justice. For example, at the Eighth Jakarta International Film Festival in 2006, the Film Censorship Institute banned three documentaries on

East Timor, which included *Tales of Crocodiles,* by Dutch filmmaker Jan van den Berg; *Passabe,* by Singaporean filmmaker James Leong; and *Timor Loro Sae,* by Brazilian filmmaker Lucélia Santos; as well as one on Aceh—William Nessen's *The Black Road,* covering clashes between the Indonesian army and Acehnese independence fighters (Reporters Without Borders 2006).

In recent years, both direct and indirect censorship of films in Indonesia has become apparent again. For example, in 2016 the Goethe Institute in Jakarta planned to screen Rahung Nasution's film *Pulau Buru Tanah Air Beta* (Buru Island My Homeland), but because of vigorous protest and threats from the FPI, the Jakarta police department indicated that it would not protect the venue, so the screening was canceled. Screenings of the film, which is about interreligious intolerance, were canceled in other cities, too, including in Bandung, where it had also provoked the outrage of the FPI, ironically bringing "into reality what the film depicts on screen" (Heryanto 2014a, p. 149).

Social Media and the Internet

According to the Indonesia Internet Service Provider Association (APJII 2018), there were an estimated 143.2 million internet users in Indonesia in 2017 (54.68 percent of the population). In urban areas, internet penetration rises above 72 percent but in the rural parts of the country is just under 50 percent. With smartphone usage estimated to reach over 90 million in 2019, it is no surprise that large numbers of Indonesians access the internet with their mobile phones only (44 percent of users). In 2018, Indonesia had 115 million Facebook users, the network's fourth-largest national community, and about 22 million Twitter accounts. For a number of years, Jakarta was considered the "Twitter capital" of the world, and Indonesia an unlikely inclusion in Twitter's top five users. A report by McKinsey and Company (2016) found that Indonesian users spend an average of 3.5 hours a day on their internet or mobile device, 2.9 of those hours on social media.

Thanks to the high penetration rate of mobile phones and very affordable data packages, Indonesians can access the internet relatively easily, which makes the country an intriguing live laboratory for anyone interested in exploring the potential of the internet and social media in politics and commerce. It has given rise to an innovative and thriving e-commerce industry, including companies such as ride-hail services and the on-demand services start-up GoJek, which was valued at over US$1 billion in 2016. Online political activism commenced more than a decade ago, when the internet was in its infancy in Indonesia and when internet users had no private access and had to rely on *warnet* (*warung internet* [internet kiosk]) (Slama 2010). The establishment of email groups provided opponents of the New Order with an important communications channel through which they could share and discuss news at home and abroad (Sen and Hill 2000). As of 2019, there has been no substantial censorship of the internet in Indonesia, apart from a brief attempt to ban online access to *Fitna*, a film made by the Dutch anti-Islam populist Geert Wilders (Slama 2010). In early 2008, the government passed the Law on Information and Electronic Transactions (ITE Law), which increased the authority of the Ministry of Communications and Information Technology to possibly censor online content. However, the ITE Law has been mainly used to convict people of online defamation, which can draw sentences of up to six years in prison. Moreover, since 2014, with the passing of the Ministerial Regulation No. 19/2014 on Internet Sites with Negative Content issued by the Ministry of Communication and Information, the government has blocked or partially restricted several hundred web pages for carrying content that is illegal under existing Indonesian laws relating to such things as pornography and child abuse, terrorism, hate speech, illegal investment, fraud, gambling, food and drugs, and copyright infringement (Freedom House 2015). Among the blocked web pages were those selling fake drugs and others offering unregistered marriage services. In May 2019, following an outbreak of rioting in Jakarta after the announcement of election results, the government used its powers to block video and photo sharing on social media and messaging sites (Tehusijarana 2019). In practice, the blocking of web pages tends to be arbitrary, because the ministerial regulation does not offer clear guidelines. Critics fear that the voices of minorities, such as LGBTQI groups, will suffer particularly from arbitrary blocking and filtering.

Although the stellar expansion of social media outlets and channels has helped to facilitate social movements and protests, as it allows for the exchange of ideas and the coordination of action, the inflation of communication and social activist platforms has also resulted in feel-good activism, or "slacktivism," which is only symbolic in that action does not go beyond pushing buttons. The Change.org petition platform was established in Indonesia in 2012 and mounted several petitions calling for the dissolution of the FPI, but to no avail. Other cases of recent online activism have had better results, especially those that also used print media and TV, eventually having an impact on the street.

An exemplary case is the clash between the Indonesian police and Komisi Pemberantasan Korupsi (Corruption Eradication Commission [KPK]), often referred to as the "gecko (*cicak*) versus crocodile (*buaya*)" fight. In April 2009, members of KPK tapped the phone of Susno Duadji, head of Bareskrim, the Indonesian Police crime investigation agency, who was investigating a corruption case involving businessman Boedi Sampoerna. Duadji had demanded Rp10 billion from Sampoerna to clear his savings stuck in the Bank Century collapse of 2008. When Duadji found out that his phone had been tapped, he was extremely angry and, in a press conference, compared the KPK to a gecko and his own institution to a crocodile, a comparison he was soon to regret. In September 2009, the KPK announced an investigation into Duadji's role in the Bank Century case, while the police charged two KPK commissioners, Bibit Samad Riyanto and Chandra Hamzah, for abuse of power. One month later, the two KPK commissioners were arrested and charged with extortion and bribery in connection with businessmen they were investigating (Gazali 2014). The arrests were clearly intended to discredit the two commissioners but also to give KPK a stern warning to stay away from the police. Once media activists and journalists had gotten hold of the case, there was no way to cover it up. Usman Yasin started a campaign on Facebook called Gerakan 1.000.000 Facebookers Dukung Chandra Hamzah & Bibit Samad Rianto (The Movement of 1,000,000 Facebookers Supporting Bibit and Chandra), and within nine days, the number of supporters had already reached 1,002,030 (Molaei 2015). Moreover, students organized demonstrations in support of KPK in several cities, several newspapers published cartoons with geckos lining up against ugly crocodiles, and TV news and talk shows reported on the issue with fervor. The significance of the case prompted President Yudhoyono to establish Team Eight, a fact-finding team, on November 2, 2009, to investigate the allegations. A day later, the police released the two commissioners, although they did not initially drop the charges.

Another case that triggered the extensive engagement of the digital community, but met with less success, is that of Prita Mulyasari, an Indonesian housewife from Tangerang Jakarta. In 2008, she had used the services of a private international hospital but found their standards poor. She wrote a letter of complaint to the hospital management about a misdiagnosis, which she shared in emails with her friends. Without her knowledge, the letter was shared widely and became a public issue. Outraged by the avalanche of negative publicity, the hospital management took legal action against Prita, who lost the court case.

The supreme court sentenced Prita to six months imprisonment for distributing a defamatory email and fined her Rp340 million (US$23,800), but the fine was subsequently reduced to Rp204 million (US$14,300) (Molaei 2015). When concerned bloggers learned about the outcome, they started protesting on their sites. Details of the case went viral in social networks, first and foremost on Facebook. One of the bloggers initiated the collection of 500 rupiah coins (US$0.05) to help Prita pay the fine, which solicited a great response (Gazali 2014). There was also substantial offline support for Prita. Even politicians, including Megawati Sukarnoputri, visited Prita in jail, partly out of sympathy, but more to mobilize Prita's popularity in her election campaign. It was not until 2012 that the supreme court overturned Prita's conviction and jail sentence.

The spread of hatred, particularly religious hatred, is not a new phenomenon in Indonesia's engagement with the digital spheres. The more encompassing cyberspace becomes as a means of message dissemination, the more alluring it is to its audiences, as their vison and hearing are engaged, thus heightening the impact of its messages. For example, a number of radical Muslim groups, such as Laskar Jihad, and Christian fundamentalists used online and offline media to disseminate images, news, (mis)information, and propaganda through their communication channels during the conflict in the Moluccas, leaving little space for moderates to voice their views (Bräuchler 2003, 2004). Birgit Bräuchler shows how the conflicting parties transferred their issues to cyberspace and instrumentalized the internet, "turning it into a weapon" (Bräuchler 2007, p. 334). Conversely, online and offline media have played a crucial role in the Moluccas since the conflict, as groups working for peace and reconciliation have embraced the fundamentals of peace journalism to reach the same audiences, but with more constructive news and information (Bräuchler 2011). The global reach of social media allows for the mobilization of activists not just within Indonesia but worldwide. In 2017, the government opted briefly to block the messenger service Telegram, as it was used to disseminate radical and terrorist propaganda. A new National Cyber and Encryption Agency was finally established in 2017, not least because Indonesia is deemed highly vulnerable to cyberattacks.

It appears likely that in Indonesia, as elsewhere, social media will continue to play a prominent role in electoral politics. Whether it has a lasting and detrimental impact on Indonesia's democratization process, or whether its potential for change is watered down by social media's many inherent limitations, such as the brevity of messages and their lack of context, remains to be seen. Online activists and defenders of online activism place hope in the potential of social media to reconfigure communicative power relations in the Indonesian media landscape by challenging monopoly control of media production and dissemination by the state and the media oligarchies. Still, quick-click activism can draw attention speedily to single cases of injustice, but it hardly ever challenges their larger context. Dependence on quantifiable indicators of success, such as high numbers of clicks, likes, or shares, puts pressure on the producers of content, such as online journalists, who depend increasingly on input from digital and social media, and thus might favor sensationalist topics and representations. Moreover, owners of mainstream media outlets have also recognized the need to embrace social media and integrate them into their services. Also, politicians, media czars, and entrepreneurs have sought to utilize the new realms for their own purposes by offering the successful Indonesian bloggers and media stars generous incentives to speak out about certain issues.

Embracing new social media has turned out to be highly influential during election campaigns, particularly for those politicians who could not afford or did not wish to rely on traditional, cost-intensive campaigns in the mainstream media. In addition to engaging sophisticated social media and publicity teams, politicians also make use of a new media campaign style that incorporates the creativity of young Indonesians and their interest in the production of pseudo-campaign material (Tapsell 2015, p. 39). Reliance on these media volunteer groups was particularly apparent during the 2014 presidential election campaigns for Joko Widodo, who used the groups to counter smear campaigns, also mounted on social media, against him (Tapsell 2015; Tomsa 2016). Widodo's opponents frequently alleged that he was not a proper Muslim and that he was of Chinese descent, in order to diminish his wide popularity among Muslim voters, which forced Widodo to undertake certain symbolic acts, such as a minor pilgrimage to Saudi Arabia just before the 2014 presidential election, to repair the damage caused by the smear campaigns. In the run-up to the 2014 election, Jokowi relied heavily on the many volunteers who gave him favorable media coverage, often for free. Nonetheless, as Tapsell (2017) argues, this alone was not enough for Jokowi to win the election; vital to his success was support from some of the mainstream media oligarchies, whose membership would then seek a share in political power, such as a position in Jokowi's cabinet.

In late 2016, another political smear campaign started on social media, which had a significant impact on Indonesian politics and arguably shifted the course of future election campaigns. In October 2016, in the run-up to Jakarta gubernatorial elections in February 2017, the incumbent governor, Basuki Tjahaja Purnama (Ahok), a Christian and of the Chinese minority, was accused of blasphemy after a video recording of him, apparently defaming the Quran, was posted on Facebook. A Facebook group managed by Buni Yani had manipulated a video of a speech by Ahok to make it appear anti-Muslim in its content and uploaded it, causing a major upheaval on social media. The video went viral and resulted in a police investigation, charges of blasphemy being laid against the governor and, finally, a trial at which he was found guilty. Before the video appeared, as an incumbent and an effective first-term leader, Ahok was a clear front-runner in the electoral race. Crucial in pushing along this legal action were mass demonstrations organized by fundamentalist Islamic groups in late 2016 and early 2017, dubbed "Aksi Bela Islam (Defending Islam Action I/II)" and attended by hundreds of thousands of people. By the time the second-round run-off election for the governor's position was held in April, Ahok's guilty verdict had been handed down and he was, somewhat inevitably, defeated. Internet and social media commentator Merlyna Lim (2017) concluded that this case shows that "social media use in electoral politics further deepens divisions among social groups and amplifies animosity and intolerance of each other." Buni Yani, who had created and posted the Ahok video online, was prosecuted in late 2017 and found guilty of breaching information and electronic transaction laws.

Ahead of the 2019 presidential elections, a rematch of the previous competition between Joko Widodo and Prabowo Subianto saw supporters from both camps deploy negative campaign advertising, fake news, and outright hoaxes. Utilizing various social media platforms and the internet, the main aim was to exploit ethnic and religious differences in an effort to stir up divisive identity politics. However, rather than being carried out by the official media teams of the two candidates, this black campaigning was often coordinated by informal campaigners (Tapsell 2019). Whereas the official TV debates between the two presidential candidates struck a measured tone, the online campaigning was characterized by passionate and polarizing content. Not unlike the 2014 presidential election, when Joko Widodo's opponents sought to cast doubt on his Muslim credentials, one social media hoax claimed that if Widodo were to win a second term, he would abolish the call for prayer and ban religious teachings at schools. In order to counter such claims, Widodo ordered the security forces to arrest people who were spreading fake news and other provocative items (Gunia 2019). His critics argued that the orders were carried out in a rather selective way, hitting Prabowo's supporters harder. The election itself proceeded smoothly and without major disturbances. However, in the weeks leading up to the recapitulation of the final vote tally Prabowo's supporters continued their calls for protest action. On 22 May this protest became violent with two days of rioting in central Jakarta. As mentioned, the government responded by blocking video and photo sharing functions on social media and messaging applications, claiming hoaxes were fuelling the unrest. As seen elsewhere in the world, post-truth politics has given rise to identity politics, and its impact will be felt for some time to come.

Conclusion

Unlike during the New Order, when the media's main role was to disseminate and endorse the "government's stances and its interpretations of news, history and the law" (Bräuchler 2011, p. 119), Indonesia's media now enjoys greater freedom of expression. Nevertheless, the legacy of the New Order is still evident. Whereas control over the media used to be in the hands of the Indonesian president, his children, and members of the military, the largest media outlets in post–New Order Indonesia are now in the hands of powerful media oligarchies, and they use their control of the media to pursue their own political and economic interests, with the help of money politics and swiftly changing alliances (Tapsell 2017). It is not surprising that Indonesians have embraced social online media with great enthusiasm in order to escape news reporting that is driven by the interests of the powerful. Despite the importance of social media and the role of "netizens" and citizen journalists trying to counter oligarchic media, the power of such interest groups persists unhindered. It must not be forgotten that digital spheres enable the circulation of even more tendentious, manipulated, and sensationalist views among Indonesians, confronting particular political, religious, and other minorities with increased online and offline oppression and hate speech.

9

Indonesia in World Affairs

IN 1953, FOUR YEARS AFTER THE FORMAL TRANSFER OF SOVER-
eignty from the Netherlands to the independent Indonesian government,
and during Indonesia's first democratic phase, Indonesian vice president
Mohammad Hatta (1953) set out the core features of the nation's foreign policy in an article for *Foreign Affairs*. Although global geopolitics
have shifted markedly over the intervening decades, and Indonesia has
transitioned from democratic to authoritarian rule and back to democracy again, Hatta's words persist as a fitting starting point to understand
Indonesia's approach to its international relations.

Hatta outlined two important geographic influences on Indonesia's
place in world affairs. Indonesia's geographic position was at once
strategic—lying between the Asian and Australian continents and at the
confluence of the Indian and the Pacific Oceans—yet at arm's length
from the main belligerents of the Cold War, as it did not share a common border with the United States, Russia, or China. Being at arm's
length from these powers enabled Indonesia to adopt what Hatta termed
an "independent and active" foreign policy. "Independent" designated
an unwillingness to permanently align either with the US-led Western
bloc of the Cold War, or with the Sino-Soviet bloc of Communist countries. Instead, Indonesia would seek good relations with all countries, an
approach Hatta noted was further necessitated both by Indonesia's
strategic location and by insufficient military might to defend the full
extent of its vast territory. "Active" indicated that Indonesia would take
steps to strengthen and preserve peace, rather than maintain neutral pas-
sivity. Although Hatta did not emphasize it in his article, this "active"

stance dovetailed with the determination of the Indonesian president of the day, Sukarno, that Indonesia would play a major role in world affairs. It also likely reflected the still recent struggle against the Dutch, when international engagement and the role of the United Nations served the Indonesian nationalists well.

All of these features are evident in twenty-first-century Indonesian thinking about its place in world affairs. Current foreign policy thinkers conceptualize Indonesia's geographic position in very similar terms to Hatta, for example. Although strategic competition between the United States, China, and Russia is rising in the second decade of this century, Indonesia's military planners see no direct threat to Indonesia's territory arising from this competition, in contrast to other Southeast Asian nations sharing common land borders or disputed islands with China. Additionally, since 2014 the current Joko Widodo government has placed Indonesia's position at the confluence of two oceans as the centerpiece of its foreign policy, outlining plans to establish Indonesia as a global maritime fulcrum, benefiting from the vital sea lanes passing through its territory and securely managing the country's maritime resources.

Each successor government to Sukarno has also declared its determination to remain "independent" (typically now called "free") and "active," even if their adherence to this principle has varied, as we will discuss below. Moreover, despite rapid economic growth over most of the intervening period, during which Indonesia's per capita GDP has increased roughly sixfold (Hill 2015, p. 286), present-day Indonesia still lacks the military capacity to secure the full extent of its territory. Nevertheless, contemporary Indonesian presidents have continued to describe the nation's international role in expansive terms, if not quite matching Sukarno's ambition. By the end of his second presidential term, Susilo Bambang Yudhoyono (2004–2014) described Indonesia as "a regional power and global player to be reckoned with" (Yudhoyono 2014). Joko Widodo, in a similar vein, has cast the shift in geopolitical and economic heft from the West to East Asia as Indonesia's opportunity to become a "great nation."

Despite such clear continuities, regime change and the transformation of domestic politics outlined in preceding chapters have inevitably also had an impact on Indonesia's foreign policy. We turn first to the impacts of this domestic political change on Indonesia's foreign policy and how it is formulated, before surveying Indonesia's key international relationships. These discussions are arranged thematically, spanning the major powers, Indonesia's Southeast Asian neighbors, the United Nations, the Muslim world, and other key partners.

Democratization and Indonesian Foreign Policy

Since the end of the authoritarian New Order in 1998, Indonesia has become more outward looking. In the preceding decades, domestic concerns such as nation building and preserving territorial sovereignty had been Indonesia's primary preoccupation, which at times fostered an island mentality. Under Sukarno and Suharto—the former known for his cosmopolitanism, the latter for his lack of it—foreign policy rested in the hands of these two strong presidential leaders and carried their personal stamp. In post-*reformasi* Indonesia, a broader range of actors has been able to influence the formulation of foreign policy, including the parliament, business interests, civil society, religious groups, and public opinion. Various examples of their influence are detailed in the subsequent sections of this chapter.

Of these newly influential groups, the national parliament (DPR) and its constituent political parties are the most important. Constitutional amendments have empowered the parliament to ratify treaties and approve ambassadorial appointments, as well as to jointly agree on legislation related to international issues with the government (Wirajuda 2014; Rüland 2009). The parliament also exerts pressure on the government through its Parliamentary Commission 1 on Defense and Foreign Affairs (Komisi 1 DPR RI), which is able to summon the foreign minister and other state officials for questioning at its meetings (Laksmana 2011). At times, the parliament has been able to alter the government's foreign policy stance or significantly delay initiatives that it opposes; overall, scholars judge it has pushed Indonesian foreign policy in a more nationalist direction (Wirajuda 2014, p. 88).

Despite the greater influence of other actors, the president continues to be able to set the direction of Indonesian foreign policy. President Yudhoyono, in particular, is considered to have restored an active role for Indonesia in international affairs, after the turbulence of the early postauthoritarian presidencies. Yudhoyono repeatedly emphasized that Indonesia must contribute to the international order and, toward the end of his rule, surmised that Indonesia had become "a regional power and a global player to be reckoned with" (Yudhoyono 2014). Yudhoyono sought to involve Indonesia in a strikingly broad range of issues, as his stated ambition for Indonesia to be "part of the solution to global problems" placed few clear limits on Indonesia's role. He also established his own special staff for foreign policy to increase his autonomy from the foreign ministry (Wirajuda 2014, pp. 74–75). Current president Joko Widodo has shown a less personal interest in foreign policy and is perhaps best known for his insistence that Indonesia's diplomacy must deliver tangible benefits to its people. His government has also placed new emphasis on the maritime domain in Indonesia's international affairs, announcing an ambition to establish Indonesia as a global maritime fulcrum. To this end, his government issued a new National Ocean Policy in 2017.

Each democratic-era foreign minister has also exerted an important influence on Indonesia's foreign policy. With the exception of Wahid-era appointee Alwi Shihab, who was a National Awakening Party (PKB) politician, each democratic-era foreign minister has been a career diplomat. Hassan Wirajuda, foreign minister from 2003 to 2009, spanning two presidencies, was especially influential. He is credited with professionalizing the foreign ministry, including fast-tracking the careers of both his successors to date as foreign minister, Marty Natalegawa and Retno Marsudi. Wirajuda also sought, without success, to leverage Indonesia's new democratic status and its emergent democracy promotion activities to lobby for a seat on the UN Security Council (Rüland 2017, p. 61). His successor, Natalegawa, foreign minister for Yudhoyono's second term, is credited with an early commitment to the idea of an Indo-Pacific imaging of Indonesia's immediate neighborhood, spanning the coastal states of both oceans, as well as for his promotion of the concept of "dynamic equilibrium" within Asia. Under this concept of dynamic equilibrium, no one power would dominate the region, although as covered below, Indonesia has been comfortable overall with a US-led regional order. As of 2019, current foreign minister Retno Marsudi has placed renewed emphasis on the Indo-Pacific, launching an Indonesian Indo-Pacific Concept in 2018 and hosting a high-level dialogue on Indo-Pacific cooperation in 2019 (Parameswaran 2019). Under her tenure, Indonesia has also utilised its temporary membership of the UN Security Council to advocate for the Palestinian cause (Tempo 2019).

Democratization has also sharpened electoral pressures on Indonesian foreign policy. In particular, given Indonesia's mostly benign security circumstances and budgetary constraints, Indonesia has not invested in strategic capabilities commensurate with its vast territory and large population and with its strategic position on some of the most important trading routes between the Indian Ocean and the Pacific Ocean connecting Asia with Australia and the Middle East. Hence, despite ambitions from its leadership for Indonesia to play a more significant role in international affairs and public expectations that Indonesia will increase its influence, Indonesia lacks the military, diplomatic, and overseas development aid profile typically associated with so-called middle powers.

Given Indonesia's limited strategic capabilities, multilateral forums have been particularly important in its diplomacy. Indonesia's leaders of

today consider it desirable that Indonesia play a more active and constructive role on the international stage, as evidenced by frequent reference in
the Foreign Ministry's Strategic Plan (2005–2025) to Indonesia's global
role, especially to international cooperation and multilateral diplomacy
(Acharya 2014, p. 99). Yudhoyono addressed these expectations with a
proactive "power of ideas" approach, in which Indonesia sought to contribute to a number of regional and global issues through multilateral
forums, such as the World Economic Forum in 2011 (McRae 2014b, p.
14). Among Yudhoyono's contributions was the establishment of the Bali
Democracy Forum in 2008, which has sought to promote democracy in
a nonaggressive manner in the Asia-Pacific region. President Yudhoyono
suggested that Indonesia should act more confidently as "a peace-maker,
confidence-builder, problem-solver, and bridge-builder" (Yudhoyono
2005, quoted in Laksmana 2011, p. 161). Although Indonesia claims to
promote peace and stability in the region and seeks to promote its model
of democratization in ASEAN countries, especially Myanmar, its efforts
have not always been effective, and limited resources have prevented more
significant outcomes in conflict resolution and peacekeeping/making.[1]
Indonesia now engages with thirty-two countries in its defense diplomacy, of which the top ten were the country's most crucial security partners (and weapons suppliers), as well as potential rivals (Laksmana
2011, p. 173). Indonesia is no longer dependent on one main supplier
for its defense strategy and equipment, having diversified its purchasing
(Acharya 2014, p. 91).

The United Nations has been one important focus. Indonesia is a
member of the UN General Assembly, has served on its Economic and
Social Council a number of times, and has been elected four times as a
nonpermanent member of the Security Council (1974–1975, 1995–1996,
2007–2008, and 2019–2020). Against long odds, Indonesia, together with
many other nations, has called for reform of the Security Council to align
it better to the contemporary balance of global power. Furthermore, its
ambassador to the United Nations served as one of four vice presidents of
the UN Human Rights Council in 2009–2010, and it has been an active
contributor to UN peacekeeping operations. Beyond the United Nations,
as the country with the world's largest Muslim population, Indonesia is a
member of the Organisation of Islamic Cooperation (OIC) and maintains
its membership in the Non-Aligned Movement, where it has been a
prominent voice on total nuclear disarmament. Since gaining membership
during the Yudhoyono era, Indonesia has also prized its membership in
the Group of 20. Yudhoyono (2014) highlighted the opportunity this
membership provided for Indonesia to participate equally with advanced

economies in determining global economic rules. At the same time, Indonesia has maintained its membership in the Group of 77 of developing countries and has sought to position itself as a bridge between developed and developing economies, as well as between the West and Muslim-majority countries (Tan 2007).

In the democratic era, there has also been new emphasis on Indonesia's diaspora. The World Bank (2017, p. 11) has estimated more than 9 million Indonesians currently work overseas, many as low-paid migrant workers, although it must be acknowledged that estimates of the size of the diaspora vary widely (Muhidin and Utomo 2015). Extending protection to its citizens living overseas has become an increasing priority for the government, particularly since the execution in Saudi Arabia in 2017 of Indonesian domestic worker Ruyati binti Satubi. The Indonesian government was not informed in advance of the execution and was excoriated domestically for its perceived inaction (McRae 2017). In recent years, efforts to mobilize the diaspora in the service of Indonesia's national interests have increased, particularly through several global conferences for the diaspora.

Indonesia and the Major Powers

Indonesia has persistently articulated independence from the major powers as a core principle of its foreign policy. In its original formulation during the Sukarno administration, Vice President Mohammad Hatta in 1948 famously described Indonesia's approach as "*mendayung di antara dua karang*" (rowing between two reefs). The reefs were the Cold War blocs of communist/socialist states and the Western capitalist states. Six decades later, in 2005, Susilo Bambang Yudhoyono updated the two-reefs metaphor to become "navigating a turbulent ocean" (Tan 2007, pp. 179–180). By this time, US-China strategic competition had replaced the Cold War as the primary source of geopolitical tension. In either formulation, this core principle of Indonesian foreign policy precludes any military alliance with a major power and prevents Indonesia from joining any power bloc led by a major power (Anwar 2018, p. 58). Each president has interpreted these restrictions on relations with the major powers somewhat differently, however, according to their perception of Indonesia's interests. In the case of Sukarno and Suharto, scholars question whether they adhered to an independent and active foreign policy at all.

The Sukarno government's adherence to independent relations with the major powers waned over the course of the two decades of his presidency, as his perception of the principal threat to Indonesian security shifted. The government's initial determination to remain disentangled from competition among the great powers was clear in its approach to China. Despite Indonesian government fears that China could destabilize Indonesia by supporting domestic communism, Indonesia nevertheless established diplomatic relations with China in 1950, in affirmation of its independent and active diplomacy (Sukma 1999). This same determination not to be trapped on either side of the Cold War was evident in 1955, when Sukarno hosted an Afro-Asian Conference in Bandung at which he initiated the Non-Aligned Movement (NAM). This arguably marked the high point of his government's free and active foreign policy, and the NAM was intended to provide a third path for newly independent countries, autonomous from the capitalist West or the communist East (Weatherbee 2009). Over time, however, the Sukarno government's perception of threats changed, and Western neoimperialism was seen as the greatest threat facing Indonesia (Anwar 2018, p. 58). Sukarno's foreign policy became increasingly radical and anti-West, in line with his radicalization of domestic politics during the Guided Democracy period (1959–1965) (Sukma 1995). Michael Leifer (2005, pp. 592–593) in fact judges Sukarno to have abandoned a free and active foreign policy stance altogether during this period, in favor of an alignment with an "anti-imperialist axis" with the governments of China, North Vietnam, and North Korea. Sukarno accordingly redefined global strategic competition in terms of a bloc of new emerging forces, with Indonesia at the forefront, pitted against the old established forces of the West (Anwar 1997, p. 21; Leifer 2005, p. 592). As part of this foreign policy shift, Sukarno rejected the formation of a federated Malaysia as an attempt at great power encirclement of Indonesia, leading him to initiate the Konfrontasi war against Indonesia's new neighbor and to withdraw Indonesia from the United Nations in 1965 in protest over Malaysia's election as a nonpermanent member of the UN Security Council. Such an alignment with this anti-imperialist axis was not absolute. Indonesia still showed an ability to astutely manipulate great-power rivalries to its advantage, notably in securing international support to remove the Dutch from Papua (Chauvel and Bhakti 2004).

The annihilation of the left in Indonesia and Suharto's seizure of the presidency put an end to Indonesia's radical foreign policy. Suharto ended Konfrontasi, restored Indonesia to the United Nations, and installed "economic development" as the focus of foreign policy in favor of Sukarno's "revolution" (Sukma 1995). This development focus and the Suharto government's anti-communist stance led it in effect to align Indonesia with the West, despite also restoring an independent and active stance as official foreign policy doctrine. Indonesia required American and Japanese aid to develop its economy (Sukma 1995) and therefore encouraged the presence of the United States in the region as the "least objectionable superpower," despite Indonesia's nominal preference for a region free of external power influence (Leifer 2005, pp. 599–600). As with Sukarno before him, Suharto's approach to the major powers also evolved over time as Indonesia's interests shifted. The final decade of Suharto's rule saw both rapprochement with a rapidly growing China and souring relations with the West, returning Indonesian foreign policy to a more free and active footing. During this decade, Indonesia reestablished diplomatic relations in 1993 with China, whereas Western restrictions on military cooperation following the 1991 Santa Cruz Massacre foreshadowed a push by Indonesia to diversify its security partnerships to lessen its reliance on the United States (Hamilton-Hart and McRae 2015).

In comparison with either Sukarno or Suharto, democratic-era presidents have been relatively consistent in seeking to maintain a semblance of equidistance between the major powers, in service of a free and active policy stance. During this period, Indonesia has concluded comprehensive and strategic partnerships with both the United States (in 2010 and 2015) and China (in 2005 and 2013), without exhibiting alignment with either. These agreements are part of a broader proliferation of such partnerships; Yudhoyono stated in his final Independence Day address as president that Indonesia had entered into such relations with "all major countries and most of the world's emerging powers." Indonesia's security partnership with the United States remains much more extensive and important than with China, but Indonesia has nevertheless demurred on several US security interests. China has emerged as the more important economic partner, but a desire to expand economic ties has been an important component of Indonesian presidential visits to the United States. Over this period, Indonesia has remained determined not to become ensnared in US-China competition. Under Yudhoyono, Indonesia promoted a so-called dynamic equilibrium among regional and global powers that would limit great-power competition to the benefit of all (Laksmana 2011, p. 162). Although the term is now rarely used, this concept has gained in prominence under Jokowi, who has spoken explicitly of approaching great-power competition from the point of view of maximizing the benefits to Indonesia's national interest.

United States

Indonesia's relationship with the United States is the closest of its ties with the major powers. The United States has long been Indonesia's most important security partner, and it remains so despite efforts by Indonesia to diversify its security interests. Indonesia has become familiar and comfortable with the American-led regional order in Asia since World War II (McRae 2014c). The United States is no longer as important an economic partner to Indonesia as it was during the initial decades of the Suharto regime, but it remains one of Indonesia's largest sources of foreign direct investment and its fourth-most-important trading partner (Hamilton-Hart and McRae 2015, p. 14). Nevertheless, Leifer's (2005, p. 599) pithy characterization of the United States as the "least objectionable superpower" in Indonesia's eyes is a reminder that the two countries' international interests have often differed in various important respects. During the democratic era in particular, various Islamic political interests have also successfully employed anti-Americanism to force the government to change policy and to constrain US-Indonesia cooperation (Murphy 2012).

In becoming Indonesia's largest security partner and establishing a reputation within Indonesia as a mostly benign power, the United States has successfully downplayed its turbulent relationship with President Sukarno (Hamilton-Hart 2012). In the late 1950s, the United States provided clandestine support to regional rebellions against Sukarno's rule and subsequently encouraged the Indonesian military to topple the president (Brands 1989, pp. 786–787; Hamilton-Hart 2012). Once Suharto took power, however, Indonesia obtained most of its military equipment from the United States and participated in regular joint military training programs. This long history of cooperation is manifest in the large share of Indonesian military equipment originating from the United States, despite a recent emphasis on procurement from other countries and on developing a defense industry in Indonesia (Gindarsah 2016, p. 348). The volume of bilateral defense diplomacy activities between Indonesia and the United States also significantly exceeds similar activities between Indonesia and other countries (Gindarsah 2016, p. 347).

Nevertheless, in many respects Indonesia's security ties with the United States remain superficial. Without a pressing, direct threat to its security, Indonesia has had no incentive to compromise its autonomy in setting its foreign policy direction by drawing closer to the United States. Indonesia does not participate in US-led global coalitions, such as that formed to oppose the Islamic State of Iraq and Syria (ISIS), even though the terror organization is a shared foe for both countries. The Indonesian government has in fact criticized military intervention as an approach to resolving the Syria conflict. Similarly, the Indonesian government has been critical on occasion of US freedom of navigation operations in the South China Sea, objecting to raised regional tensions despite a shared opposition to China's advancement of its claims outside the framework of international law. Nor has Indonesia invested in military capabilities that would enable interoperability with the United States, even were it inclined to cooperate so closely. It was in fact initially critical of the deployment of United States Marines to Darwin in Australia's Northern Territory in 2011, with some nationalist figures suggesting the deployment could be used to protect US mining interests in Indonesia's Papua Province. Indonesia also lacks an intelligence relationship with the United States of the depth of that between the United States and its so-called Five Eyes partners—Australia, Canada, New Zealand, the United Kingdom, and the United States.

Moreover, although the United States enjoys an overall positive image among Indonesians, US foreign policy has on occasion provoked public outpourings of anti-Americanism. Many Indonesians perceived George W. Bush's post–September 11 global war on terror to be a war on Islam, for example, a view encouraged by various Islamic leaders within the country. The Megawati government refrained from direct criticism of the US-led war on Afghanistan, in the interests of restoring bilateral ties to a normal footing after restrictions on security cooperation in the 1990s, but Megawati's visit to the United States soon after September 11 was controversial at home because it was seen as implicitly supportive of the war (Anwar 2003, pp. 84–86).

Reflecting such sensitivities, the Indonesian government has generally not publicized American support for domestic counterterrorism. US-led sanctions against Iran over its nuclear program also became a political issue within Indonesia, causing an about-face in government policy, as discussed in more detail later in this chapter (Murphy 2012). Public perceptions of the United States improved significantly during the presidency of Barack Obama, who spent three years in Indonesia as a child. The United States did not become the target of public opprobrium over foreign espionage in 2013 in the way that Australia did, for example, even though this espionage came to light through a leak from US intelligence.

Renegotiation of the contract agreement for the giant Freeport gold and copper mine was the main source of public anti-Americanism during this period, provoking deep veins of public suspicion that foreign resource companies are exploiting Indonesia's wealth on unfair terms. Such public sentiment, as well as competition between different coalitions of domestic politico-business interests seeking to benefit from the mine, greatly complicated Indonesian government efforts to conclude new arrangements with the company (Budiartie and Warburton 2015). The Trump presidency has not been as controversial in Indonesia as in many parts of the world (Mantong 2017), despite moves to restrict immigration from various majority-Muslim countries, but his administration's decision to move its embassy in Israel from Tel Aviv to Jerusalem did provoke large public protests.

China

Changes in Indonesia's domestic politics and China's sustained economic boom have helped to thaw Indonesia-China relations from their long, deep chill. The resultant changes to the bilateral relationship have been striking. Although direct trade between the two countries was banned until 1985 (Sukma 1999, pp. 183–186), China is now Indonesia's largest trading partner, and successive Indonesian governments have actively sought to attract more Chinese investment in large-scale infrastructure projects in Indonesia. Reflecting the importance of the Chinese economy to Indonesia, China's Belt and Road Initiative (BRI), a policy aimed at improving China's connectivity with the rest of the world through the development of sea and land routes, was announced in Jakarta, and Indonesia unsuccessfully sought to have the Chinese-led Asian Infrastructure Investment Bank headquartered in Jakarta. Security ties have been slower to defrost but have also expanded since the mid-2000s.

After Sukarno brought Indonesia into close alignment with China in the final years of his presidency, the stridently anti-communist Suharto government suspended diplomatic ties in 1967, following tit-for-tat attacks on the Indonesian Embassy in Beijing in 1967 and the Chinese Embassy in Jakarta (Storey 2013, p. 195). For most of Suharto's New Order regime, Sino-Indonesian political and economic relations lay dormant. Ethnic Chinese in Indonesia—who compose about 1.2 percent of the population—faced widespread institutionalized ethnic and religious discrimination (Tjhin 2012; Coppel 2017) and were excluded from many professions, leaving business the only option for most of them to earn a living. Those who succeeded suffered from the envy of other Indonesians, which sporadically gave rise to violent anti-Chinese riots (Purdey 2006). Chinese-language newspapers and schools were shut down by the Indonesian authorities after the 1965 coup, which meant that Indonesia was for almost three decades without significant knowledge of developments in China (Tjhin 2012, p. 312; He 2008, p. 60).

Even after the Suharto government normalized ties in 1990, enduring suspicions and fresh tensions over China's territorial claims in the South China Sea constrained ties for the remainder of Indonesia's authoritarian period. Only under democratic rule did ties genuinely improve, as Wahid eased discrimination against the ethnic Chinese and made his first international visit to China, and the Indonesian government faced the imperative to grow the economy following the 1997 financial crisis (Fukuoka and Verico 2016).

The expansion of China-Indonesia ties during the democratic era is clearly visible in trade statistics. Average annual trade was almost four times higher in 1998–2007 than during the preceding decade of authoritarian rule; in 2008–2012, it was fourfold higher again, in part reflecting a massive increase after the ASEAN-China Free Trade Agreement came into full effect in 2010 (Fukuoka and Verico 2016, p. 58). By 2016, two-way trade with China had reached US$47 billion, making China easily Indonesia's largest trading partner (World Bank 2018). Consistent with the scale of trade with China, Indonesia has been involved in negotiations involving China for a Regional Comprehensive Economic Partnership (RCEP), but not in negotiations for the Trans-Pacific Partnership (TPP), widely perceived as a US-led economic bloc prior to the Trump administration's withdrawal from the deal. President Jokowi stated Indonesia's "intention" to join the TPP during a trip to Washington, DC, in 2015, but this did not appear to be a firm commitment.

Investment is more difficult to quantify, owing to single-digit realization rates on pledged investments and informal flows of capital. Nevertheless, Indonesia has actively pursued Chinese investment in infrastructure and resource extraction since the early 2000s (Hamilton-Hart and McRae 2015, p. 10), reflecting a perception that Chinese money is more readily available and comes with fewer strings than investment from other sources such as the United States. The Jokowi government in particular has sought to capitalize on the Belt and Road Initiative to attract Chinese investment in port development, and also opted for Chinese state-owned enterprises over a Japanese bid to develop high-speed rail between Jakarta and Bandung. Particularly given the tumultuous history of Indonesia-China ties, a striking feature of such investments is the absence—at least in public discourse—of the security concerns aired in Western countries over similar proposals. Instead, as reviewed below, the main concern with Chinese investment involves the labor force for projects.

Nevertheless, various business and political actors who see the expansion of China-Indonesia economic ties as a threat to their interests have sought to resuscitate the China threat discourse and have lobbied for greater protectionism (Fukuoka and Verico 2016, p. 54). A fear of being outcompeted arises from a pattern of China-Indonesia trade that involves the export of manufactured goods to Indonesia and unprocessed or semiprocessed commodities to China, with China benefiting from a large trade surplus (Booth 2011b, p. 150). Fukuoka and Verico (2016, p. 58) observe that China's comparative advantage in most trading products has led to deindustrialization in Indonesia, particularly after the volume of trade has increased in the wake of the ASEAN-China Free Trade Agreement, which came into force in 2010. More recently, the alleged use of Chinese laborers by Chinese investors in construction projects in Indonesia has become politically controversial in Indonesia, spurring sometimes racist and xenophobic coverage and commentary.

Enduring suspicion that China poses a long-term threat to Indonesia has been more pronounced again in the security sphere. China's long-term strategic ambitions in the South China Sea are the clearest point of friction. Indonesia is not a direct party to the territorial disputes over the Spratly and Paracel island groups, which receive the lion's share of international media coverage, although Chinese militarization of these islands concerns Indonesia to the extent that it impinges on freedom of navigation or observance of international law. In February 2014, for example, Indonesia issued a clear warning to China about installing an air defense identification zone in the South China Sea, which it had done in the East China Sea in 2013 (Acharya 2014, p. 80). Of greater concern to Indonesia is the apparent overlap between China's so-called nine-dashed line on its maps, enclosing most of the South China Sea, and the 200-nautical-mile exclusive economic zone (EEZ) projecting into the South China Sea that Indonesia claims in the vicinity of its Natuna Islands, northeast of Singapore. This overlap has led to periodic confrontations between the two countries over Indonesia's attempts to apprehend Chinese fishing vessels within waters it claims as its EEZ, as these vessels are often accompanied by Chinese patrol boats. Tensions flared in particular under the Jokowi administration, which has taken a hard line on illegal fishing, including sinking seized vessels with explosives in carefully staged media events. Three confrontations at sea took place around the Natunas in 2016 as Indonesia attempted to seize Chinese fishing boats, culminating in President Jokowi involving himself personally in the dispute by holding a limited cabinet meeting aboard a warship in the vicinity of the incidents (McRae 2019).

Much as such incidents fuel Indonesian anxieties that China's rise will not remain peaceful, since the Yudhoyono government came into power, Indonesia's approach has been to attempt to build trust with China by developing more comprehensive collaboration across a range of sectors, including the security sphere. Following the signing of the Indonesia-China strategic partnership in 2005, Indonesia and China have held several bilateral and multilateral military exercises, albeit at a much lower volume than equivalent exercises with the United States, and Indonesia has sought to acquire from or jointly produce some defense equipment with China (Tjhin 2012, p. 306). Despite such plans, China has remained only a minor supplier of defense equipment to Indonesia, with Russian military products generally preferred to Chinese weapon systems, which have had a reputation of being of poor quality and durability (Storey 2013, p. 207; Gindarsah 2016). Nevertheless, late in the Yudhoyono administration, Indonesia and China upgraded the 2005 strategic partnership into a comprehensive strategic partnership during President Xi Jinping's visit to Indonesia in 2013 (McRae 2014c, p. 7). Despite the incidents in the Natunas, China-Indonesia relations are widely perceived to have become closer again under Joko Widodo, who has frequently met with his Chinese counterpart.

Indonesia and ASEAN

Indonesia's Ministry of Foreign Affairs has explained its diplomatic cooperation in terms of a series of concentric circles. The implicit assumption is that Indonesia's interests are greatest in its immediate region. This imagining of Indonesia's foreign relationships places the Association of Southeast Asian Nations (ASEAN) and its member states within the innermost circle, whereas the next circle out contains the main East Asian economic drivers—Japan, China, and South Korea. This central position for ASEAN is consistent with then foreign minister Adam Malik's characterization of the regional organization soon after its formation in 1967 as the "cornerstone of Indonesian foreign policy" (Heiduk 2016, p. 7).

Indonesia's priority within ASEAN has been to maintain regional stability (Emmers 2014; Heiduk 2016, p. 6). In particular, Indonesia has sought to limit the influence of external powers in Southeast Asia by enmeshing them in so-called ASEAN-centered multilateral forums. Latterly, as Indonesia's desire to exert extraregional influence has grown during the democratic era, these ASEAN-centered forums such as the East Asia Summit have provided a stepping-stone for Indonesia to attempt a broader global role (McRae 2014c). Regional economic integration has been a lesser priority; indeed, Indonesia has obstructed this goal (Emmers 2014; Heiduk 2016, p. 8).

Despite these various interests, doubts persist about the importance of ASEAN to Indonesian diplomacy. Such doubts encompass both Indonesia's commitment to the grouping and its ability to set the agenda within ASEAN. Both issues are discussed in more detail below, along with Indonesia's often turbulent relations with selected individual ASEAN member states.

Association of Southeast Asian Nations

For Indonesia, the formation of ASEAN in 1967 was an opportunity to promote regional stability by limiting great-power influence in its immediate environs. The military's rise to power under the presidency of General Suharto meant that communist powers were seen as the primary threat. Dewi Fortuna Anwar (1997, p. 24) observes that the Indonesian military supported ASEAN because it perceived that the non-communist membership of the group—the other founding members were Singapore, Malaysia, the Philippines, and China—would provide a buffer against China. Concern about maintaining a buffer against China underpinned Indonesia's leading role in ASEAN efforts to bring about a diplomatic solution to the Cambodia conflict during the Vietnamese occupation. By brokering peace, Indonesia hoped that Vietnam could play this role for the region (Weatherbee 2013, p. 60). Indonesia has also lent support to various ASEAN declarations and statements aimed at establishing Southeast Asia's strategic autonomy, including the 1967 Bangkok Declaration deeming foreign military bases in the region to be temporary, the 1971 Zone of Peace, Freedom and Neutrality (ZOPFAN), and the Southeast Asia Nuclear Weapon Free Zone Treaty in 1995 (Anwar 1997, p. 25; Weatherbee 2013, p. 59).

The other founding members saw ASEAN as an avenue to incorporate Indonesia into the region as a nonexpansionist power, following the end of Sukarno's Konfrontasi war against Malaysia (which had involved the Philippines because of its territorial claims in Sabah) and his campaign to gain control of Papua (Weatherbee 2013, p. 59). This context limited Indonesia's ability to exert leadership within ASEAN, despite being the largest country. Although Indonesia perceived itself as first among equals on account of its size—a status reflected in the location of the ASEAN secretariat and six important sub-offices in Jakarta—self-restraint was also an important initial priority for Indonesia to regain its neighbors' trust (Heiduk 2016, p. 7; Anwar 1997, p. 21;

Weatherbee 2005, pp. 150, 161). Indonesia's ability to impose an agenda on the grouping is further inhibited by ASEAN's internal operating principles, which include noninterference in the affairs of other member countries, a preference for nonbinding instruments of cooperation, peaceful resolution of conflicts, and consensus decisionmaking (Heiduk 2016, p. 7). The organization's critics suggest that the requirement for the assent of all members has caused Indonesia to compromise its own foreign policy interests to adhere to "lowest common denominator consensus and inaction" (Weatherbee 2013, p. 83).

Under democratic rule, Indonesia has pushed for ASEAN to become a robust political and security community (Laksmana 2011, p. 158; Sukma 2011). Both ideas have gained only limited traction. Other ASEAN members, mostly authoritarian states, have largely rebuffed Indonesian proposals for greater observance of democratic principles in the region. Where these have been adopted, such as Jakarta's proposal for an ASEAN Intergovernmental Commission on Human Rights, the original Indonesian proposal has been substantially watered down (Sukma 2011, p. 114). Indonesian calls for an ASEAN peacekeeping force were also rejected, although Indonesia did invite an EU-ASEAN monitoring mission to oversee implementation of its peace agreement with the Free Aceh Movement (GAM) in 2005. A proposal in 2011 to provide Indonesian truce observers in an ASEAN attempt to resolve a border dispute between Thailand and Cambodia also foundered, because of Thai objections (International Crisis Group 2011; Acharya 2014, p. 57).

ASEAN's contemporary contribution to regional security comes primarily through so-called ASEAN-centered forums, which bring together ASEAN as a bloc with various external dialogue partners. Notable among these forums are the East Asia Summit—comprising ASEAN, the United States, China, Russia, India, Japan, South Korea, Australia, and New Zealand—and the twenty-seven-member ASEAN Regional Forum (ARF) security dialogue. To function effectively, however, such forums require the ASEAN countries to reach a consensus position. Such consensus has proven increasingly difficult to achieve as China has increased its influence on mainland Southeast Asian states, particularly Cambodia and also Laos. The divisive influence of China and the disparate interests of member states became obvious in 2012, when ASEAN foreign ministers failed to produce a joint communiqué on a territorial dispute in the South China Sea. Only Indonesian foreign minister Marty Natalegawa's shuttle diplomacy restored temporary consensus. ASEAN is currently focusing on negotiating a code of conduct for the South

China Sea with China but faces Chinese reluctance to engage with the process and the challenge of maintaining its own unity as a grouping.

If Indonesia has been frustrated with other ASEAN members' response to its political and security proposals, it has been Indonesia that has frustrated ASEAN efforts to achieve greater regional economic integration (Heiduk 2016, p. 6). Singapore, Malaysia, and Thailand have exercised the most economic leadership within ASEAN (Emmers 2014, p. 550), with Singapore proposing both the ASEAN Free Trade Area, which came into force in 2003, and the ASEAN Economic Community, established in 2015. By contrast, Felix Heiduk (2016, pp. 6, 8) sets out a history of Indonesian obstruction of regional economic integration dating back to the Suharto era, underpinned by limited economic interdependence with ASEAN states, a desire to develop economic partners outside the region, and concerns that Indonesian firms would be unable to compete with their regional peers on a truly level playing field.

Nevertheless, Indonesia's limited ability to corral ASEAN states to a common position that serves Indonesian interests has spurred calls within Indonesia to diminish its role within Indonesian foreign policy. The most famous advocate for such a diminution has been Rizal Sukma, who as executive director of the Centre for Strategic and International Studies (CSIS), a Jakarta think tank, called for a post-ASEAN foreign policy in a *Jakarta Post* opinion piece in 2009. Under the Jokowi government, Sukma has transitioned from think-tank observer to policy adviser and ambassador; his influence and Jokowi's overall focus on tangible outcomes from Indonesia's diplomacy have each fueled predictions that Indonesia may turn away from ASEAN. Such predictions have not yet been borne out, however. Despite ASEAN's shortcomings, Indonesia has no clear alternative to engage effectively with the major powers on regional security issues.

Malaysia and Singapore

Indonesia's relations with its immediate neighbors, Malaysia and Singapore, are difficult yet ultimately amicable. Indeed, Indonesia's relations with Malaysia in particular are often likened to those of siblings, marked both by rivalry but also closeness. Sukarno's Konfrontasi military campaign from 1963 to 1966 and its aftermath marked a low point in ties between the two nations, and bilateral relations have frequently been beset by public controversies over a broad range of issues ever since. Despite such tensions, Malaysia and Singapore are among Indonesia's closest economic partners and share common security interests with their much larger neighbor. Along with Australia, Malaysia and Singapore are the only countries to have leader-level annual meetings with Indonesia.

Tensions with Malaysia have centered on territorial disputes, cultural identity, and cross-border labor issues (Weiss 2010, p. 173; Clark and Pietsch 2014). Sections of Indonesia and Malaysia's maritime boundary are yet to be demarcated, owing to protracted disputes, especially regarding the Ambalat block, northeast of Kalimantan, believed to contain vast oil and natural gas supplies. Each country lodges overlapping claims to the area, which result in periodic naval standoffs. Within Indonesia, the political context for negotiations over Ambalat and other border sections is a perception that Indonesia "lost" two disputed islands, Sipidan and Ligitan, to Malaysia in 2002 in an International Court of Justice ruling, a loss that must not be repeated. Another bone of contention is what Indonesia perceives as the cultural theft of songs, recipes, dance choreographies, and textile printing (batik), when Malaysia began to patent material and nonmaterial cultural artifacts (Clark and Pietsch 2014). Malaysia may indeed have gone too far in some cases, but Indonesia has done little to promote its cultural treasures or to prevent many of its cultural artifacts and heritage from being sold, destroyed, or even simply forgotten.

The treatment of Indonesian labor migrants in Malaysia gives rise to disagreement and discontent. By one estimate, 1.2 million Indonesians work in Malaysia, more than in any other country (Weiss 2010, p. 171). Repeated media reports of denigrating treatment, physical and sexual abuse, and quasi-serfdom of female domestic workers at the hands of their employers, and of the treatment of male workers in construction and agriculture, indicate a denial of their basic rights and fairness in employment. In 2009, after a series of abuse cases had hit the news, Indonesia banned the sending of domestic workers to Malaysia. The formal 2011 Memorandum of Understanding between Indonesia and Malaysia, crafted to protect the basic rights of Indonesian domestic workers in Malaysia, has not, according to labor activists in both countries, brought fundamental change. The issue is periodically of high political salience in Indonesia; presidential hopeful Prabowo Subianto made a highly publicized personal intervention in the case of a female migrant worker facing a potential death sentence in Malaysia in the lead-up to the 2014 elections, for example—she was ultimately acquitted of the murder of her employer.

Singapore shares many similar sources of tension with Indonesia. Although the number of Indonesians working in Singapore is far fewer than in Malaysia, cases of maltreatment spur protests in Indonesia from time to time. Issues of territory manifest between the two countries regarding the boundary between Singapore and the island of Batam, as well as Singapore's control of airspace over Indonesia's Riau Archipelago as part of the former's Flight Information Region, an arrangement the Indonesian military reportedly aspires to reverse. Singapore's land reclamation efforts have also given rise to territorial concerns in Indonesia. Singapore has imported vast amounts of sand and granite from Indonesia for land reclamation, but fearing that the extension of Singapore's shores would change sea boundaries, Indonesia banned the export of these materials from 2007 to 2011, although they continued to be smuggled out of the country.

Singapore's reputation as a safe haven for corrupt Indonesians and their money underpins a further diplomatic quarrel. Natasha Hamilton-Hart (2009, p. 264) quotes a Merrill Lynch estimate that "up to one third of the investors with assets of more than US$1 million in Singapore are of Indonesian origin"; this situation spurs resentment within Indonesia that Singapore's economic development is in significant part underpinned by illicit funds sourced from Indonesia. Indonesia and Singapore attempted to resolve this issue in 2007 when a Defence Cooperation Agreement and Extradition Treaty were signed as a package, but neither agreement came into force after parliamentary objections in Indonesia to the terms of the defense agreement (Hamilton-Hart 2009, p. 257). The absence of an operation extradition treaty still remains a bone of contention.

History and Singapore's perceived insecurities as a small island state also provide a recurring source of tension. President Habibie famously dismissed Singapore as a "little red dot" on the map, although the term's enthusiastic adoption by Singaporean diplomats may indicate little genuine offense was caused (Hamilton-Hart 2009, p. 251). A diplomatic spat also resulted in 2014 from Indonesia's decision to name a new naval frigate in honor of two marines executed in Singapore in 1968 for a Konfrontasi-era bombing attack. Indonesia's military chief apologized, but the frigate's name was not changed.

A final point of tension between Indonesia and Singapore (and Malaysia) is the regular occurrence of haze (transborder pollution) from forest fires. Every year, during the dry season, Indonesian planters burn large parts of the forests in Sumatra, generating smoke that crosses the Straits of Melaka and has a negative impact on tourism, aviation, and maritime activities in Singapore and Malaysia. Indonesia admits only partial responsibility for the problem, laying much of the blame on Singaporean and Malaysian investors for the slash-and-burn land clearance for their new oil palm plantations (Acharya 2014, p. 60).

Hamilton-Hart (2009, pp. 260–266) cautions against viewing Indonesia-Singapore ties as especially fractious, noting that the two countries' interests are in large part complementary and that even high-level emotional political disputes are often underpinned only by minor conflicts of interest. Certainly, Indonesia's interests align much more closely with Singapore within ASEAN than with those of mainland Southeast Asian states such as Laos and Cambodia. The same point holds true regarding shared interests between Indonesia and Malaysia.

Timor-Leste

The relationship between Indonesia and Timor-Leste is defined by the history of Indonesian annexation. Indonesia invaded Timor-Leste in December 1975, shortly after the former Portuguese colony declared independence but never gained UN recognition for the territory's annexation (Fernandes 2010). Upon democratization, President Habibie perceived an opportunity to remove what Foreign Minister Ali Alatas had famously described as a "pebble in Indonesia's shoe" and arranged for a referendum on the territory's future. The September 1999 referendum led to Timor-Leste's independence, in response to a large majority (78.5 percent) vote, but it also precipitated a murderous scorched-earth campaign by pro-Indonesia militia, actively supported by the Indonesian military. Around 2,000 people were killed, approximately 400,000 were displaced, and 60–80 percent of East Timor's underdeveloped infrastructure was destroyed (Strating 2014, p. 233). This campaign of violence followed a long history of human rights violations during Indonesian occupation, including a period of mass killings in the first five years of the occupation (Cribb 2001b). Among subsequent incidents, the 1991 Santa Cruz Massacre gained particular international notoriety.

Indonesian governments have shown no interest in confronting their nation's role as a colonizer, or in bringing Indonesian perpetrators to justice (see Chapter 7). Within Indonesia, the dominant perception is that the East Timorese opted voluntarily to join Indonesia in 1976, and that Timor-Leste's eventual separation was the outcome of foreign meddling (Hidayat 2011, pp. 24–25). The Indonesian government stance has posed a dilemma for successive governments of independent Timor-Leste—to pursue justice and reparations for the history of violence, or to prioritize good bilateral ties. This dilemma is sharpened by Timor-Leste's dependence on Indonesia for food imports, especially during the dry season, as well as Timor-Leste's need for Indonesian support for its security and defense. Illustrating these security interests, in 2011 and 2014, the two countries signed security and defense agreements that encompassed border control and smuggling issues and the supply of military equipment to Timor-Leste. Timor-Leste also aspires to join the Association of Southeast Asian Nations, for which it requires Indonesia's endorsement (Strating 2014, p. 235). Under these circumstances, Timor-Leste governments have opted for reconciliation rather than pressing the issue of past abuses with Indonesia. Timor-Leste opposed a recommendation by a UN Commission of Experts in 2005 that an international tribunal be established if domestic justice protesters failed to bring perpetrators of the 1999 violence to account (Hidayat 2011, p. 18). Indeed, the two governments established a bilateral Commission for Truth and Friendship (CTF) in 2005 with the express purpose of heading off any new international process (Hidayat 2011, p. 17). Both governments accepted the commission's recommendations in 2008, which unexpectedly included an acknowledgment of Indonesian responsibility for crimes, but there has been little follow-up since (Strating 2014, p. 251).

The Muslim World

Much as Indonesia is a majority Muslim country but not an Islamic state, Indonesia's foreign policy takes up Muslim concerns but is not driven by Islamic principles; nor does Indonesia place special importance on the countries of the Muslim world as international partners. In response to domestic pressures, advocacy for conflict-affected Muslim populations abroad has been a particular feature of Indonesian foreign policy, albeit conducted under an explicitly nonreligious banner.

Indonesia has not been uniformly proactive in responding to international conflicts that involve Muslim populations but has been more likely to become involved when these conflicts grab the attention of its domestic public. The Israeli-Palestinian conflict has been a particular focus of Indonesian diplomacy. Indonesia has consistently assisted the cause for the establishment of an independent Palestinian state and maintains a policy of not recognizing Israel. Among its recent steps in support of Palestinian statehood, in 2012 Indonesia cosponsored the Palestinian bid to become a full member of the United Nations and of UNESCO, and in 2016 Indonesia opened an honorary consulate in Ramallah. Indonesia also condemned the US decision under President Trump to move its embassy from Tel Aviv to Jerusalem. Within its own region, violence against Rohingya Muslims in Myanmar has gained the greatest public attention, including from Indonesian jihadis who have occasionally attempted retaliatory terror attacks. Indonesia has issued periodic statements of concern and submitted a "4+1 Formula" plan to Myanmar in 2017 in response to large-scale ethnic cleansing in Rakhine State. In practice, however, Indonesia has been able to exert little influence on events in Myanmar and has generally failed to extend sustained protection to Rohingya who are fleeing Myanmar (Missbach 2016).

On Bosnia, and later Kosovo, by contrast, each of which have much less public salience within Indonesia, the Indonesian government has been more circumspect. Indonesia initially resisted approaches to provide peacekeepers during the Bosnian crisis in the early 1990s, relenting only after Islamic organizations began to recruit Muslim volunteers to travel to the conflict (Suryadinata 1995, pp. 300–302). On Kosovo, the Indonesian government has rejected domestic calls to extend recognition following the Muslim majority territory's 2008 declaration of independence, wary of giving oxygen to Indonesia's own secessionist movements (Al-Anshori 2016). In each instance, the Indonesian government has explained its involvement in nonreligious terms rather than as the product of Islamic solidarity. It casts its support for a Palestinian state as opposition to colonialism and has described its diplomacy for other conflicts in humanitarian terms (Smith 2000, p. 523; Perwita 2007, p. 172; Suryadinata 1995; Al-Anshori 2016).

Because of the importance of domestic pressure, the influence of Islam on Indonesia's foreign policy has fluctuated in line with the influence of Islamic political groups within Indonesia. Suharto initially marginalized political Islam as a political threat to his regime, before ultimately embracing Islam as an alternate power base to the military during the 1990s. Since Suharto's fall, champions of political Islam have faced few formal restrictions in campaigning for greater incorporation of Islamic principles in public life, but they have not established themselves as a dominant force in domestic politics, as noted in Chapter 5.

Although the influence of Islam on foreign policy has increased (Al-Anshori 2016), Islam primarily acts as a constraint on the range of foreign policy positions available to the government, according to prominent foreign policy observer and adviser Dewi Fortuna Anwar. No Indonesian government has been able to extend diplomatic recognition to Israel, for example, despite efforts by Abdurrahman Wahid in particular to normalize ties (Smith 2000). The Yudhoyono government was also forced in 2007 to reverse its initial support for a UN resolution imposing sanctions on Iran for its enrichment of uranium, following criticism from domestic Muslim groups and the parliament. In this case, the government could not support a measure seen as "unfairly targeting a Muslim country," even though it was consistent with its broader policy of denuclearization and nonproliferation (Anwar 2010b, p. 48; Al-Anshori 2016).

The Muslim world has also been of periodic importance to Indonesia because of domestic security implications. Dating at least to the 1980s, jihadi terrorist networks operating within Indonesia have gained training, weapons, funds, and ideological inspiration from their counterparts in overseas theaters of conflict in Afghanistan, the Southern Philippines, Syria, and Iraq. The Indonesian government has typically had little ability to influence events in these conflict areas, but the history of their impact within Indonesia demonstrates the need for Indonesian authorities to monitor their citizens' involvement and understand new developments in jihadi ideology emanating from these conflict zones (Solahudin 2013b).

Several hundred members of Darul Islam trained in Afghanistan in the 1980s, laying the groundwork for Jemaah Islamiyah's bombing campaign of the early 2000s, in itself inspired by a fatwa issued by Osama bin Laden (Solahudin 2013a). The Southern Philippines also subsequently provided jihadi groups in Indonesia with an arena to obtain training and weaponry, some of which was used in the large-scale interreligious conflict areas in eastern Indonesia during the early postauthoritarian period. Concerted law enforcement greatly reduced the risk posed by these networks, but the emergence of the Islamic State in Iraq and Syria then reinvigorated Indonesian jihadis. Over 1,000 Indonesians are thought to have traveled to Iraq and Syria to join various groups, and more than 500 Indonesians have since returned to Indonesia.

Despite fears that such returnees would perpetrate violence at home, to date the greater risk has emanated from Indonesian ISIS sympathizers who were unable to travel to Syria and Iraq and have instead chosen to conduct attacks in Indonesia (Jones 2018). The success of pro-ISIS fighters in occupying the Philippines city of Marawi for several months in 2017 also created new security risks for Indonesia (Institute for Policy Analysis and Conflict 2017b). Beyond such influences, radical Muslims in Indonesia have launched fierce anti-Western protests on a number of occasions in reaction to global events, such as the 2005 publication of cartoons in the Danish newspaper *Jyllands Posten* that were deemed blasphemous. Additionally, in retaliation for the violence against and displacement of thousands of Rohingya in Myanmar by Buddhist extremists, two bombs were set off at a Buddhist temple in Jakarta in August 2013, injuring three people.

The one exception to Indonesia's avoidance of a religious image in its international relations has been its explicit positioning as a "model

Muslim democracy" during the post-Suharto era. Such a description fits with Indonesia's self-conception as a "bridge builder" between different worlds—in this case the mostly authoritarian Islamic world and the democratic West (Anwar 2010b, p. 45). It has also underpinned democracy promotion efforts and soft-power projects in Egypt, Tunisia, Iraq, Afghanistan, and other Muslim majority nations (Acharya 2014, p. 111). As with Indonesia's periodic attempts to mediate conflicts between Islamic countries, such a positioning has been undercut by the view of Middle Eastern countries that Indonesia holds only a peripheral place in the Muslim world, not least because Indonesian versions of Islam and the teachings of Indonesian Muslim scholars have never been exported widely (Bruinessen 2012, p. 134). Indeed, Anwar (2010b, p. 53) sees the construction and successful dissemination by Indonesian scholars of an "alternative model of Islam and society" as a precondition for Indonesia to effectively function either as a bridge builder or as a model for others.

The sheer scale of Indonesia's Muslim population—more Muslims live in Southeast Asia, primarily in Indonesia, than in the Middle East (Anwar 2010b, p. 53)—has also facilitated explicitly religious ties between Indonesia and donors in Saudi Arabia, Kuwait, Yemen, and Qatar. Such support has seen thousands of mosques built throughout the country, opening new paths for conservative Islamic ideas and for the radical ideas of Wahhabi and Salafi thinkers (Bruinessen 2012, p. 134). Saudi Arabia is also the main exporter of religious education to Indonesia, thereby promoting Salafism and Saudi Arabian versions of Islam, which tend to be openly antipluralist, anti-Semitic, and antidemocratic (Kovacs 2014).

Other International Partners

European Union

The European Union (EU) and its member states are of secondary importance to Indonesia as international partners. Their significance is diminished by geographic distance, as well as the imprint that the former colonial powers—the Netherlands and, to a lesser extent, Great Britain and Portugal—left in Indonesia. David Camroux and Annisa Srikandini (2013, p. 555) characterize the Indonesia-EU relationship as one in which "expectations on both sides are low," leading each side to commit only modest capabilities to developing ties. Nevertheless, the two sides have established a range of institutions to support bilateral relations. A European Community–ASEAN Cooperation Agreement was concluded in 1980, a EU delegation to Indonesia was opened in 1988, and an EU-Indonesia Partnership and Cooperation Agreement was signed in 2009, for example.

Human rights issues have placed a recurrent strain on the EU-Indonesia relationship, particularly with regard to Indonesia's annexation of East Timor in 1975. At first, the EU was acquiescent, but when Timor's former colonial power, Portugal, joined the European Community in 1986, it regularly spoke out in the European Parliament and the Council of Ministers against the annexation and against human rights violations. Like the United States, the EU imposed an arms embargo on Indonesia after the Santa Cruz Massacre in 1991. Prior to the embargo, Germany had sold large quantities of discarded military equipment from the inventory of the former East German military to Indonesia. During the democratic era, since the EU-Indonesia Human Rights Dialogue was launched in 2009—which initiated projects to promote freedom of religion, support human rights defenders, protect vulnerable minorities and women and children, increase human rights accountability, and prevent torture—the EU-Indonesia relationship has suffered severe setbacks. Not the least of these came with the execution of fourteen people for drug crimes in 2015, most of whom were foreigners. The EU and others have long pressed Indonesia to remove the death penalty from its sentencing laws, and the executions took place despite extensive international entreaties. A Dutch citizen was among those executed, and a French citizen received an eleventh-hour reprieve. The Netherlands temporarily recalled its ambassador in response. Beyond human rights issues, the EU has imposed various restrictions on Indonesian products for failing to meet EU regulations. In 2005, Indonesian fishery products were not admitted into EU markets because they were suspected of containing hazardous chemical substances, and in 2007, all Indonesian airlines were banned from European airspace because of their poor aviation safety standards (Luhulima, Panjaitan, and Widiana 2009, pp. 96, 109). In 2018, announcements by the EU to introduce a ban on Indonesian palm oil caused new tensions. In June 2019, following the EU's final decision to reduce and ban palm oil biofuel altogether by 2030, major producers Indonesia and Malaysia announced they would challenge the decision at the World Trade Organization (WTO) (*New Straits Times*, "Malaysia and Indonesia to Jointly Fight EU's Palm Oil Ban at WTO," July 16, 2019).

Despite disagreements over human rights, the EU played a major role in the resolution of the seemingly intractable secessionist civil war in Aceh, following successful peace talks in 2005 facilitated by the

Finnish Crisis Management Initiative. The EU provided funding for these talks between the Indonesian government and the Free Aceh Movement (GAM). Following the conclusion of a memorandum of understanding, the EU and ASEAN also deployed the Aceh Monitoring Mission (AMM) to oversee the implementation of the peace agreement. The AMM monitored the decommissioning of GAM's weapons, the redeployment of 25,890 Indonesian soldiers and 5,791 police who had been fighting GAM in Aceh, the reintegration of former GAM combatants, and the drafting of new legislation for the governance of Aceh (Schulze 2010, p. 12). The monitoring mission was deemed a great success; those seeking to resolve other regional secessionist conflicts have often sought to emulate the Aceh peacemaking process.

Development cooperation has constituted a major part of EU-Indonesia relations, particularly since democratization in Indonesia. From 1992 to 2007, the EU was a donor to Indonesia through the Consultative Group for Indonesia (CGI), a forum set up by the Indonesian government and the World Bank to alleviate Indonesia's foreign debt. Democratic-era EU assistance to Indonesia has been wide-ranging and has included support for good governance, public administration, natural resource management, justice and security, counterterrorism, and climate change (European Union External Action 2001, pp. 3–4; Heiduk 2014, p. 708). From 2013, Indonesia was deemed by the EU to have moved beyond needing development assistance. It currently enjoys preferential treatment in trading with the EU, as one of the developing countries whose imports have tax-free or tax-reduced entry into the EU. Indonesia exports agricultural products and processed resources to the EU—mainly palm oil, fuel, minerals, textiles, and furniture—whereas the EU primarily exports high-tech machinery, transport equipment, chemicals, and manufactured goods to Indonesia.

Australia

As with Indonesia's volatile relationships with Singapore and Malaysia, Indonesia-Australia relations have also been subject to a "tyranny of proximity" (Mackie 2007; Purdey and Missbach 2015; Ward 2015; Lindsey and McRae 2018). Despite being neighbors, the two countries differ in almost every respect, including ethnic and religious composition, language, per capita income, and until 1998, political system. Indonesia's democratization has not lessened the episodic turbulence of bilateral ties. During the post-Suharto era, Indonesia has withdrawn its ambassador twice and Australia once, in disputes over sovereignty, espionage, and transnational crime. In fact, as a democratic Indonesia has returned to an outward footing, a sense that Australia pays its northern neighbor insufficient respect as a rising power has further complicated bilateral ties. And yet, as with Indonesia's relations with its other neighbors, despite this turbulence, Australia-Indonesia relations have expanded incrementally and in some respects warmed since 1998.

The most persistent source of tension in bilateral ties has been the perception of Australian support for separatists within Indonesia. Despite Australia's tolerance of the Indonesian invasion of East Timor in 1975 and its recognition of Indonesian sovereignty over the territory—Australia was one of few Western countries to do so—the question of East Timor's status ultimately ruptured bilateral ties temporarily. Many Indonesian nationalists blame Australia for the loss of East Timor, because Australian prime minister John Howard wrote to Habibie in 1998 suggesting a period of autonomy followed by a referendum, after which Australia also led the international peacekeeping force sent to restore security. To such nationalists, Australia's change of position on East Timor reveals its support for Indonesian territorial integrity as inherently suspect, even as Australian leaders ritually express such support in bilateral meetings. Australia's decision to grant temporary protection visas in 2006 to a group of Papuan asylum seekers who had arrived in Australia by boat only reinforced the perception of Australian unreliability (Neumann and Taylor 2009). Indonesia withdrew its ambassador in response to the granting of these visas, but bilateral relations were soon repaired by the conclusion of a new security treaty, the Lombok Treaty, in November 2006. Ironically, this treaty replaced a 1995 security treaty that Indonesia had unilaterally abrogated in 1999 in response to the East Timor episode.

Transnational crime in its various manifestations has been another recurrent source of friction; people smuggling, the international drug trade, and terrorism have all loomed large in the bilateral relationship. Indonesia is typically the final point of transit for asylum seekers attempting to reach Australia, assisted by people smugglers who arrange their journey in whole or in part. The arrival of such asylum seekers is highly politicized within Australia, and most Australian governments have adopted hard-line policies to try to prevent asylum seekers from departing Indonesia. The continued long-term presence of more than 10,000 asylum seekers in Indonesia is in itself a minor irritant to the country's authorities, but it has been Australian enforcement actions that have been periodically incendiary. Asylum boat turn-backs have been especially resented, and Australian maritime authorities have on at least six occasions violated Indonesia's twelve-nautical-mile territorial waters (Missbach 2018). Australia's insistence that Indonesia take back asylum seekers rescued by the MV *Tampa* freighter in 2001 and by the Australian customs vessel *Oceanic Viking* in 2009 also aggrieved Indonesian officials (Missbach 2018, p. 130).

The international drug trade has typically affected bilateral relations when Australians have received stern penalties for trafficking drugs in Indonesia. The most notable cases have been the twenty-year sentence handed down to Schapelle Corby in 2005 for importation of marijuana, and the execution in 2015 of two members of the "Bali Nine" heroin smuggling ring, Andrew Chan and Myuran Sukumaran. Indonesians were angered when Australian prime minister Tony Abbott appeared to link Australia's $1 billion in aid to Indonesia following the 2004 Boxing Day tsunami to his government's entreaties for clemency for the two men. Ultimately, Widodo remained aloof to Australia's advocacy for Chan and Sukumaran, precipitating the recall of Australia's ambassador upon their execution.

For its part, the primary impact of jihadi terrorism on bilateral ties has been its influence on Australian perceptions of Indonesia. Successive Australian governments have approached Islam in Indonesia primarily through a prism of contrasts between moderate and radical Islam (Fealy 2018), whereas the death of eighty-eight Australians in the 2002 Bali bombings have helped entrench Australian public perceptions of Indonesia as a dangerous destination. Ironically, at the same time, counterterrorism cooperation has also emerged as a central, mutually appreciated area of bilateral security cooperation in the wake of the Bali bombings. Such cooperation was impacted only minimally by a suspension order from President Yudhoyono in 2013 in the wake of revelations of Australian spying on the president's family and inner circle, and it has been further energized by the emergent threat of ISIS (McKenzie 2018).

A perception that the Australian government disrespects and belittles Indonesia further complicates bilateral relations (McRae 2014b, p. 18). Episodes such Prime Minister Abbott's comments regarding the tsunami fuel this perception, spurring an impression that Australia believes it can buy policy outcomes in Indonesia. Emblematic of this perception, at times of bilateral controversy it is common to hear Indonesians express the view that Australia needs Indonesia more than the reverse.

Nevertheless, as with Indonesia's bilateral relations with several countries, to focus solely on sources of friction would be to overlook important dynamics in bilateral ties with Australia. Both sides recognize the importance of maintaining a functioning relationship, and the leaders of the day have typically intervened to mend fences when ties have been seriously strained (McRae 2018). Apart from pragmatism, such efforts draw upon reserves of goodwill within bilateral ties, for which Australia's long-running scholarship program to support tertiary study for Indonesians is one source (Purdey and Missbach 2015). Since the ten-year tenure of Susilo Bambang Yudhoyono in particular, bilateral relations have broadened and, in some respects, have warmed, underpinned by a range of new institutions (McRae 2018; Lindsey and McRae 2018). During this period, as well as through concluding the Lombok Treaty, Australia and Indonesia have established an annual leaders' meeting and an annual two-plus-two defense and foreign minister's meeting, entered the informal MIKTA (Mexico, Indonesia, South Korea, Turkey, Australia) middle-power grouping, and concluded an Indonesia-Australia Comprehensive Economic Partnership Agreement (IA-CEPA) in 2019.

The Pacific Islands

The members of the eighteen-nation Pacific Islands Forum and the smaller subregion, four-nation Melanesian Spearhead Group (MSG) have emerged as key diplomatic interlocutors for Indonesia, owing to advocacy within these regional organizations by Papuan independence activists. Pro-independence activists attained observer status in the MSG in 2015 for the United Liberation Movement for West Papua (ULMWP), an umbrella group representing Papuans living abroad (Lawson 2016, p. 518). The leaders of Pacific Island nations have also repeatedly raised the issue of the status of Papua in their speeches at the United Nations (Chauvel 2018).

Indonesia has been direct in its opposition to Pacific Island nations raising the issue of Papua. It opposed ULMWP membership of the MSG, succeeding in limiting the organization to observer status and simultaneously gaining observer status for itself (Lawson 2016, pp. 507–508). It has also lobbied to keep Papua off the agenda of the Pacific Islands Forum, reportedly receiving support from Australia to water down language on Papua in the forum's 2015 communiqué (Chauvel 2018, p. 274). In 2016, Indonesia directly refuted the speeches of the Pacific nations' leaders at the United Nations, presenting a junior diplomat to rebuke these leaders for supporting separatism in Papua, purportedly for their own domestic political aims (Chauvel 2018, p. 260). Arguably, Indonesia's use of a young diplomat to rebuke Pacific Island leaders reflects its power advantage over much smaller Pacific

Island states, an imbalance Indonesia enjoys in few of its international relations. Consistent with this imbalance, the Pacific has been one of the first areas of Indonesian aid provision, with the government providing ad hoc development assistance to seek, albeit ineffectively, to head off support for Papua (Chauvel 2018; Wangge 2016).

* * *

Indonesia has yet to play a role in international politics commensurate with its vast territory, strategic position, and large population. Nevertheless, its free and active foreign policy and the expectation of a rapid increase in its international capabilities and influence have seen several larger powers devote increasing resources to deepening their ties with the archipelagic nation.

Note

1. Between 1957 and 2009, Indonesia participated in twenty-four peacekeeping operations (Acharya 2014, p. 112). In 2010, with 1,765 peacekeepers, Indonesia was among the top twenty contributors of uniformed personnel—a sharp increase from 2005, when it ranked forty-seventh in terms of its military contribution (Laksmana 2011, p. 170). In 2013, Indonesia was part of six United Nations peacekeeping missions, ranking as the sixteenth-largest contributor (Acharya 2014, p. 112).

Glossary

ABRI Angkatan Bersenjata Republik Indonesia (Indonesian Armed Forces)
adat custom, tradition
agama religion
Aliansi Jurnalis Independen Alliance for Independent Journalists
ANFREL Asian Network for Free Elections
Angkatan Muda Youth Association
antargolongan intergroup relations
APEC Asia-Pacific Economic Cooperation
APJII Asosiasi Penyelenggara Jasa Internet Indonesia (Indonesia Internet Service Provider Association)
ARF ASEAN Regional Forum
ASEAN Association of Southeast Asian Nations
ASNLF Acheh-Sumatra National Liberation Front
asuransi kesehatan masyarakat miskin social insurance for poor households
azas kekeluargaan family principle
Baperki Badan Permusjawaratan Kewarganegaraan Indonesia (Indonesian Citizenship Consultative Council)
Bersiap campaign against the Dutch return to Indonesia in 1945 and 1946; literally, "Be Ready"
BIN Badan Intelijen Negara (State Intelligence Agency)
Bintang Kejora Morning Star flag (Papuan independence)
BLT Bantuan Langsung Tunai (unconditional cash transfers)
BNN Badan Narkotika Nasional (National Narcotics Agency)
BOS Bantuan Operasional Sekolah (School Operational Assistance Grant)
BRA Badan Reintegrasi-Damai Aceh (Aceh Peaceful Reintegration Agency)
BSM *bantuan siswa miskin* (assistance programs for poor school pupils)

223

BTI Barisan Tani Indonesia (Indonesian Peasants Front)
bupati district head, mayor
CAVR Comissão de Acolhimento, Verdade e Reconciliação de Timor Leste
  (Commission for Reception, Truth and Reconciliation in East Timor)
CTF Commission for Truth and Friendship
cukong Chinese businessmen in relationships with elites in the military,
  police
Cultuurstelsel Dutch-imposed Cultivation System
dakwah proselytization
Darul Islam Islamic Armed Forces of Indonesia
Dewan Nasional National Council
Dewan Papua Papuan Council
Dharma Pertiwi armed forces' wives' organization
Dharma Wanita civil servants' wives' organization
diyat compensation for the family of people killed (Acehnese)
DOM *daerah operasi militer* (designated militarized zones)
DPD Dewan Perwakilan Daerah (Regional Representative Assembly)
DPR Dewan Perwakilan Rakyat (People's Representative Assembly)
dua anak cukup "two children are enough" (population-control slogan)
dwifungsi dual-function doctrine of the military
ELSAM Lembaga Studi dan Advokasi Masyarakat (Institute for Policy
  Research and Advocacy)
ethici middle-class Dutch advocates of a more ethical colonial policy
FORERI Forum Rekonsiliasi Masyarakat Irian Jaya (Forum for
  Reconciliation for the People from Irian Jaya)
FPI Front Pembela Islam (Islamic Defenders Front)
Fretilin Frente Revolucionária de Timor-Leste Independente (Revolutionary
  Front for an Independent East Timor)
GAM Gerakan Aceh Merdeka (Free Aceh Movement)
GBHN Garis-garis Besar Haluan Negara (State Policy Guidelines)
Gerakan Pemuda Ansor Nahdlatul Ulama youth wing
Gerindra Partai Gerakan Indonesia Raya (Great Indonesia Movement Party)
Gerwani Gerakan Wanita Indonesia (Indonesian Women's Movement)
GOC United Nations' Committee of Good Offices
Golkar Golongan Karya (Functional Groups)
golput *golongan putih* (white group)
gotong royong mutual/communal decisionmaking and cooperation
guru honorer teachers appointed and paid by individual schools
Hanura Partai Hati Nurani Rakyat (People's Conscience Party)
Heiho Indonesian auxiliary troops formed by the Japanese occupying forces
Himpunan Waria Djakarta Waria Association for Jakarta

HTI Hizbut Tahrir Indonesia

ICMI Ikatan Cendekiawan Muslim Indonesia (Association of Indonesian Muslim Intellectuals)

Indos Eurasian people descended from Indonesian ethnic groups and Dutch settlers

IPKI Partai Ikatan Pendukung Kemerdekaan Indonesia (League of Supporters of Indonesian Independence)

islah traditional Islamic practice for resolving a dispute (Arabic)

Jamkesda Jaminan Kesehatan Daerah (regional health insurance)

Jamsostek Jaminan Sosial Tenaga Kerja (workers' social insurance)

janda widow or divorcée

Jawa Hokokai Javanese Service Association

JKN Jaminan Kesehatan Nasional (universal social health-insurance scheme)

JPS Jaring Pengaman Sosial (Social Safety Net)

Kabinet Karya Working Cabinet

kabupaten districts

KAMI Kesatuan Aksi Mahasiswa Indonesia (Indonesian Student Action Unit)

KAPPI Kesatuan Aksi Pelajar Pemuda Indonesia (Indonesian Youth and Students' Action Front)

kartu Indonesia pintar smart card

Kartu Jakarta Sehat Jakarta Health Card

Kawal Pemilu Guard the Election movement

kekaryaan principle underpinning the military dual function

kekerasan dalam rumah tangga domestic violence

KIP Komisi Informasi Pusat (Central Information Commission)

KKR Komisi Kebenaran dan Rekonsiliasi (Commission for Truth and Reconciliation)

KNPB Komite Nasional Papua Barat (West Papua National Committee)

Komnas HAM Komisi Nasional Hak Asasi Manusia (National Commission on Human Rights)

koneksitas civil-military courts

Konfrontasi confrontation with Malaysia

Konstituante Constitutional Assembly

KontraS Komisi untuk Orang Hilang dan Korban Tindak Kekerasan (Commission for the Disappeared and Victims of Violence)

Kopassus Komando Pasukan Khusus (Army Special Forces Command)

Kostrad Komando Candangan Strategis Angkatan Darat (Army Strategic Command)

kota city or municipality

KPK Komisi Pemberantasan Korupsi (Corruption Eradication Commission)
KPP-HAM Komisi Penyelidik Pelanggaran Hak Asasi Manusia di Timor Timur (Commission for Human Rights Violations in East Timor)
LBH Lembaga Bantuan Hukum (Legal Aid Institute)
LDPD Lembaga Pengelola Dana Pendidikan (Endowment Fund for Education)
Lekra Lembaga Kebudayaan Rakyat (Institute for the People's Culture)
liwath sodomy (Arabic)
LSF Lembaga Sensor Film (Film Censorship Institute)
LSM *lembaga swadaya masyarakat* (civil society organizations)
madrasah Muslim religious school at primary and secondary levels
makar treason, or rebellion
Manipol USDEK Political Manifesto of the Republic
Masyumi Partai Majelis Syuro Muslimin Indonesia (Council of Indonesian Muslim Associations)
MFA Movimento das Forcas Armadas (Portuguese Armed Forces Movement)
MNCTV Media Nusantara Citra Televisi
MPR Majelis Permusyawaratan Rakyat (People's Consultative Assembly)
MPRS Majelis Permusyawaratan Rakyat Sementara (Provisional People's Consultative Assembly
MSG Melanesian Spearhead Group
MUI Majelis Ulama Indonesia (Council of Indonesian Ulama)
NAM Non-Aligned Movement
NASAKOM Nasionalisme, Agama, Komunisme (Nationalism, Religion, Communism)
Nasdem Partai Nasional Demokrat (National Democratic Party)
Nekolim neocolonialism and imperialism
NU Nahdlatul Ulama (Revival of the Muslim Scholars)
OECD Organisation for Economic Co-operation and Development
OPM Organisasi Papua Merdeka (Free Papua Movement)
OSVIA Opleiding School voor Inlandsche Ambtenaren (Training School for Native Officials)
PAN Partai Amanat Nasional (National Mandate Party)
Pancasila (Pantja Sila) five principles for the Indonesian nation
Panitia Persiapan Kemerdekaan Indonesia Preparatory Committee for Indonesian Independence
Parindra Partai Indonesia Raya (Great Indonesia Party)
Partindo Partai Indonesia (Indonesia Party)
pasung physical restraint, or shackling
PDI Partai Demokrasi Indonesia (Indonesian Democratic Party)

PDI-P Partai Demokrasi Indonesia Perjuangan (Indonesian Democratic Struggle Party)

PDSM Pacific Decolonization Solidarity Movement

pemekaran blossoming (lit.) division of districts, municipalities, and provinces into new administrative units

pemuda youth

Pemuda Rakyat People's Youth, the PKI youth wing

PEPERA Penentuan Pendapat Rakyat (Act of Free Choice)

perda sharia regional government regulations informed by Islamic Law

Permesta Piagam Perjuangan Semesta (Universal Struggle Charter)

Perti Persatuan Tarbiyah Islamiyah (Tarbiyah Islamiyah Union)

pesantren Islamic boarding school

Peta Pembela Tanah Air (Defenders of the Fatherland)

peusijuek ritual to symbolize reconciliation (Acehnese)

Piagam Jakarta Jakarta Charter

PK Partai Keadilan (Justice Party)

PKB Partai Kebangkitan Bangsa (National Awakening Party)

PKH Program Keluarga Harapan (conditional cash transfer program)

PKI Partai Komunis Indonesia (Indonesian Communist Party)

PKS Partai Keadilan Sejahtera (Prosperous Justice Party)

PNI Partai Nasional Indonesia (Indonesian National Party)

PPP Partai Persatuan Pembangunan (Development Unity Party)

pribumi indigenous people

priyayi lower aristocracy

PRRI Pemerintah Revolusioner Republik Indonesia (Revolutionary Government of the Republic of Indonesia)

PSI Partai Sosialis Indonesia (Indonesian Socialist Party)

PSII Partai Syarikat Islam Indonesia (Indonesian Islamic Union Party)

puskesmas *pusat kesehatan masyarakat* (community health centers)

Putera Pusat Tenaga Rakyat (Center of People's Power)

Ran HAM Rancangan Hak Asasi Manusia (National Human Rights Plan of Action)

ras race

RCTI Rajawali Citra Televisi Indonesia

SARA *suku, agama, ras, antargolongan* (ethnic, religious, racial, and intergroup diversity of topics banned for religious discussion under the New Order)

SCTV Surya Citra Televisi

SEAC Allied Southeast Asia Command

sinetron television soap operas

SMK *sekolah menengah kejuruan* (vocational education)

SOBSI   Sentral Organisasi Buruh Seluruh Indonesia (Central Labor Organization of the Republic of Indonesia)

STOVIA   School tot Opleiding voor Indische Artsen (School for Training Native Doctors)

suku   ethnicity

Supersemar   Surat Perintah Sebelas Maret (Order of the Eleventh March)

tarbiyah   education (Arabic)

TKR   Tentara Keamanan Rakyat (People's Security Army)

TNI   Tentara Nasional Indonesia (Indonesian National Army)

TPI   Televisi Pendidikan Indonesia (Educational Television Indonesia)

TPN   Tentara Pembebasan Nasional (National Liberation Army)

TPN–PB   Tentara Pembebasan Nasional–Papua Barat (West Papuan National Liberation Army)

Trikora   Tri Komando Rakyat (Peoples' Triple Command)

TVRI   Televisi Republik Indonesia

ULMWP   United Liberation Movement for West Papua

UNCI   United Nations Commission on Indonesia

UNTAET   United Nations Transitional Administration in East Timor

VOC   Vereenigde Oostindische Compagnie (Dutch East India Company)

waria   transgender male-to-female

warnet   *warung internet* (internet kiosk)

YLBHI   Yayasan Lembaga Bantuan Hukum (Indonesian Legal Aid Foundation)

YPKP   Yayasan Penelitian Korban Pembunuhan 1965–1966 (Foundation for Research into Victims of the 1965–1966 Killings)

zakat   religious tax (Arabic)

zina   sexual relations outside of marriage (Arabic)

References

Acharya, Amitav. 2014. *Indonesia Matters: Asia's Emerging Democratic Power.* Singapore: World Scientific.

Adrison, Vid. 2013. *Deforestation in Decentralized and Democratic Indonesia.* LPEM-FEUI Working Paper no. 1. Jakarta: LPEM-FEUI.

Afrianti, Dina. 2016. "The Implementation of Perda Syari'at in Aceh and West Sumatra." In T. Lindsey and H. Pausacker, eds., *Religion, Law and Intolerance in Indonesia*, 335–352. London: Routledge.

Aisyah, Rachmadea. 2019. "Poverty Rate Down." *Jakarta Post*, January 15. https://www.thejakartapost.com/news/2019/01/15/poverty-rate-down-to-9-66-percent-gini-ratio-improves-to-0-384.html.

Aisyah, Siti, and Lyn Parker. 2014. "Problematic Conjugations: Women's Agency, Marriage and Domestic Violence in Indonesia." *Asian Studies Review* 38, no. 2: 205–223.

Aiyar, Pallavi. 2015. "In Indonesia, Madrassas of Moderation." *New York Times*, February 10.

Aji, Priasto. 2015. *Summary of Indonesia's Poverty Analysis.* ADB Papers on Indonesia no. 4. Manila: Asian Development Bank.

Al-Anshori, Mohamad Zakaria. 2016. "The Role of Islam in Indonesia's Contemporary Foreign Policy." PhD diss., Victoria University of Wellington.

Allen, Pam. 2007. "Challenging Diversity? Indonesia's Anti-Pornography Bill." *Asian Studies Review* 31: 101–115.

Alwi, Des. 2008. *Friends and Exiles: A Memoir of the Nutmeg Isles and the Indonesian Nationalist Movement.* Edited by Barbara Harvey. Ithaca: SEAP Publications, Cornell University Press.

Amnesty International. 2018. *Indonesia Report 2017/2018.* https://www.amnesty.org/en/countries/asia-and-the-pacific/indonesia/report-indonesia/.

Amnesty International Indonesia. 2018. *"Don't Bother, Just Let Him Die": Killing with Impunity in Papua.* Jakarta.

Ananta, A., Evu Nurvidya Arifin, M. Sairi Hasbullah, Nur Budi Handayani, and Agus Pramono. 2015. *Demography of Indonesia's Ethnicity.* Singapore: Institute of Southeast Asian Studies.

Anderson, B. 1961. *Some Aspects of Indonesian Politics Under the Japanese Occupation, 1944–1945.* Modern Indonesia Project Interim Reports series. Ithaca: Cornell University, Department of Far Eastern Studies.

Anderson, Bobby. 2013. "The Failure of Education in Papua's Highlands." *Inside Indonesia* 113.

Anwar, Dewi Fortuna. 1997. "ASEAN and Indonesia: Some Reflections." *Asian Journal of Political Science* 5, no. 1: 20–34.

———. 2003. "Megawati's Search for an Effective Foreign Policy." In H. Soesastro, A. L. Smith, and H. M. Ling, eds., *Governance in Indonesia: Challenges Facing the Megawati Presidency*, 70–90. Singapore: ISEAS.

———. 2010a. "The Habibie Presidency: Catapulting Towards Reform." In E. Aspinall and G. Fealy, eds., *Suharto's New Order and Its Legacy: Essays in Honour of Harold Crouch*, 99–118. Canberra: ANU E-Press.

———. 2010b. "Foreign Policy, Islam and Democracy in Indonesia." *Journal of Indonesian Social Sciences and Humanities* 3: 37–54.

———. 2018. "Indonesia's Vision of Regional Order in East Asia amid US–China Rivalry: Continuity and Change." *Asia Policy* 13, no. 2: 57–63.

APJII. 2018. *Survei APJII: Penetrasi Internet di Indonesia Capai 143 Juta Jiwa.* May.

Aragon, L. 2007. "Elite Competition in Central Sulawesi." In H. S. Nordholt and G. van Klinken, eds., *Renegotiating Boundaries: Local Politics in Post-Suharto Indonesia*, 39–66. Leiden: Brill.

Armando, Ade. 2014. "The Greedy Giants: Centralized Television in Post-Authoritarian Indonesia." *International Communication Gazette* 76, no. 4–5: 390–406.

Aspinall, E. 2005a. *Opposing Suharto: Compromise, Resistance and Regime Change in Indonesia.* Stanford: Stanford University Press.

———. 2005b. *The Helsinki Agreement: A More Promising Basis for Peace in Aceh?* Washington, DC: East-West Center.

———. 2008a. "Ethnic and Religious Violence in Indonesia: A Review Essay." *Australian Journal of International Affairs* 62, no. 4 (December): 558–572.

———. 2008b. *Peace Without Justice? The Helsinki Peace Process in Aceh.* Geneva: HD Centre for Humanitarian Dialogue.

———. 2013a. "How Indonesia Survived: Comparative Perspectives on State Disintegration and Democratic Integration." In M. Künkler and A. Stepan, eds., *Democracy and Islam in Indonesia*, 126–147. New York: Columbia University Press.

———. 2013b. "A Nation in Fragments." *Critical Asian Studies* 45, no. 1: 27–54.

———. 2014. "Health Care and Democratization in Indonesia." *Democratization* 21, no. 5: 803–823.

———. 2015. "The Surprising Democratic Behemoth: Indonesia in Comparative Asian Perspective." *Journal of Asian Studies* 74, no. 4 (November): 889–902.

Aspinall, E., and M. T. Berger. 2002. "The Break-Up of Indonesia? Nationalisms After Decolonisation and the Limits of the Nation-State in Post–Cold War Southeast Asia." *Third World Quarterly* 22, no. 6 (December): 1003–1024.

Aspinall, E., N. Rohman, A. Z. Hamdi, Rubaidi, and Z. E. Triantini. 2017. "Vote Buying in Indonesia: Candidate Strategies, Market Logic and Effectiveness." *Journal of East Asian Studies* 17, no. 1 (March): 1–27.

Aspinall, E., and M. Uhaib As'ad. 2016. "Understanding Family Politics: Successes and Failures of Political Dynasties in Regional Indonesia." South East Asia Research 24, no. 3 (September): 420–435.

Aspinall, E., and E. Warburton. 2013. "A Healthcare Revolution in the Regions." *Inside Indonesia* 111 (January–March).

Aswicahyono, Haryo, Hal Hill, and Dionisius Narjoko. 2010. "Industrialisation After a Deep Economic Crisis: Indonesia." *Journal of Development Studies* 46, no. 6: 1084–1108.

Austin, Anne, Jonathan Barnard, and Nicola Hutcheon. 2015. *Media Consumption Forecast 2015.* London: ZenithOptimedia.

Avonius, Leena. 2009. "Reconciliation and Human Rights in Post-Conflict Aceh." In B. Bräuchler, ed., *Reconciling Indonesia: Grassroots Agency for Peace*, 121–137. London: Routledge.

Azhar, Haris. 2014. "The Human Rights Struggle in Indonesia: International Advances, Domestic Deadlocks." *SUR: International Journal on Human Rights* 11, no. 20 (June–December): 226–234.

Badan Pusat Statistik. 2017. "Number of General Hospitals, Special Hospitals and *Puskesmas* by Province, 2012 and 2013." https://www.bps.go.id/linkTableDinamis /view/id/933.

Barker, Thomas. 2015. "Sex on Indonesia's Screens." In S. G. Davies and L. R. Bennett, eds., *Sex and Sexualities in Contemporary Indonesia: Sexual Politics, Health, Diversity and Representations*, 253–272. London: Routledge.

Barkin, Gareth. 2014. "Commercial Islam in Indonesia: How Television Producers Mediate Religiosity Among National Audiences." *International Journal of Asian Studies* 11, no. 1: 1–24.

Barron, P., S. Jaffrey, and A. Varshney. 2016. "When Large Conflicts Subside: The Ebbs and Flows of Violence in Post-Suharto Indonesia." *Journal of East Asian Studies* 16, no. 2 (July): 191–217.

Batu, Safrin La. 2017. "Jokowi's Commitment to Rights Questioned, Again," *Jakarta Post,* September 12.

Baumgardner, Jennifer. 2014. "A Multi-Level, Integrated Approach to Ending Female Genital Mutilation/Cutting in Indonesia." *Journal of Global Justice and Public Policy* 1, no. 1 (Fall): 267–291.

Bertrand, Jacques. 2004. *Nationalism and Ethnic Conflict in Indonesia*. Cambridge: Cambridge University Press.

———. 2007. "Indonesia's Quasi-Federalist Approach: Accommodation amid Strong Integrationist Tendencies." *International Journal of Constitutional Law* 5, no. 4 (October): 576–605.

Bevins, Vincent. 2017. "What the United States Did in Indonesia." *Atlantic*, October 20.

Blackburn, Susan. 1999. "Gender Violence and the Indonesian Political Transition." *Asian Studies Review* 23, no. 4: 433–448.

Boellstorff, Tom. 2004a. "Playing Back the Nation: *Waria*, Indonesian Transvestites." *Cultural Anthropology* 19, no. 2: 159–196.

———. 2004b. "The Emergence of Political Homophobia in Indonesia: Masculinity and National Belonging." *Ethnos* 69, no. 4: 465–486.

Booth, Anne. 2011a. "Splitting, Splitting and Splitting Again: A Brief History of the Development of Regional Government in Indonesia Since Independence." *Bijdragen tot de Taal-, Land- en Volkenkunde* 167, no. 1: 31–59.

———. 2011b. "China's Economic Relations with Indonesia: Threats and Opportunities." *Journal of Current Southeast Asian Affairs* 30, no. 2: 141–160.

Bourchier, D. 1987. "The Petition of Fifty." *Inside Indonesia* 10 (April): 7–10.

———. 1999. "Skeletons, Vigilantes and the Armed Forces' Fall from Grace." In A. Budiman, B. Hatley, and D. Kingsbury, eds., *Reformasi: Crisis and Change in Indonesia*, 149–171. Melbourne: Monash Asia Institute.

———. 2008. "Positivism and Romanticism in Indonesian Legal Thought." In T. Lindsey, ed., *Indonesia: Law and Society*, 94–104. Leichardt, New South Wales: Federation Press.

Brands, H. W. 1989. "The Limits of Manipulation: How the United States Didn't Topple Sukarno." *Journal of American History* 76, no. 3: 785–808.

Bräuchler, Birgit. 2003. "Cyberidentities at War: Religion, Identity, and the Internet in the Moluccan Conflict." *Indonesia* 75: 123–151.

————. 2004. "Islamic Radicalism Online: The Moluccan Mission of Laskar Jihad in Cyberspace." *Australian Journal of Anthropology* 15, no. 3: 253–271.

————. 2007. "Religious Conflicts in Cyberage." *Citizenship Studies* 11, no. 4: 329–347.

————. 2011. "The Transformation of the Media Scene: From War to Peace in the Moluccas, Eastern Indonesia." In K. Sen and David Hill, *Politics and Media in Twenty-First Century Indonesia*, 119–140. London: Routledge.

Britnell, Mark. 2015. *In Search of the Perfect Health System*. London: Palgrave.

Brown, C. 2003. *A Short History of Indonesia: The Unlikely Nation?* Crows Nest, New South Wales: Allen and Unwin.

Bruinessen, Martin van. 2012. "Indonesian Muslims and Their Place in the Larger World of Islam." In A. Reid, ed., *Indonesia Rising: The Repositioning of Asia's Third Giant*, 117–140. Singapore: ISEAS.

Budiartie, Gustidha, and Eve Warburton. 2015. "Indonesia's Freeport Saga." *New Mandala*, December 22. http://www.newmandala.org/indonesias-freeport-saga/.

Buehler, Michael. 2013a. "Married with Children." *Inside Indonesia* 112 (April–June).

————. 2013b. "Subnational Islamization Through Secular Parties: Comparing Shari'a Politics in Two Indonesian Provinces." *Comparative Politics* 46, no. 1 (October): 63–82.

————. 2018. "The Ephemeral Nature of Local Political Monopolies." In R. W. Hefner, ed., *Handbook of Contemporary Indonesia*, 106–117. New York: Routledge.

Bush, Robin. 2008. "Regional *Sharia* Regulations in Indonesia: Anomaly or Symptom?" In G. Fealy and S. White, eds., *Expressing Islam: Religious Life and Politics in Indonesia*, 173–191. Singapore: Institute of Southeast Asian Studies.

Camroux, David, and Annisa Srikandini. 2013. "EU-Indonesia Relations: No Expectations–Capability Gap?" In T. Christiansen, E. Kirchner, and P. Murray, eds., *The Palgrave Handbook of EU–Asia Relations*, 554–570. Basingstoke, Hants: Palgrave Macmillan.

Caraway, Teri. 2007. *Assembling Women: The Feminization of Global Manufacturing*. Ithaca: Cornell University Press.

Chauvel, Richard. 2005. *Constructing Papuan Nationalism: History, Ethnicity and Adaptation*. Policy Studies 14. Washington, DC: East-West Center.

————. 2008. "Rulers in Their Own Country?" *Inside Indonesia* 94 (October–December).

————. 2009. "Between Guns and Dialogue: Papua After the Exile's Return." *APSNet Policy Forum* 23 (April). https://nautilus.org/apsnet/between-guns-and -dialogue-papua-after-the-exiles-return/.

————. 2015. "Grandstanding on Papua: Where People-to-People Engagement Is Not Encouraged." In A. Missbach and J. Purdey, eds., *Linking People: Connections and Encounters Between Australians and Indonesians*, 73–90. Berlin: Regiospectra.

————. 2017. "Self-Determination and Rights Abuses: Papua Petitions the UN." *Indonesia at Melbourne*, November 8. http://indonesiaatmelbourne.unimelb .edu.au/self-determination-and-rights-abuses-papua-petitions-the-un/.

————. 2018. "Papua as a Multilateral Issue for Indonesia." In T. Lindsey and D. McRae, eds., *Strangers Next Door? Indonesia and Australia in the Asian Century*, 259–286. Oxford: Hart.

Chauvel, Richard, and Ikrar Nusa Bhakti. 2004. *The Papua Conflict: Jakarta's Perceptions and Policies*. Washington, DC: East-West Center.

Choi, I., and Y. Fukuoka. 2015. "Co-opting Good Governance Reform: The Rise of a Not-so-Reformist Leader in Kebumen, Central Java." *Asian Journal of Political Science* 23, no. 1: 83–101.

Clark, Marshall, and Juliet Pietsch. 2014. *Indonesia-Malaysia Relations: Cultural Heritage, Politics and Labour Migration*. Abingdon, Oxon: Routledge.

Clarke, R., G. Wandita, Samsidar, and International Center for Transitional Justice (ICTJ). 2008. *Considering Victims: The Aceh Peace Process from a Transitional Justice Perspective*. Jakarta: ICTJ.

Cochrane, J. 2018. "Indonesia Clamps Down on Simmering Independence Effort in Papua." *New York Times*, June 3. https://www.nytimes.com/2018/06/03/world/asia/indonesia-papua-independence-human-rights.html.

Coedès, G. 1975. *The Indianized States of Southeast Asia*. 3rd ed. Edited by Walter F. Vella; translated by Susan Brown Cowing. Canberra: Australian National University Press.

Colbran, Nicola. 2010. "Realities and Challenges in Realising Freedom of Religion or Belief in Indonesia." *International Journal of Human Rights* 14, no. 5: 678–704.

Colombijn, Freek, and Joost Coté, eds. 2014. *Cars, Conduits and Kampongs; Modernization of the Indonesian City, 1920–1960*. Leiden: Brill.

Committee to Protect Journalists. 2018. "Journalists Killed in Indonesia Since 1992." https://www.cpj.org/killed/asia/indonesia/.

Coppedge, Michael, et al. 2019. "V-Dem [Country-Year/Country-Date] Dataset v9." Varieties of Democracy (V-Dem) Project.

Coppel, C. 1983. *Indonesian Chinese in Crisis*. Kuala Lumpur: Oxford University Press.

———. 2017. "Reassessing Assumptions About Chinese Indonesians." *Indonesia at Melbourne Blog*, October 26. https://indonesiaatmelbourne.unimelb.edu.au/reassessing-assumptions-about-chinese-indonesians/.

Coutas, Penelope. 2006. "Fame, Fortune, *Fantasi: Indonesia Idol* and the New Celebrity." *Asian Journal of Communication* 16, no. 4: 371–392.

Cribb, R. 1994. *The Late Colonial State in Indonesia: Political and Economic Foundations of the Netherlands Indies, 1880–1942*. Leiden: KITLV Press.

———. 1999. "Nation: Making Indonesia." In D. K. Emmerson, ed., *Indonesia Beyond Suharto*, 3–38. Armonk, NY: M. E. Sharpe.

———. 2000. *Historical Atlas of Indonesia*. Honolulu: University of Hawai'i Press.

———. 2001a. "Genocide in Indonesia, 1965–1966." *Journal of Genocide Research* 3, no. 2: 219–239.

———. 2001b. "How Many Deaths? Problems in the Statistics of Massacre in Indonesia (1965–1966) and East Timor (1975–1980)." In I. Wessel and G. Wimhofer, eds., *Violence in Indonesia*, 82–89. Hamburg: Abera-Ver.

Cribb, R., and A. Kahin. 2004. *Historical Dictionary of Indonesia*. 2nd ed. Lanham, MD: Scarecrow Press.

Crouch, H. 1978. *The Army and Politics in Indonesia*. Ithaca: Cornell University Press.

———. 2000. "Indonesia: Democratization and the Threat of Disintegration." *Southeast Asian Affairs*, January 1, 2000, Vol. 27: 115–133.

———. 2010. *Political Reform in Indonesia After Soeharto*. Singapore: ISEAS.

Crouch, Melissa. 2012. *Indonesia's Blasphemy Law: Bleak Outlook for Minority Religions*. Washington, DC: East-West Center.

———. 2014. *Law and Religion in Indonesia: Conflict and the Courts in West Java*. Abingdon, Oxon: Routledge.

Davidson, Jamie S. 2008. *From Rebellion to Riots: Collective Violence on Indonesian Borneo*. Madison: University of Wisconsin Press.

De Silva, Indunil, and Sudarno Sumarto. 2014. "Does Economic Growth Really Benefit the Poor? Income Distribution Dynamics and Pro-Poor Growth in Indonesia." *Bulletin of Indonesian Economic Studies* 50, no. 2: 227–242.

Dettman, Sebastian, Thomas B. Pepinsky, and Jan H. Pierskalla. 2017. "Incumbency Advantage and Candidate Characteristics in Open-List Proportional

Representation Systems: Evidence from Indonesia." *Electoral Studies* 48 (August): 111–120.

Diamond, L. 2009. "Is a 'Rainbow Coalition' a Good Way to Govern?" *Bulletin of Indonesian Economic Studies* 45, no. 3: 337–340.

———. 2015. "Facing Up to the Democratic Recession." *Journal of Democracy* 26, no. 1 (January): 141–155.

Dibley, Thushara. 2014. "Able to Choose." *Inside Indonesia* 117 (July–September).

———. 2016. "Keeping Promises." *Inside Indonesia* 123 (January–March).

Dick, Howard, and Jeremy Mulholland. 2011. "The State as Marketplace: Slush Funds and Intra-Elite Rivalry." In E. Aspinall and G. van Klinken, eds., *The State and Illegality in Indonesia*, 65–85. Leiden: KITLV Press.

———. 2016. "The Politics of Corruption in Indonesia." *Georgetown Journal of International Affairs* 17, no. 1: 43–49.

di Gropello, Emanuela. 2013. "Role of the Education and Training Sector in Addressing Skill Match in Indonesia." In D. Suryadarma and G. W. Jones, eds., *Education in Indonesia*, 236–266. Singapore: ISEAS.

Diplomasi: Australia and Indonesia's Independence. 1994. Edited by Philip Dorling. Documents on Australian Foreign Policy 1937–1949. Canberra: AGPS.

Doeppers, Daniel F. 1972. "An Incident in the PRRI/Permesta Rebellion of 1958." *Indonesia,* no. 14 (October): 182–195.

Easter, D. 2015. "Active Soviet Military Support for Indonesia During the 1962 West New Guinea Crisis." *Cold War History* 15, no. 2: 201–220.

The Economist Intelligence Unit. 2017. *The Economist Intelligence Unit's Democracy Index.* https://infographics.economist.com/2018/DemocracyIndex/.

Ehito, Kimura. 2015. "The Struggle for Justice and Reconciliation in Post-Suharto Indonesia." *Southeast Asian Studies* 4, no. 1: 73–93.

Ellis, A. 2002. "The Indonesian Constitutional Transition: Conservatism or Fundamental Change?" *Singapore Journal of International and Comparative Law* 6: 116–153.

———. 2004. "Indonesia: Transition and Change but Electoral System Continuity." In J. M. Colomer et al., eds., *The Handbook of Electoral System Choice*, 497–511. Basingstoke: Palgrave Macmillan.

———. 2005. "Constitutional Reform in Indonesia: A Retrospective." International Institute for Democracy and Electoral Assistance. https://www.idea.int/news-media/media/constitutional-reform-indonesia-%C2%A0retrospective.

Elson, R. 2008. *The Idea of Indonesia: A History*. Cambridge: Cambridge University Press.

Emmers, Ralf. 2014. "Indonesia's Role in ASEAN: A Case of Incomplete and Sectoral Leadership." *Pacific Review* 27, no. 4: 543–562.

Erman, Erwiza. 2005. "Illegal Coalmining in West Sumatra: Access and Actors in the Post-Soeharto Era." In B. P. Resosudarmo, ed., *The Politics and Economics of Indonesia's Natural Resources*, 206–215. Singapore: Institute of Southeast Asian Studies.

European Union External Action. 2001. *Indonesia Country Strategy Paper, 2002–2006.* http://eeas.europa.eu/indonesia/csp/02_06_en.pdf.

Fealy, Greg. 2018. "Islam in Australia-Indonesia Relations: Fear, Stereotypes and Opportunity." In T. Lindsey and D. McRae, eds., *Strangers Next Door? Indonesia and Australia in the Asian Century*, 149–168. Oxford: Hart.

Feillard, A., and R. Madinier. 2011. *The End of Innocence? Indonesian Islam and the Temptations of Radicalism*. Singapore: NUS.

Feith, H. 1962. *The Decline of Constitutional Democracy in Indonesia*. Ithaca: Cornell University Press.

————. 1964. "President Soekarno, the Army and the Communists: The Triangle Changes Shape." *Asian Survey* 4, no. 8 (August): 969–980.

Fernandes, Clinton. 2010. "East Timor and the Struggle for Independence." In L. Barria and S. Roper, eds., *The Development of Institutions of Human Rights: A Comparative Study*, 163–178. New York: Palgrave Macmillan.

Finnane, A., and D. McDougall. 2010. *Bandung 1955: Little Histories*. Monash Papers on Southeast Asia 69. Caulfield East, Victoria: Monash University Press.

Fossati, Diego. 2017. "Support for Decentralization and Political Islam Go Together in Indonesia." *ISEAS Perspective* 69 (September 12).

Fox, James J., D. S. Adhuri, and I. A. P. Resosudarmo. 2005. "Unfinished Edifice or Pandora's Box? Decentralisation and Resource Management in Indonesia." In B. P. Resosudarmo, ed., *The Politics and Economics of Indonesia's Natural Resources,* 92–108. Singapore: Institute of Southeast Asian Studies.

Frakking, R. 2012. "'Who Wants to Cover Everything, Covers Nothing': The Organization of Indigenous Security Forces in Indonesia, 1945–50." *Journal of Genocide Research* 14, no. 3–4: 337–358.

Freedom House. 2015. *Indonesia: Freedom on the Net*. https://freedomhouse.org /sites/default/files/resources/FOTN%202015_Indonesia.pdf.

————. 2018. *Freedom in the World 2018: Democracy in Crisis*. https://freedomhouse .org/report/freedom-world/freedom-world-2018.

Fuad, Bahrul. 2018. "City of Traps." *Inside Indonesia* 132 (April–June).

Fukuoka, Yuki, and Kiki Verico. 2016. "Indonesia-China Economic Relations in the Twenty-First Century: Opportunities and Challenges." In Y.-C. Kim, ed., *Chinese Global Production Networks in ASEAN*, 53–75. Cham, Switzerland: Springer International.

Gandataruna, Kosim, and Kirsty Haymon. 2011. "A Dream Denied? Mining Legislation and the Constitution in Indonesia." *Bulletin of Indonesian Economic Studies* 47, no. 2: 221–231.

Gazali, Effendi. 2014. "Learning by Clicking: An Experiment with Social Media Democracy in Indonesia." *International Communication Gazette* 76, no. 4–5: 425–439.

Gellert, Paul K. 2015. "Optimism and Education: The New Ideology of Development in Indonesia." *Journal of Contemporary Asia* 45, no. 3: 371–393.

Gelman Taylor, J. 2003. *Indonesia: Peoples and Histories*. New Haven: Yale University Press.

————. 2013. *Global Indonesia*. Abingdon, Oxon; New York: Routledge.

Gindarsah, Iis. 2016. "Strategic Hedging in Indonesia's Defense Diplomacy." *Defense and Security Analysis* 32, no. 4: 336–353.

Gunia, Amy. 2019. "Social Media Gets a Bad Rap in Elections." *Time*, April 17. http://time.com/5567287/social-media-indonesia-elections-kawal-pemilu/.

Hadiprayitno, Irene Istiningsih. 2010. "Defensive Enforcement: Human Rights in Indonesia." *Human Rights Review* 11, no. 3 (September): 373–399.

Hadiz, V. R. 2003. "Reorganizing Political Power in Indonesia: A Reconsideration of So-called 'Democratic Transitions.'" *Pacific Review* 16, no. 4: 591–611.

————. 2010. *Localising Power in Post-Authoritarian Indonesia: A Southeast Asia Perspective*. Stanford: Stanford University Press.

————. 2014. "The Organizational Vehicles of Islamic Political Dissent: Social Bases, Genealogies and Strategies." In B. T. Khoo, V. R. Hadiz, and Y. Nakanishi, eds., *Between Dissent and Power: The Transformation of Islamic Politics in the Middle East and Asia*, 42–65. New York: Palgrave Macmillan.

————. 2017a. "Indonesia's Year of Democratic Setbacks: Towards a New Phase of Deepening Illiberalism?" *Bulletin of Indonesian Economic Studies* 53, no. 3: 261–278.

————. 2017b. "Behind Indonesia's Illiberal Turn." *New Mandala,* October 20.

Hadiz, V. R., and R. Robison. 2013. "The Political Economy of Oligarchy and the Reorganization of Power in Indonesia." *Indonesia* 96: 35–57.

Hamid, Usman. 2009. Letter to the UN Special Rapporteur of the Human Rights Council on the Independence of Judges and Lawyers, KontraS, September 11.

Hamilton-Hart, Natasha. 2012. *Hard Interests, Soft Illusions: Southeast Asia and American Power.* Ithaca: Cornell University Press.

————. 2009. "Indonesia and Singapore: Structure, Politics and Interests." *Contemporary Southeast Asia* 31, no. 2: 249–271.

Hamilton-Hart, Natasha, and Dave McRae. 2015. *Indonesia: Balancing the United States and China, Aiming for Independence.* Sydney: United States Studies Centre.

Hanan, David. 2010. "Innovation and Tradition in Indonesian Cinema." *Third Text* 24, no. 1: 107–121.

Harsono, Andreas. 2017a. "Public Floggings in Indonesia Top 500: *Sharia* Punishment, Including for Same-Sex Relations, Imposed in Aceh." *Human Rights Watch*, October 24. https://www.hrw.org/news/2017/10/24/public-floggings-indonesia-top-500.

————. 2017b. "Indonesia Ruling Lifts Blasphemy Prosecution Threat to Religious Minorities." *Human Rights Watch*, November 7. https://www.hrw.org/news/2017/11/07/indonesia-ruling-lifts-blasphemy-prosecution-threat-religious-minorities.

Hatta, M. 1951. "Legend and Reality Surrounding the Proclamation of 17th August." *Mimbar Indonesia* 32/33 (August).

————. 1953. "Indonesia's Foreign Policy." *Foreign Affairs* 31, no. 3 (April): 441–452.

He, Kai. 2008. "Indonesia's Foreign Policy After Soeharto: International Pressure, Democratization, and Policy Change." *International Relations of the Asia-Pacific* 8: 47–72.

Hedman, E. 2008. *Conflict, Violence and Displacement in Indonesia.* Ithaca: Southeast Asia Program, Cornell University.

Heiduk, Felix. 2014. "In It Together yet Worlds Apart? EU-ASEAN Counter-Terrorism Cooperation After the Bali Bombing." *Journal of European Integration* 36, no. 7: 697–714.

————. 2016. *Indonesia in ASEAN: Regional Leadership Between Ambition and Ambiguity.* SWP Research Paper. Berlin: Stiftung Wissenschaft und Politik.

Herbert, Jeff. 2008. "The Legal Framework of Human Rights in Indonesia." In T. Lindsey, ed., *Indonesia: Law and Society*, 456–482. Leichardt, New South Wales: Federation Press.

Hernawan, Budi J. 2018. *Torture and Peacebuilding in Indonesia: The Case of Papua.* Abingdon, Oxon: Routledge.

Heryanto, A. 2006. *State Terrorism and Political Identity in Indonesia: Fatally Belonging.* New York: Routledge.

————. 2011. "Upgraded Piety and Pleasure: The New Middle Class and Islam in Indonesian Popular Culture." In A. N. Weintraub, ed., *Islam and Popular Culture in Indonesia and Malaysia*, 60–82. Abingdon, Oxon: Routledge.

————. 2014a. "The Cinematic Contest of Popular Post-Islamism." In J. Schlehe and E. Sandkühler, eds., *Religion, Tradition and the Popular: Transcultural Views from Asia and Europe*, 139–156. Bielefeld: Transcript.

————. 2014b. *Identity and Pleasure: The Politics of Indonesian Screen Culture.* Singapore: NUS Press and Kyoto University Press.

Hewett, Rosalind. 2016. "The Forgotten Killings." *Inside Indonesia* 125 (July–September). http://www.insideindonesia.org/the-forgotten-killings.

Hidayat, Papang. 2011. *Transitional Justice for Two Countries? The Commission for Truth and Friendship Between Indonesia and Timor-Leste.* Lambert Academic.

Hill, D. T. 2007. *The Press in New Order Indonesia.* Jakarta: Equinox Publishing.

Hill, Hal. 2014. "An Introduction to the Issues." In H. Hill, ed., *Regional Dynamics in a Decentralized Indonesia*, 1–22. Singapore: ISEAS.

———. 2015. "The Indonesian Economy During the Yudhoyono Decade." In E. Aspinall, M. Mietzner, and D. Tomsa, eds., *The Yudhoyono Presidency: Indonesia's Decade of Stability and Stagnation*, 281–302. Singapore: ISEAS.

Hillman, Ben. 2017. "Increasing Women's Parliamentary Representation in Asia and the Pacific: The Indonesian Experience." *Asia and the Pacific Policy Studies* 4, no. 1: 38–49.

Hindley, D. 1964. *The Communist Party of Indonesia, 1951–1963*. Berkeley: University of California Press.

Hoesterey, James B., and Marshall Clark. 2012. "*Film Islami*: Gender, Piety and Pop Culture in Post-Authoritarian Indonesia." *Asian Studies Review* 36, no. 2: 207–226.

Honna, Jun. 2013. "Security Challenges and Military Reform in Post-Authoritarian Indonesia: The Impact of Separatism, Terrorism and Communal Violence." In J. Rüland, M-G. Manea, and H. Born, eds., *The Politics of Military Reform: Experiences from Indonesia and Nigeria*, 185–200. Heidelberg: Springer.

Horowitz, Donald L. 2013. *Constitutional Change and Democracy in Indonesia*. New York: Cambridge University Press.

Hughes-Freeland, Felicia. 2011. "Women's Creativity in Indonesian Cinema." *Indonesia and the Malay World* 39, no. 115: 417–444.

Hull, T. H. 2012. "Indonesia's Demographic Mosaic." In H. Groth and A. Sousa-Poza, eds., *Population Dynamics in Muslim Countries: Assembling the Jigsaw*, 195–209. Berlin: Springer.

———. 2016. "Indonesia's Fertility Levels, Trends and Determinants: Dilemmas of Analysis." In C. Guilmoto and G. W. Jones, eds., *Contemporary Demographic Transformations in China, India and Indonesia*, 133–153. Berlin: Springer.

Hull, T. H., and N. Widyantoro. 2010. "Abortion and Politics in Indonesia." In A. Whittaker, ed., *Abortion in Asia: Local Dilemmas, Global Politics*, 175–198. New York: Berghahn Books.

Human Rights Watch (HRW). 2007a. *Out of Sight: Endemic Abuse and Impunity in Papua's Central Highlands*. New York: Human Rights Watch.

———. 2007b. *Protest and Punishment: Political Prisoners in Papua*. New York: Human Rights Watch.

———. 2013. *In Religion's Name: Abuses Against Religious Minorities in Indonesia*. New York: Human Rights Watch.

———. 2016. *Living in Hell: Abuses Against People with Psychosocial Disabilities in Indonesia*. New York: Human Rights Watch.

———. 2018. "Indonesia's Blasphemy Law Survives Court Challenge." *HRW Despatches,* July 26. https://www.hrw.org/news/2018/07/26/indonesias-blasphemy-law-survives-court-challenge.

Huntington, S. P. 1991. "Democracy's Third Wave." *Journal of Democracy* 2, no. 2 (Spring): 12–34.

Ibn Battuta. 1929. *Travels in Asia and Africa, 1325–1354*. Translated and selected by H. A. R. Gibb. London: Routledge.

Index Mundi. 2000. "Millennium Development Goals: Indonesia." http://www.indexmundi.com/indonesia/millennium-development-goals.html.

Indikator. 2016. *Revisi UU KPK dan Pertaruhan Modal Politik Jokowi: Temuan Survei Nasional, 18–29 Januari 2016*. Jakarta. https://indikator.co.id/uploads/20160208141409.Bahan_Rilis_Indi_KPKJOKOWI.pdf.

Indonesia. 2017. National Report submitted to United Nations, Human Rights Council, Working Group on the Universal Periodic Review, Twenty-Seventh session, May 1–12, 2017. Doc: A/HRC/WG.6/27/IDN/1.

Indonesia Investments. 2017. "Unemployment in Indonesia." https://www.indonesia
-investments.com/finance/macroeconomic-indicators/unemployment/item255?.
Institute for Policy Analysis of Conflict (IPAC). 2016. *Update on the Indonesian
Military's Influence.* Jakarta.
———. 2017a. *Policy Miscalculations on Papua.* IPAC Report no. 40. Jakarta.
———. 2017b. *Marawi, the "East Asia Wilayah," and Indonesia.* IPAC Report no.
38. Jakarta.
———. 2018. *After Ahok: The Islamist Agenda in Indonesia.* IPAC Report no. 44.
Jakarta.
Intan, Benyamin F. 2012. "Religious Violence in Indonesia: The Role of State and
Civil Society." *International Journal for Religious Freedom* 5, no. 2: 63–77.
International Centre for Transitional Justice (ICTJ) and Komisi untuk Orang Hilang
dan Korban Tindak Kekerasan (KontraS). 2011. *Derailed: Transitional Justice
in Indonesia Since the Fall of Soeharto.* Jakarta.
International Coalition for Papua (ICP). 2017. *Human Rights in West Papua 2017:
The Fifth Report Covering Events from January 2015 Until December 2016.*
Wuppertal.
International Crisis Group (ICG). 2003. *Jemaah Islamiyah in South East Asia:
Damaged but Still Dangerous.* Asia Report no. 63. Jakarta.
———. 2011. *Waging Peace: ASEAN and the Thai-Cambodian Border Conflict.*
Report no. 215. Jakarta.
———. 2013. *Dividing Papua: How Not to Do It.* Briefing/Asia no. 24. Jakarta.
International Labour Organization, International Monetary Fund, Organisation for
Economic Co-operation and Development, and World Bank Group. 2015.
*Income Inequality and Labour Income Share in G20 Countries: Trends, Impacts
and Causes.* http://www.ilo.org/wcmsp5/groups/public/—-europe/—-ro-geneva
/—-ilo-ankara/documents/meetingdocument/wcms_398774.pdf.
International Organisation for Migration (IOM). 2010. *Labour Migration from
Indonesia: An Overview of Indonesian Migration to Selected Destinations in
Asia and the Middle East.* Jakarta.
International Peoples Tribunal (IPT). 2017. *Final Report of the IPT 1965: Findings
and Documents of the IPT 1965.* Bandung: Ultimus.
Irawanto, Budi. 2011. "Riding Waves of Change: Islamic Press in Post-Authoritarian
Indonesia." In K. Sen and D. Hill, eds., *Politics and the Media in Twenty-First
Century Indonesia*, 67–84. Hoboken, NJ: Taylor and Francis.
I-Tsing. 1894. *Mémoire Composé àl'Époque de la Grande Dynastie T'ang sur les
Religieux Éminents qui Allèrent Chercher la Loi dans les Pays d'Occident.*
Translated into French by Édouard Chavannes. Paris: E. Leroux.
Jacq-Hergoualc'h, Michel. 2002. *The Malay Peninsula, Crossroads of the Maritime
Silk Road (100 BC–1300 AD).* Leiden: E. J. Brill.
Joint Commission International. 2017. "JCI-Accredited Organizations: Indonesia."
http://www.jointcommissioninternational.org/about-jci/jci-accredited-organizations
/?c=Indonesia.
"Jokowi Launches Indonesia Health Card and Smart Card." 2014. *Jakarta Globe,*
November 3.
Jolliffe, Jill. 2005. "Jakarta's Timor Trials 'a Sham.'" *Age,* June 19.
Jones, Sidney. 2018. "How ISIS Has Changed Terrorism in Indonesia." *New York
Times,* May 22.
Junaedi. 2016. "Usut Korupsi dana BOS Rp 400 Juta, Guru dan Kepsek di Polewale
Diperiksa Polisi." *Kompas.com,* July 27. http://internasional.kompas.com/read
/2016/07/27/08442021/usut.korupsi.dana.bos.rp.400.juta.guru.dan.kepsek.di
.polewali.diperiksa.polisi.

Jung, Eunsook. 2016. "Campaigning for All Indonesians: The Politics of Healthcare in Indonesia." *Contemporary Southeast Asia* 38, no. 3 (December): 476–494.

Junge, J. Fabian. 2008. *Kesempatan yang Hilang, Janji yang tak Terpenuhi. Pengadilan HAM Ad Hoc untuk Kejahatan di Tanjung Priok 1984.* Jakarta: KontraS /Watch Indonesia!.

Jurriëns, Edwin. 2016. "'TV or Not TV': Spelling the Indonesian Media with Veven Sp. Wardhana." *Bijdragen tot de Taal-, Land- en Volkenkunde* 172: 33–65.

Juwono, V. 2016. "Berantas Korupsi: A Political History of Governance Reform and Anti-corruption Initiatives in Indonesia 1945–2014." PhD diss., London School of Economics and Political Science.

Kahin, A. 1985. *Regional Dynamics of the Indonesian Revolution: Unity from Diversity.* Honolulu: University of Hawaii Press.

———. 1999. *Rebellion to Integration: West Sumatra and the Indonesian Polity, 1926–1998.* Amsterdam: Amsterdam University Press.

———. 2015. *Historical Dictionary of Indonesia.* 3rd ed. Lanham, MD: Rowman and Littlefield.

Kahin, A., and G. McT. Kahin. 1995. *Subversion as Foreign Policy: The Secret Eisenhower and Dulles Debacle in Indonesia.* New York: New Press.

Kahin, G. McT. 1952. *Nationalism and Revolution in Indonesia.* Ithaca: Cornell University Press.

Kammen, Douglas. 2003. "Security Disorders." *Inside Indonesia* 73 (January–March). https://www.insideindonesia.org/security-disorders.

"Kemenristekdikti Terima Laporan 141 Pejabat Berijazah palsu." 2017. *Tempo.co,* February 2.

Kementerian Dalam Negeri Republik (Kemendagri). 2014. *Pembentukan Daerah-Daerah Otonom di Indonesia Sampai Dengan tahun 2014* (The establishment of autonomous regions up to 2014). Jakarta.

Kent, Lia. 2009. "The Politics of Remembering and Forgetting." *Inside Indonesia* 96 (April–June).

Kent, Lia, and Rizki Amalia Affiat. 2017. "Gambling with Truth." *Inside Indonesia* 129 (July–September). https://www.insideindonesia.org/gambling-with-truth.

Khanis, Suvianita. 2013. "Human Rights and the LGBTI Movement in Indonesia." *Asian Journal of Women's Studies* 19, no. 1: 127–138.

King, Dwight Y. 2000. "The 1999 Electoral Reforms in Indonesia: Debate, Design and Implementation." *Southeast Asian Journal of Social Science* 28, no. 2: 89–110.

———. 2003. *Half-Hearted Reform: Electoral Institutions and the Struggle for Democracy in Indonesia.* Westport, CT: Praeger.

Kingham, Robert, and Jemma Parsons. 2013. "Integrating Islamic Schools into Indonesian National Education System: A Case of Architecture Over Implementation?" In D. Suryadarma and G. W. Jones, eds., *Education in Indonesia,* 68–81. Singapore: ISEAS.

Kitley, Philip. 2000. *Television, Nation, and Culture in Indonesia.* Athens: Ohio University Press.

Komnas Perempuan. 2012. *Stagnansi Sistem Hukum: Menggantung asa Perempuan Korban. Catatan Tahunan Tentang Kekerasan Terhadap Perempuan 2011.* Jakarta.

Kovacs, Amanda. 2014. *Saudi Arabia Exporting Salafi Education and Radicalizing Indonesia's Muslims.* GIGA Focus no. 7. Hamburg: German Institute of Global and Area Studies. https://www.giga-hamburg.de/en/system/files/publications/gf _international_1407.pdf.

KPK. 2017. "Lampiran Siaran Pers Kinerja KPK tahun 2017." https://www.kpk.go .id/images/pdf/Lampiran_Siaran_Pers_Kinerja_KPK_2017_rev.pdf.

Kumar, Ann. 2012. "Dominion over Palm and Pine: Early Indonesia's Maritime Reach." In Geoff Wade and Li Tana, eds., *Anthony Reid and the Study of the Southeast Asian Past*, 101–124. Singapore: ISEAS.

Kusuma, Hendra. 2018. "Angka Kemiskinan Terbesar RI Ada di Maluku-Papua 21.2%." *Detik*, July 16. https://finance.detik.com/berita-ekonomi-bisnis/d-4117175 /angka-kemiskinan-terbesar-ri-ada-di-maluku-papua-212.

Laksmana, Evan. 2011. "Indonesia's Rising Regional and Global Profile: Does Size Really Matter?" *Contemporary Southeast Asia* 33, no. 2: 157–182.

Lawson, Stephanie. 2016. "West Papua, Indonesia and the Melanesian Spearhead Group: Competing Logics in Regional and International Politics." *Australian Journal of International Affairs* 70, no. 5: 506–524.

Leifer, Michael. 2005. *Selected Work on Southeast Asia*. Singapore: ISEAS.

Lev, Daniel S. 1966. *The Transition to Guided Democracy: Indonesian Politics, 1957–1959*. Ithaca: Modern Indonesia Project, Southeast Asia Program, Cornell University.

Lewis, Blane D. 2014. "Twelve Years of Fiscal Decentralization: A Balance Sheet." In H. Hill, ed., *Regional Dynamics in a Decentralized Indonesia*, 135–155. Singapore: ISEAS.

Lim, Merlyna. 2017. "Freedom to Hate: Social Media, Algorithmic Enclaves, and the Rise of Tribal Nationalism in Indonesia." *Critical Asian Studies* 49, no. 3: 411–427.

Lindsay, Jennifer. 2011. "Media and Morality: Pornography Post Suharto." In K. Sen and D. Hill, eds., *Politics and the Media in Twenty-First Century Indonesia*, 172–194. Hoboken, NJ: Taylor and Francis.

Lindsey, Tim. 2002. "Indonesian Constitutional Reform: Muddling Towards Democracy?" *Singapore Journal of International and Comparative Law* 6: 244–301.

Lindsey, Tim, and Simon Butt. 2016. "State Power to Restrict Religious Freedom: An Overview of the Legal Framework." In T. Lindsey and H. Pausacker, eds., *Religion, Law and Intolerance in Indonesia*, 19–41. London: Routledge.

Lindsey, Tim, and Dave McRae, eds. 2018. *Strangers Next Door? Indonesia and Australia in the Asian Century*. Oxford: Hart.

Linton, Suzannah. 2004. "Unravelling the First Three Trials at Indonesia's Ad Hoc Court for Human Rights Violations in East Timor." *Leiden Journal of International Law* 17, no. 2 (June): 303–361.

Locher-Scholten, Elsbeth. 2004. *Sumatran Sultanate and Colonial State: Jambi and the Rise of Dutch Imperialism, 1830–1907*. Translated by Beverley Jackson. Ithaca: Southeast Asia Program, Cornell University.

Luhulima, C. P. F., E. M. L. Panjaitan, and A. Widiana. 2009. "EU Images in Indonesia." In M. Holland, N. Chaban, and P. Ryan, eds., *EU Through the Eyes of Asia. Volume 2: New Cases, New Findings*, 93–124. World Scientific Publishing.

Lustig, N. 2016. "Inequality and Fiscal Redistribution in Middle Income Countries: Brazil, Chile, Colombia, Indonesia, Mexico, Peru and South Africa." *Journal of Globalization and Development* 7, no. 1 (June): 17–60.

Mackie, J. 1975. *Konfrontasi: The Indonesia-Malaysia Dispute, 1963–1966*. Kuala Lumpur: Oxford University Press for the Australian Institute of International Affairs.

———. 2005. *Bandung 1955: Non-Alignment and Afro-Asian Solidarity*. Singapore: Editions Didier Millet.

———. 2007. *Australia and Indonesia: Current Problems, Future Prospects*. Lowy Institute Paper 19. Sydney: Lowy Institute for International Policy.

———. 2010. "The Bandung Conference and Afro-Asian Solidarity: Indonesian Aspects." In A. Finnane and D. McDougall, eds., *Bandung 1955: Little Histories*. Caulfield East, Victoria: Monash University Press.

Mahbubani, Kishore. 2018. "Kishore Mahbubani on China's Rise and America's Myopia." *Sinica podcast*, February 8. https://supchina.com/podcast/kishore -mahbubani-chinas-rise-americas-myopia/.

"Majority of Disabled Lack Access to Education." 2013. *Jakarta Post*, March 19. http://www.thejakartapost.com/news/2013/03/19/majority-disabled-lack-access-education.html.

Malley, Michael. 2009. "Decentralization and Democratic Transition in Indonesia." In G. Bland and C. J. Arnson, eds., *Democratic Deficits: Addressing Challenges to Sustainability and Consolidation Around the World*, 135–146. Washington, DC: Woodrow Wilson International and RTI International.

Manning, Chris, and Sudarno Sumarto, eds. 2011. *Employment, Living Standards and Poverty in Contemporary Indonesia*. Singapore: ISEAS.

Mantong, Andrew. 2017. "Why Is There No Serious Opposition to Trump in Indonesia?" *Indonesia at Melbourne*, April 4. http://indonesiaatmelbourne.unimelb.edu.au/why-is-there-no-serious-opposition-to-trump-in-indonesia/.

Maralani, Vida. 2008. "The Changing Relationship Between Family Size and Educational Attainment over the Course of Socioeconomic Development: Evidence from Indonesia." *Demography* 45, no. 3: 693–717.

Mas'udi, Wawan. 2017. "Creating Legitimacy in Decentralized Indonesia: Joko 'Jokowi' Widodo's Path to Legitimacy in Solo, 2005–2012." PhD diss., University of Melbourne.

McCarthy, John F. 2011. "The Limits of Legality: State, Governance and Resource Control in Indonesia." In E. Aspinall and G. van Klinken, eds., *The State and Illegality in Indonesia*, 89–106. Leiden: KITLV Press.

McCulloch, Lesley. 2005. *Aceh: Then and Now*. London: Minority Rights Group International.

McDonald, Peter. 2014. "The Demography of Indonesia in Comparative Perspective." *Bulletin of Indonesian Economic Studies* 50, no. 1: 29–52.

McGibbon, Rod. 2004. *Secessionist Challenges in Aceh and Papua: Is Special Autonomy the Solution?* Washington, DC: East-West Center.

McGrath, K. 2016. "Australia's Recognition of the Indonesian Annexation of East Timor: The Timor Sea Boundary Negotiation Nexus (1976–1978)." In S. Smith, A. B. da Silva, N. Canas Mendes, A. da Costa Ximenes, C. Fernandes, and M. Leach, eds., *Timor-Leste: The Local, the Regional and the Global*, vol. 1, 296–305. Dili: Timor-Leste Studies Association.

McGregor, K. 2007. *History in Uniform: Military Ideology and the Construction of Indonesia's Past*. Singapore: ASAA, in association with NUS Press.

McGregor, K., J. Melvin, and A. Pohlman. 2018. "New Interpretations of the Causes, Dynamics and Legacies of the Indonesian Genocide." In K. McGregor, J. Melvin, and A. Pohlman, eds., *The Indonesian Genocide of 1965: Causes, Dynamics and Legacies*, 1–26. Basingstoke: Palgrave Macmillan.

McGregor, K., and J. Purdey. 2016. "The IPT 1965 Is a Historic Moral Intervention: Will It Finally Lead to Action?" *Indonesia at Melbourne*, July 29.

McGregor, K., and K. Setiawan. 2019. "The Shift from International to 'Indonesian' Justice Measures for Addressing Past Human Rights Violations in the Post-Suharto Era." *Journal of Contemporary Asia* (7 March): 1–25.

McIntyre, A. 2005. *The Indonesian Presidency: The Shift from Personal Toward Constitutional Rule*. Lanham, MD: Rowman and Littlefield.

McKenzie, Michael. 2018. "A Common Enemy: Police Cooperation Between Australia and Indonesia." In T. Lindsey and D. McRae, eds., *Strangers Next Door? Australia and Indonesia in the Asian Century*, 211–234. Oxford: Hart.

McKinsey and Company. 2016. *Unlocking Indonesia's Digital Opportunity*. Jakarta: McKinsey Indonesia.

McLeod, Ross H. 2000. "Soeharto's Indonesia: A Better Class of Corruption." *Agenda* 7, no. 2: 99–112.

McRae, Dave. 2002. "A Discourse on Separatists." *Indonesia* 74 (October): 37–58.

————. 2017. "Indonesian Capital Punishment in Comparative Perspective." *Bijdragen tot de Taal-, Land- en Volkenkunde* 173, no. 1: 1–22.

————. 2013a. *A Few Poorly Organised Men: Interreligious Violence in Poso, Indonesia.* Leiden: Brill.

————. 2013b. "Indonesian Politics in 2013: The Search for New Leadership." *Bulletin of Indonesian Economic Studies* 49, no. 3: 289–304.

————. 2014a. "Prabowo Continues His Anti-Democratic Rhetoric." *Indonesia at Melbourne*, June 30.

————. 2014b. *The 2014 Indonesian Elections and Australia-Indonesia Relations.* CILIS Policy Paper 7. Melbourne: Centre for Indonesian Law, Islam and Society, University of Melbourne.

————. 2014c. *More Talk Than Walk: Indonesia as a Foreign Policy Actor.* Lowy Institute Analysis. Sydney: Lowy Institute for International Policy.

————. 2018. "A Fair Dinkum Partnership? Australia-Indonesia Ties During the Yudhoyono Era." In U. Fiona, ed., *Million Friends, Zero Enemies: Indonesia's Global Role Under Susilo Bambang Yudhoyono.* Singapore: ISEAS.

————. 2019. "Indonesia's Foreign Policy Takes an Illiberal Turn? Indonesia's South China Sea Diplomacy." *Journal of Contemporary Asia*, 24 April, https://doi.org/10.1080/00472336.2019.1601240.

McRae, Dave, and Diane Zhang. 2015. "Local Elections: The Power of Incumbency." *Indonesia at Melbourne*, December 8. http://indonesiaatmelbourne.unimelb.edu.au/local-elections-the-power-of-incumbency/.

Melvin, Jess. 2017. "Mechanics of Mass Murder: A Case for Understanding the Indonesian Killings as Genocide." *Journal of Genocide Research* 19, no. 4: 487–511.

————. 2018. *The Army and the Indonesian Genocide: Mechanics of Mass Murder.* London, New York: Routledge.

Mietzner, Marcus. 2010. "Indonesia's Direct Elections: Empowering the Electorate or Entrenching the New Order Oligarchy?" In E. Aspinall and G. Fealy, eds., *Soeharto's New Order and Its Legacy: Essays in Honour of Harold Crouch*, 173–190. Canberra: ANU ePress.

————. 2011. "Funding *Pilkada*: Illegal Campaign Financing in Indonesia's Local Elections." In E. Aspinall and G. van Klinken, eds., *The State and Illegality in Indonesia*, 123–138. Leiden: KITLV Press.

————. 2013. *Money, Power, and Ideology: Political Parties in Post-Authoritarian Indonesia.* Singapore: NUS Press.

————. 2014. "Indonesia's Decentralization: The Rise of Local Identities and the Survival of the Nation-State." In H. Hill, ed., *Regional Dynamics in a Decentralized Indonesia*, 45–67. Singapore: ISEAS.

————. 2015. "Dysfunction by Design: Political Finance and Corruption in Indonesia." *Critical Asian Studies* 47, no. 4: 587–610.

————. 2016. "The Sukarno Dynasty in Indonesia: Between Institutionalisation, Ideological Continuity and Crises of Succession." *South East Asia Research* 24, no. 3 (September): 355–368.

Mietzner, Marcus, and Burhanuddin Muhtadi. 2017. "Ahok's Satisfied Non-Voters: An Anatomy." *New Mandala*, May 5. http://www.newmandala.org/ahoks-satisfied-non-voters-anatomy/.

Misnaniarti, and Dumilah Ayuningtyas. 2016. "Unmet Need for Family Planning in Indonesia and the Policy Strategy of Intervention in Several Countries." *International Journal of Reproduction, Contraception, Obstetrics and Gynecology* 5, no. 6: 1680–1685.

Misol, Lisa. 2006. *Too High a Price: The Human Rights Cost of the Indonesian Military's Economic Activities.* New York: Human Rights Watch.

Missbach, Antje. 2016. "The Rohingya in Aceh: Displaced, Exploited and Nearly Forgotten." *Indonesia at Melbourne*, March 14. http://indonesiaatmelbourne .unimelb.edu.au/the-rohingya-in-aceh-displaced-exploited-and-nearly-forgotten/.

———. 2018. "Big Fears About Small Boats: How Asylum Seekers Keep Upsetting the Indonesia–Australia Relationship." In T. Lindsey and D. McRae, eds., *Strangers Next Door? Indonesia and Australia in the Asian Century*, 125–148. Oxford: Hart.

Molaei, Hamideh. 2015. "Discursive Opportunity Structures and the Contribution of Social Media to the Success of Social Movements in Indonesia." *Information, Communication and Society*, 18, no. 1: 94–108.

Morfit, M. 1981. "Pancasila: The Indonesian State Ideology According to the New Order Government." *Asian Survey* 21, no. 8 (August): 838–851.

Mortimer, R. 1974. *Indonesian Communism Under Sukarno: Ideology and Politics, 1959–1965*. Ithaca: Cornell University Press.

Muhidin, Salut, and Ariane Utomo. 2015. "Global Indonesian Diaspora: How Many Are There and Where Are They?" *Journal of ASEAN Studies* 3, no. 2: 93–101.

Munro, Jenny. 2013. "The Violence of Inflated Possibilities: Education, Transformation, and Diminishment in Wamena, Papua." *Indonesia* 95: 25–46.

Murphy, Ann Marie. 2012. "Democratization and Indonesian Foreign Policy: Implications for the United States." *Asia Policy,* no. 13 (January): 83–111.

Naafs, Suzanne. 2013. "Youth, Gender, and the Workplace: Shifting Opportunities and Aspirations in an Indonesian Industrial Town." *Annals of the American Academy of Political and Social Science* 646 (March): 233–250.

National Democratic Institute for International Affairs (NDI). 1999. *The 1999 Presidential Election and Post-Election Developments in Indonesia: A Post-Election Assessment Report*. Washington, DC: NDI.

National Security Archive. 2017. "US Embassy Tracked Indonesia Mass Murder." Briefing Paper no. 607. October 17.

Neumann, Klaus, and Savitri Taylor. 2009. "Australia, Indonesia, and West Papuan Refugees, 1962–2009." *International Relations of the Asia-Pacific* 10, no. 1: 1–31.

Nurjannah, I., J. Mills, T. Park, and K. Usher. 2015. "Human Rights of the Mentally Ill in Indonesia." *International Nursing Review* 62, no. 2: 153–161.

OECD/ADB. 2015. *Education in Indonesia: Rising to the Challenge*. Paris: OECD Publishing.

Oxfam International. 2017. *Towards a More Equal Indonesia.* Oxfam Briefing Paper. February. Oxford. https://www.oxfam.org/sites/www.oxfam.org/files/bp -towards-more-equal-indonesia-230217-en_0.pdf.

Padmo, Dewi, T. Belawati, O. Idrus, and L. S. Ardiasih. 2017. "The State of Practice of Mobile Learning in Universitas Terbuka Indonesia." In A. Murphy, H. Farley, and L. E. Dyson, eds., *Mobile Learning in Higher Education in the Asia-Pacific Region: Harnessing Trends and Challenging Orthodoxies*, 173–193. Singapore: Springer.

Palatino, Mong. 2013. "More Religion, Less Science for Indonesian Students." *Diplomat*, August 21. http://thediplomat.com/2013/08/more-religion-less-science -for-indonesian-students/.

Palmer, Wayne. 2012. "Discretion and the Trafficking-Like Practices of the Indonesian State." In M. Ford, L. Lyons, and W. van Schendel, eds., *Labour Migration and Human Trafficking in Southeast Asia: Critical Perspectives*, 149–166. London: Routledge.

Parameswaran, Prashanth. 2019. "Indonesia's Indo-Pacific Approach: Between Promises and Perils." *Diplomat,* March 15. https://thediplomat.com/2019/03 /indonesias-indo-pacific-approach-between-promises-and-perils/.

Parker, Lyn, and Pam Nilan. 2013. *Adolescents in Contemporary Indonesia*. Abingdon, Oxon: Routledge.

Parks, T., N. Colletta, and B. Oppenheim. 2013. *The Contested Corners of Asia: Subnational Conflict and International Development Assistance.* San Francisco: Asia Foundation.

Parsons, Nicholas, and Marcus Mietzner. 2009. "Sharia By-laws in Indonesia: A Legal and Political Analysis." *Australian Journal of Asian Law* 11, no. 2: 190–217.

Pausacker, Helen. 2014. "Sanctions Against Popstars . . . and Politicians? Indonesia's 2008 Pornography Law and Its Aftermath." In B. Platzdasch and J. Saravanamuttu, eds., *Religious Minorities in Muslim-Majority Localities of Southeast Asia: Areas of Toleration and Conflict*, 89–112. Singapore: Institute for Southeast Asian Studies.

Pepinsky, T. 2014. "Is Indonesia an Unusual Muslim Country?" November 2. https://tompepinsky.com/2014/11/02/is-indonesia-an-unusual-muslim-country/.

Perdana, Ari, and John Maxwell. 2011. "The Evolution of Poverty Alleviation Policies: Ideas, Issues and Actors." In C. Manning and S. Sumarto, eds., *Employment, Living Standards and Poverty in Contemporary Indonesia*, 272–290. Singapore: ISEAS.

Perwita, Anak Agung Banyu. 2007. *Indonesia and the Muslim World: Islam and Secularism in the Foreign Policy of Soeharto and Beyond.* Copenhagen: NIAS.

Pichler, Melanie. 2015. "Legal Dispossession: State Strategies and Selectivities in the Expansion of Indonesian Palm Oil and Agrofuel Production." *Development and Change* 46, no. 3 (May): 508–533.

Pisani, E. 2013. "A Nation of Dunces?" *Inside Indonesia* 114 (October–December).

Pisani, E., and M. Buehler. 2017. "Why Do Indonesian Politicians Promote Shari'a Laws? An Analytic Framework for Muslim-Majority Democracies." *Third World Quarterly* 38, no. 3: 734–752.

Pisani, E., M. O. Kok, and K. Nugroho. 2017. "Indonesia's Road to Universal Health Coverage: A Political Journey." *Health Policy and Planning* 32, no. 2 (March): 267–276.

Pohlman, A. 2015. *Women, Sexual Violence and the Indonesian Killings of 1965–66.* Abingdon, Oxon: Routledge.

———. 2017. "The Spectre of Communist Women, Sexual Violence and Citizenship in Indonesia." *Sexualities* 20, no. 1–2: 196–211.

Postill, J., and K. Saputro. 2017. "Digital Activism in Contemporary Indonesia: Victims, Volunteers and Voices." In E. Jurriëns and R. Tapsell, eds., *Digital Indonesia: Connectivity and Divergence*, 127–145. Singapore: ISEAS.

Pramono, Stafanus Teguh Edi. 2019. "Rusuh di Ujung Pemilu." *Tempo*, May 26. https://majalah.tempo.co/read/157782/rusuh-di-ujung-pemilu.

Purdey, J. 2006. *Anti-Chinese Violence in Indonesia, 1996–1999.* Honolulu: University of Hawai'i Press.

———. 2016a. "Political Families in Southeast Asia." *South East Asia Research* 24, no. 3 (September): 319–327.

———. 2016b. "Narratives to Power: The Case of the Djojohadikusumo Family Dynasty over Four Generations." *South East Asia Research* 24, no. 3 (September): 369–385.

Purdey, J., and A. Missbach. 2015. "Australia-Indonesia Relations: How to Stop the Roller Coaster?" In A. Missbach and J. Purdey, eds., *Linking People: Connections and Encounters Between Australians and Indonesians*, 1–24. Berlin: Regiospectra.

Rahadian, Lalu. 2017. "Pemerintah Tegaskan Tidak Ada Pemekaran Wilayah Hingga 2018." *CNN Indonesia,* June 20. https://www.cnnindonesia.com/nasional/20170620140423-20-223003/pemerintah-tegaskan-tidak-ada-pemekaran-wilayah-hingga-2018.

Rakhmani, Inaya. 2014a. "Mainstream Islam: Television Industry Practice and Trends in Indonesian *Sinetron*." *Asian Journal of Social Science* 42: 435–466.

————. 2014b. "The Commercialization of *Da'wah*: Understanding Indonesian *Sinetron* and Their Portrayal of Islam." *International Communication Gazette* 76, no. 4–5: 340–359.

Rasyid, M. Ryaas. 2004. "The Policy of Decentralization in Indonesia." In J. Alm, J. Martinez-Vazquez, and S. M. Indrawati, eds., *Reforming Intergovernmental Fiscal Relations and the Rebuilding of Indonesia: The "Big Bang" Program and Its Economic Consequences*, 65–74. Cheltenham, UK: Edward Elgar.

Reid, Anthony. 2005. *An Indonesian Frontier: Acehnese and Other Histories of Sumatra.* Singapore: Singapore University Press.

Reporters Without Borders. 2006. "Four Films on Aceh and East Timor Censored." *News*, November 27.

————. 2018. "Indonesia." https://rsf.org/en/indonesia.

Reuters. 2017. "Graft Suspected in Indonesian Anti-Corruption Monument Project." November 9. https://www.reuters.com/article/us-indonesia-corruption/graft-suspected -in-indonesian-anti-corruption-monument-project-idUSKBN1D91CQ?il=0.

Ricklefs, M. C. 2001. *A History of Modern Indonesia Since c. 1200.* 3rd ed. Stanford: Stanford University Press.

Rinaldo, Rachel. 2008. "Envisioning the Nation: Women Activists, Religion and the Public Sphere in Indonesia." *Social Forces* 86, no. 4: 1781–1804.

Ristianto, Christofous. 2019. "Riset Puskapol UI: Persentase Caleg Terpilih Perempuan Bertambah Jadi 20,05 persen." *Kompas.com*, May 27. https://nasional .kompas.com/read/2019/05/27/13174291/riset-puskapol-ui-persentase-caleg -terpilih-perempuan-bertambah-jadi-2005.

Robison, Richard, and V. Hadiz. 2004. *Reorganising Power in Indonesia: The Politics of Oligarchy in an Age of Markets.* Abingdon, Oxon: Taylor and Francis.

Rompies, Karuni, and Jewel Topsfield. 2017. "Two Men Receive 83 Lashes for Gay Sex in Indonesian Province of Aceh." *Sydney Morning Herald*, May 23.

Roosa, J. 2006. *Pretext for Mass Murder: The September 30th Movement and Suharto's Coup d'État in Indonesia.* Madison: University of Wisconsin Press.

Rosser, Andrew. 2012. "Realising Free Health Care for the Poor in Indonesia: The Politics of Illegal Fees." *Journal of Contemporary Asia* 42, no. 2: 255–275.

————. 2018. *Beyond Access: Making Indonesia's Education System Work.* Lowy Institute Analyses. February. https://www.lowyinstitute.org/publications/beyond -access-making-indonesia-s-education-system-work.

Rothenberg, A., A. Gaduh, N. E. Burger, C. Chazali, I. Tjandraningsih, R. Radikun, C. Sutera, and S. Weilant. 2016. "Rethinking Indonesia's Informal Sector." *World Development* 80 (April): 96–113.

Rüland, Jürgen. 2009. "Deepening ASEAN Cooperation Through Democratization? The Indonesian Legislature and Foreign Policymaking." *International Relations of the Asia Pacific* 9, no. 3: 373–402.

————. 2017. "Democratizing Foreign-Policy Making in Indonesia and the Democratization of ASEAN: A Role Theory Analysis." *TRaNS* 5, no. 1: 49–73.

Rutherford, D. 1999. "Waiting for the End in Biak: Violence, Order, and a Flag Raising." *Indonesia* 67: 39–59.

Safitri, Dewi. 2011. "Twenty Ribu Penderita Sakit Jiwa Dipasung." *BBC Indonesia*, October 5. http://www.bbc.com/indonesia/laporan_khusus/2011/10/111004_mental6.

Saltford, John. 2003. *The United Nations and the Indonesian Takeover of West Papua, 1962–1969: The Anatomy of Betrayal.* London: RoutledgeCurzon.

Schaefer, B., and B. T. Wardaya, eds. 2013. *1965: Indonesia and the World, Indonesia Dan Dunia.* Jakarta: Gramedia Pustaka Utama.

Schulze, Kirsten. 2010. "The AMM and the Transition from Conflict to Peace in Aceh, 2005–2006." In M. Martin and M. Kaldor, eds., *The European Union and*

Human Security: External Interventions and Missions, 12–34. London: Taylor and Francis.

Schut, Thjis. 2015. "Underemployed Ambitions." *Inside Indonesia* 120 (April–June).

Sebastian, L., and I. Gindarsah. 2013. "Taking Stock of Military Reform in Indonesia." In J. Rüland, M.-G. Manea, and H. Born, eds., *The Politics of Military Reform: Experiences from Indonesia and Nigeria*, 29–56. Heidelberg: Springer.

Sedgh, Gilda, and Haley Ball. 2008. *Abortion in Indonesia*. In Brief no. 2. New York: Guttmacher Institute. https://www.guttmacher.org/sites/default/files/report _pdf/ib_abortion_indonesia_0.pdf.

Sen, Krishna, and David T. Hill. 2000. *Media, Culture and Politics in Indonesia.* Melbourne: Oxford University Press.

Setiawan, H. 2004. *Memoar Pulau Buru* (Cet. 1). Magelang: IndonesiaTera.

Setiawan, Ken. 2016. "The Politics of Compromise." *Inside Indonesia* 123 (January–March). https://www.insideindonesia.org/the-politics-of-compromise.

Sherlock, Stephen. 2009. "SBY's Consensus Cabinet—Lanjutkan?" *Bulletin of Indonesian Economic Studies* 45, no. 3: 341–343.

———. 2012. "Made by Committee and Consensus: Parties and Policy in the Indonesian Parliament." *South East Asia Research* 20, no. 4 (December): 551–568.

Sidel, John T. 2006. *Riots, Pogroms, Jihad; Religious Violence in Indonesia*. Ithaca: Cornell University Press.

Simpson, B. 2008. *Economists with Guns: Authoritarian Development and U.S.-Indonesian Relations, 1960–1968.* Stanford: Stanford University Press.

———. 2013. "The United States and the International Dimension of the Killings in Indonesia." In B. Schaefer and B. T. Wardaya, eds., *1965: Indonesia and the World, Indonesia Dan Dunia*, 43–60. Jakarta: Gramedia Pustaka Utama.

Slama, Martin. 2010. "The Agency of the Heart: Internet Chatting as Youth Culture in Indonesia." *Social Anthropology* 18, no. 3: 316–360.

Slater, Dan. 2018. "Party Cartelization, Indonesian-style: Presidential Power-Sharing and the Contingency of Democratic Opposition." *Journal of East Asian Studies* 18, no. 1 (March): 23–46.

Slater, May. 2013. "Teaching Remote Indonesia." *Inside Indonesia* 111 (January–March).

Smith, Anthony L. 2000. "Indonesia's Foreign Policy Under Abdurrahman Wahid: Radical or Status Quo State?" *Contemporary Southeast Asia* 22, no. 3: 498–526.

Smith, Benjamin. 2008. "The Origins of Regional Autonomy in Indonesia: Experts and the Marketing of Political Interests." *Journal of East Asian Studies* 8, no. 2 (May–August): 211–234.

Solahudin. 2013a. *The Roots of Terrorism in Indonesia: From Darul Islam to Jema'ah Islamiyah*. Translated by Dave McRae. Sydney: NewSouth Publishing.

———. 2013b. "Salafi Terror in Indonesia Is Still a Threat." *Australian*, August 19.

Southeast Asia and the Middle East: Islam, Movement, and the Longue Durée. 2009. Edited by Eric Tagliacozzo. Singapore: NUS Press.

Sparrow, R., S. Budiyati, A. Yumna, N. Warda, A. Suryahadi, and A. S. Bedi. 2017. "Sub-National Health Care Financing Reforms in Indonesia." *Health Policy and Planning* 32, no. 1 (February): 91–101.

"Standar Garis Kemiskinan Kita Terlalu Rendah." 2018. *Sinar Harapan*, July 19. http://sinarharapan.co/opinidaneditorial/read/2638/standar_garis_kemiskinan _kita_terlalu_rendah.

Statista. 2017. "Indonesia: Distribution of Employment by Economic Sector from 2007 to 2017." https://www.statista.com/statistics/320160/employment-by-economic -sector-in-indonesia/.

Steele, Janet. 2011. "Indonesian Journalism Post-Suharto: Changing Ideals and Professional Practices." In K. Sen and D. Hill, eds., *Politics and the Media in*

Twenty-First Century Indonesia, 85–108. London: Routledge.

Stepan, S. 1990. *Credibility Gap: Australia and Timor Gap Treaty.* Development dossier no. 28. Canberra: Australian Council for Overseas Aid.

Stoler, Ann Laura. 1995. *Capitalism and Confrontation in Sumatra's Plantation Belt, 1870–1979.* Ann Arbor: University of Michigan Press.

Storey, Ian. 2013. *Southeast Asia and the Rise of China: The Search for Security.* London: Routledge.

Strating, Rebecca. 2014. "The Indonesia-Timor-Leste Commission of Truth and Friendship: Enhancing Bilateral Relations at the Expense of Justice." *Contemporary Southeast Asia* 36, no. 2: 232–261.

Suharti. 2013. "Trends in Education in Indonesia." In D. Suryadarma and G. W. Jones, eds., *Education in Indonesia*, 15–52. Singapore: ISEAS.

Sukarno. 1965. *Sukarno: An Autobiography as Told to Cindy Adams.* Indianapolis, IN: Bobbs-Merrill.

Sukma, Rizal. 1995. "The Evolution of Indonesia's Foreign Policy: An Indonesian View." *Asian Survey* 35, no. 3: 304–315.

———. 1999. *Indonesia and China: The Politics of a Troubled Relationship.* London: Routledge.

———. 2009. "Indonesia Needs a Post-ASEAN Foreign Policy." *Jakarta Post*, June 30.

———. 2011. "Indonesia Finds a New Voice." *Journal of Democracy* 22, no. 4: 110–123.

Sumarto, S., A. Suryahadi, and S. Bazzi. 2008. "Indonesia's Social Protection During and After the Crisis." In A. Barrientos and D. Hulme, eds., *Social Protection for the Poor and Poorest: Concepts, Policies and Politics*, 121–145. New York: Palgrave Macmillan.

Sumner, Cate, and Tim Lindsey. 2010. *Courting Reform: Indonesia's Islamic Courts and Justice for the Poor.* Lowy Institute paper no. 31. Woollahra, New South Wales: Lowy Institute for International Policy.

Sundawa, Shela Putri. 2014. "Why Indonesia Should Legalize Abortion." *Jakarta Post*, August 24.

"Survey of Recent Developments." 1965. *Bulletin of Indonesian Economic Studies* 1, no. 1: 1–12.

———. 1972. *Bulletin of Indonesian Economic Studies* 8, no. 3: 1–32.

Suryadarma, D. 2015. "Quantity but Not Quality." *Inside Indonesia* 119 (January–March).

Suryadarma, D., and G. W. Jones, eds. 2013. *Education in Indonesia.* Singapore: ISEAS.

Suryadinata, L. 1995. "Islam and Suharto's Foreign Policy: Indonesia, the Middle East, and Bosnia." *Asian Survey* 35, no. 3: 293–303.

Suryadinata, L., E. N. Arifin, and A. Ananta. 2003. *Indonesia's Population: Ethnicity and Religion in a Changing Political Landscape.* Singapore: ISEAS.

Suryahadi, Asep. 2018. "Is Higher Inequality the New Normal for Indonesia?" *Indonesia at Melbourne,* November 27. https://indonesiaatmelbourne.unimelb.edu.au/is-higher-inequality-the-new-normal-for-indonesia/.

Swift, Ann. 1989. *The Road to Madiun: The Indonesian Communist Uprising of 1948.* Ithaca: Cornell Modern Indonesia Project, Southeast Asia Program.

Tadjoeddin, Mohammad Zulfan. 2014. "Decent Work: On the Quality of Employment in Indonesia." *Asian Journal of Social Science* 42, no. 1–2: 9–44.

Tan, Charlene. 2012. *Islamic Education and Indoctrination: The Case in Indonesia.* Hoboken, NJ: Taylor and Francis.

Tan, Paige Johnson. 2007. "Navigating a Turbulent Ocean: Indonesia's Worldview and Foreign Policy." *Asian Perspective* 31, no. 3: 147–181.

Tapsell, Ross. 2012a. "Old Tricks in a New Era: Self-Censorship in Indonesian Journalism." *Asian Studies Review* 36, no. 2: 227–245.

————. 2012b. "Politics and the Press in Indonesia." *Media Asia* 39, no. 2: 109–116.

————. 2015. "Indonesia's Media Oligarchy and the 'Jokowi Phenomenon.'" *Indonesia* 99: 29–50.

————. 2017. *Media Power in Indonesia: Oligarchs, Citizens and the Digital Revolution*. London: Rowman and Littlefield.

————. 2019. "When They Go Low, We Go Lower." *New York Times*, April 16. https://www.nytimes.com/2019/04/16/opinion/indonesia-election-fake-news.html.

Team of *Tempo* journalists. 2009. "Why Was *Tempo* Banned?" In T. Hellwig and E. Tagliacozzo, eds., *The Indonesia Reader: History, Culture, Politics*, 398–401. Durham, NC: Duke University Press.

Tehusijarana, K. 2019. "Jakarta Riot: Government Temporarily Limits Access to Social Media, Messaging Apps." *Jakarta Post*, May 22. https://www.thejakartapost.com/life/2019/05/22/jakarta-riot-government-temporarily-limits-access-to-social-media-messaging-apps.html.

Tempo. 2019. "Kami Hanya Mengingatkan Dunia Soal Palestina." May 26. https://majalah.tempo.co/read/157756/menteri-luar-negeri-retno-lestari-priansari-marsudi-kami-hanya-mengingatkan-dunia-soal-palestina.

Thee, Kian Wie. 2009. "Indonesia's Two Deep Economic Crises: The Mid 1960s and Late 1990s." *Journal of the Asia Pacific Economy* 14, no. 1: 49–60.

Thristiawati, S., H. Booth, T. Hull, and I. D. Utomo. 2015. "Self-Rated Health of Older Persons in Indonesia: Sex and Ethnic Differences." *Asian Population Studies* 11, no. 1: 44–66.

Tjhin, Christine Susanna. 2012. "Indonesia's Relations with China: Productive and Pragmatic, but Not Yet a Strategic Partnership." *China Report* 48, no. 3: 303–315.

Tomsa, D. 2007. "Party Politics and the Media in Indonesia: Creating a New Dual Identity for Golkar." *Contemporary Southeast Asia* 29, no. 1 (April): 77–96.

————. 2008. *Party Politics and Democratization in Indonesia: Golkar in the Post-Suharto Era*. Hoboken, NJ: Taylor and Francis.

————. 2016. "Not Just Another Local Election." *Asian Currents*, October 6.

————. 2018. "Parties and the Party Room in Post-Reformasi Politics." In R. W. Heffner, ed., *Routledge Handbook of Contemporary Indonesia*, 95–105. New York: Routledge.

Topsfield, Jewel, and Karuni Rompies. 2017. "Court Recognises Indonesian Native Faiths in Victory for Religious Freedom." *Sydney Morning Herald*, November 8.

"Treat Rape Victim as Victim." 2018. *Jakarta Post*, July 24. http://www.thejakartapost.com/academia/2018/07/24/treat-rape-victim-as-victim.html.

Tribunnews. 2013. "Three Aceh Local Parties Officially Become Election Participants." January 10. http://www.tribunnews.com/regional/2013/01/10/tiga-partai-lokal-aceh-resmi-jadi-peserta-pemilu.

Trisnantoro, L., S. Soemantri, B. Singgih, K. Pritasari, E. Mulati, F. H. Agung, and M. W. Weber. 2010. "Reducing Child Mortality in Indonesia." *Bulletin of the World Health Organization* 88: 642.

Ufen, Andreas. 2010. "The Legislative and Presidential Elections in Indonesia in 2009." *Electoral Studies* 29, no. 2 (June): 281–285.

UNICEF. 2015. "Child Marriage in Indonesia." https://www.unicef.org/indonesia/UNICEF_Indonesia_Child_Marriage_Factsheet_.pdf.

United Nations Human Rights Council, Working Group on the Universal Periodic Review. 2017. *National Report . . . Indonesia* (A/HRC/WG.6/27/IDN/1). New York: United Nations. https://www.ohchr.org/EN/HRBodies/UPR/Pages/IDIndex.aspx.

United States Department of State, Office of the Historian. 1995. *95/03/06 Foreign Relations, 1961–63, Vol. XXIII, Southeast Asia*, March 6. https://wpik.org/Src/950306_FRUS_XXIII_1961-63.html.

Utomo, A., A. Reimondos, I. Utomo, P. McDonald, and T. H. Hull. 2014. "What Happens After You Drop Out? Transition to Adulthood Among Early School-Leavers in Urban Indonesia." *Demographic Research* 30 (April): 1189–1218.

van Baardewijk, Frans. 1994. "Rural Response to Intensifying Colonial Exploitation: Coffee, State and Society in Central and East Java, 1830–1880." In G. J. Schutte, ed., *State and Trade in the Indonesian Archipelago.* Working papers (Koninklijk Instituut voor Taal-, Land- en Volkenkunde) 13, pp. 151–176. Leiden: KITLV Press.

van der Eng, Pierre. 2012. *All Lies? Famines in Sukarno's Indonesia, 1950s–1960s.* Canberra: Indonesia Project, Crawford School of Public Policy, Australian National University.

van der Wolf, W. J., C. Tofan, and D. de Ruiter. 2011. *National Truth and Reconciliation Commissions: Facts and Materials.* Oisterwijk, The Netherlands: International Courts Association.

van Heeren, Katinka. 2007. "Return of the Kyai: Representations of Horror, Commerce, and Censorship in Post-Suharto Indonesian Film and Television." *Inter-Asia Cultural Studies* 8, no. 2: 211–226.

———. 2012. *Contemporary Indonesian Film: Spirits of Reform and Ghosts from the Past.* Leiden: KITLV.

van Klinken, Gerry. 2007. *Communal Violence and Democratization in Indonesia: Small Town Wars.* London: Routledge.

Vickers, Adrian. 2013. *A History of Modern Indonesia.* New York: Cambridge University Press.

Wahyuningroem, Ayu. 2016. "Justice Denied?" *Inside Indonesia* 125 (July–September). https://www.insideindonesia.org/justice-denied.

Wangge, H. Y. R. 2016. "Clumsy Diplomacy: Indonesia, Papua and the Pacific." *Indonesia at Melbourne*, October 12. http://indonesiaatmelbourne.unimelb.edu.au/clumsy-diplomacy-indonesia-papua-and-the-pacific/.

Ward, K. 1974. *The 1971 Election in Indonesia: An East Java Case Study.* Monash papers on Southeast Asia no. 2. Clayton, Victoria: Centre of Southeast Asian Studies, Monash University.

———. 2009. "Non-Violent Extremists? Hizbut Tahrir Indonesia." *Australian Journal of International Affairs* 63, no. 2: 149–164.

Ward, Ken. 2015. *Condemned to Crisis?* Lowy Institute Paper. Sydney: Lowy Institute.

Waterson, Roxana. 2009. "Reconciliation as Ritual: Comparative Perspectives on Innovation and Performance in Processes of Reconciliation." *Humanities Research* 15, no. 3: 27–47.

Weatherbee, Donald. 2005. "Indonesian Foreign Policy: A Wounded Phoenix." *Southeast Asian Affairs 2005.* Singapore: ISEAS–Yusof Ishak Institute, pp. 150–170.

———. 2009. *International Relations in Southeast Asia: The Struggle for Autonomy.* Lanham, MD: Rowman and Littlefield.

———. 2013. *Indonesia in ASEAN: Vision and Reality.* Singapore: ISEAS.

Weintraub, A. 2008. "'Dance Drills, Faith Spills': Islam, Body Politics, and Popular Music in Post-Suharto Indonesia." *Popular Music* 27, no. 3: 367–392.

Weiss, Meredith L. 2010. "Malaysia-Indonesia Bilateral Relations: Sibling Rivals in a Fraught Family." In N. Ganesan and Ramses Amer, eds., *International Relations in Southeast Asia: Between Bilateralism and Multilateralism*, 171–198. Singapore: ISEAS.

Wieringa, S. E. 1998. "Sexual Metaphors in the Change from Soekarno's Old Order to Soeharto's New Order in Indonesia." *Review of Indonesian and Malaysian Affairs* 32, no. 2: 143–178.

Wieringa, Saskia. 2017. "When a History Seminar Becomes Toxic." *Inside Indonesia* 130 (October–December). https://www.insideindonesia.org/when-a-history-seminar -becomes-toxic.

Wilson, Chris. 2008. *Ethno-Religious Violence in Indonesia: From Soil to God.* Abingdon, Oxon: Routledge.

Wilson, Ian. 2014. "Morality Racketeering: Vigilantism and Populist Islamic Militancy in Indonesia." In B. T. Khoo, V. R. Hadiz, and Y. Nakanishi, eds., *Between Dissent and Power: The Transformation of Islamic Politics in the Middle East and Asia*, 248–274. New York: Palgrave Macmillan.

———. 2017. "Jakarta: Inequality and the Poverty of Elite Pluralism." *New Mandala*, April 19. http://www.newmandala.org/jakarta-inequality-poverty-elite-pluralism/.

Wilson, Lee, and Eryanto Nugroho. 2012. "For the Good of the People?" *Inside Indonesia* 109 (August).

Winters, J. 2011. *Oligarchy.* Cambridge: Cambridge University Press.

Winters, J. A. 2013. "Oligarchy and Democracy in Indonesia." *Indonesia* 96: 99–121.

Wirajuda, Muhammad Hadianto. 2014. "The Impact of Democratisation on Indonesia's Foreign Policy: Regional Cooperation, Promotion of Political Values, and Conflict Management." PhD diss., London School of Economics and Political Science.

World Atlas. 2017. "Leading Causes of Death in Indonesia." Updated March 16. http://www.worldatlas.com/articles/leading-causes-of-death-in-indonesia.html.

World Bank. 2010. *Transforming Indonesia's Teaching Force. Volume II: From Pre-Service Training to Retirement: Producing and Maintaining a High-Quality, Efficient, and Motivated Workforce.* Jakarta: World Bank.

———. 2015. "The Double Burden of Malnutrition in Indonesia." April 23.

———. 2016. *Indonesia's Rising Divide.* Jakarta: World Bank.

———. 2017. *Indonesia's Global Worker: Juggling Opportunities and Risks.* Jakarta: World Bank.

———. 2018. "Indonesia Trade at a Glance: Most Recent Values." https://wits .worldbank.org/CountrySnapshot/en/IDN/textview.

World Economic Forum. 2016. "The Global Gender Gap Report 2016: Results and Analysis." http://reports.weforum.org/global-gender-gap-report-2016/results-and -analysis/.

World Health Organization. 2017a. "Hospital Beds (per 1,000 People)." http:// data.worldbank.org/indicator/SH.MED.BEDS.ZS.

———. 2017b. "Indonesia." http://www.who.int/countries/idn/en/.

Yudhoyono, Susilo Bambang. 2014. "Indonesian President's State Address for the 69th Anniversary of the Proclamation of Indonesian Independence." Jakarta.

Yusuf, A. A., and A. Sumner. 2015. "Growth, Poverty and Inequality Under Jokowi." *Bulletin of Indonesian Economic Studies* 51, no. 3: 323–348.

Yusuf, M., and C. Sterkens. 2015. "Analysing the State's Laws on Religious Education in Post–New Order Indonesia." *Al-Jamiah: Journal of Islamic Studies* 53, no. 1: 105–130.

Zainu'ddin, A. 1980. *A Short History of Indonesia.* 2nd ed. Stanmore, New South Wales: Cassell Australia.

Zhang, Diane. 2014. "What Is the Basis for Jokowi's Claim to the Presidency?" *Election Watch Indonesia*, July 12. http://past.electionwatch.edu.au/indonesia -2014/what-basis-jokowis-claim-presidency.

Zhang, Diane, and Dave McRae. 2015. *Policy Diffusion: A Four District Study of the Replication of Health Insurance (JAMKESDA) and BOSDA in Indonesia.* Jakarta: AIPD.

Index

About the Book

INDONESIA REMAINS A COUNTRY IN TRANSITION EVEN NOW, SOME two decades after its extraordinary shift from authoritarianism to democracy and from economic crisis to a rapidly growing economy. What explains the trajectory of that shift? What challenges does this island nation of 270 million people—with the world's largest Muslim population—face now, as the quality of democratic life erodes and it grapples with profound social and economic inequalities?

Addressing these questions, the authors comprehensively explore the dynamics of Indonesia's politics, society, political economy, and culture, as well as its role in the international order.

Jemma Purdey is a research fellow at the Australia-Indonesia Centre at Monash University and adjunct fellow in Deakin University's Faculty of Arts and Education. **Antje Missbach** is senior research fellow in the School of Social Sciences at Monash University and senior research fellow at the Arnold Bergstraesser Institute. **Dave McRae** is senior lecturer at the University of Melbourne's Asia Institute.